JEAN-JACQUES ROUSSEAU

Jean-Jacques Rousseau

IN TWO VOLUMES

VOLUME ONE 1712–1758
VOLUME TWO 1758–1778

JEAN-JACQUES
ROUSSEAU

By

JEAN GUÉHENNO

Translated from the French by

JOHN AND DOREEN WEIGHTMAN

VOLUME TWO 1758—1778

LONDON: Routledge and Kegan Paul
NEW YORK: Columbia University Press
1967

Translated from the French
JEAN-JACQUES: HISTOIRE D'UNE CONSCIENCE
© *Editions Gallimard 1962*

This edition published 1966
in Great Britain
by Routledge & Kegan Paul Ltd
Broadway House, 68-74 Carter Lane
London, E.C.4
and in the United States of America
by Columbia University Press
Columbia University, New York

Printed in Great Britain by
Richard Clay (The Chaucer Press) Ltd
Bungay, Suffolk

English translation
© *Copyright Routledge & Kegan Paul Ltd 1966*

Second Printing 1967

Library of Congress Catalog Card No: 66-12112

Contents

THE GREATNESS AND WRETCHEDNESS
OF A HUMAN MIND

'Alas, grant me therefore madness, O divine powers! Madness so that I may finally believe in myself! Grant me outbursts of delirium and convulsions, sudden moments of clarity and obscurity, terrify me with shivering-fits and burning sensations such as no mortal has ever experienced, surround me with noise and spectres! Let me howl and moan and crawl like a beast, provided I succeed in having faith in myself.'

Nietzsche (*Dawn*, Aph. 14)

Prologue

WHEN I UNDERTOOK to retell the story of Jean-Jacques' life day by day, I wondered if the whole project was not absurd. For years I have been reading and re-reading that admirable book, the *Confessions*. More than once, I have felt that Jean-Jacques was sitting opposite me, a great, ranting, marvellously eloquent ghost, and so sincere that I could not but feel ridiculous as his opponent in the kind of game we were playing, which was the contest for truth. I picked holes in his statements, produced my petty proofs, pushed forward my little bits of paper. 'You are mistaken,' I would murmur, 'here, and here again. I am not suggesting that you are actually telling lies, but you certainly know how to cover up. You do so unconsciously. You claim to be describing yourself *intus et in cute*, but you are clothed in your virtue and so muffled up in it, indeed, that you can no longer see your own skin.' . . . Whereupon there would be another outburst from him; I would look him full in the face; his eyes were as in the portrait by Ramsay and I could see such torment and pain in them that I, in my turn, no longer knew what to think. I should have liked to let the whole enquiry drop, and wait for 'the trumpet on the day of the Last Judgement', when he could come forward, as he said he wished to do, with his *Confessions* in his hand, 'and present himself before the sovereign judge'!

I came back to him anew every morning. I had got used to living with an enigma. The days, the years went by. It is impossible to live with people if you are constantly sitting in judgement on them. The trouble is that he himself insists on being judged. From 1760 onwards, which is the period of his life we have now reached, he keeps demanding to be judged, as if he were a prisoner whose case was failing to come up for examination. He wants to be either acquitted or convicted and he urges us to make up our minds. The Dostoievskian hero has become Kafkaesque. But, for my part, I no longer feel any desire to pass judgement on him. I would be content to understand him, and I am aware that I shall never be able to do so fully. Curiously enough, he is the only man, in the entire history of ideas—apart from the saints—with whom his fellow-men have been anxious to maintain a bond by referring to him by his christian name: Jean-Jacques, rather than by his surname. Obviously, I did not want to write a biography of 'Rousseau' but of 'Jean-Jacques', and it had to be coloured by that ironical tenderness which made his contemporaries use his name for the chorus of a song, and which we no doubt always feel when we recognise ourselves in another man. Rousseau poses both a literary and a political problem, but it is not with them that I am most concerned. I was chiefly interested in Jean-Jacques because he had not wanted to become a writer, or had only become one reluctantly. He was both a poor fellow and a great man, as all men are, and in fact, because of this mixture, one of the most authentic witnesses of the human race; it is his testimony which I have tried to elucidate. I sensed that in him we could see how greatness can spring from a great deal of wretchedness.

In approaching him from this angle, I can at least be sure of having avoided certain biased attitudes and prejudices. There may be said to be two schools of Rousseau criticism, both as regards his work, and his life, and one is as passionate as the other. Even before his death, people had begun to take sides about him once and for all, and inevitably made him into a sort of monster, or a sort of saint. People still insist on seeing him either as a prophet or a madman. Those who are opposed to his 'ideas' and his 'system' have studied the disreputable aspects of his life to find reasons to condemn his work, while his supporters who proclaim their solidarity with his work, maintain that everything in his life can be justified. It is difficult to find any critics who are not slanderers or adulators. He himself, by his confidences, provided both friends and enemies with all the material required for a pointless controversy. . . . But, when all is said and done, he was only a man and, like everybody else, he had more ways than one of being a man, containing within himself as he did those difficulties and contradictions which define us

all, although in him they were magnified by his genius. People
have been constantly misled by the notorious statement on the
first page of his *Confessions*; he defies the reader—indeed he defies
all men—to dare to claim, at the bar of Heaven, that they were
'better' than he was. But this is not tantamount to saying that
he himself is good. He knew better than anyone what a mixture
of good and bad is to be found in every individual. What he was
profoundly conscious of was his struggle to attain virtue and
truth, and for us the whole interest of the matter lies in the story
of this struggle.

In the first part of this work I tried to describe his efforts and
strivings. Rousseau eventually became Jean-Jacques. For forty
years he had sought to become himself. But for his genius, he
might have been no more than one of those literary adventurers
who were so common in the eighteenth century. He was helped
by the adventures, the set-backs, the misfortunes and the
humiliations he experienced during his first forty years. Although
born a son of Geneva, the 'new Zion', a citizen and a member of
'the race of the just', for a long time he had the good fortune to
be no more than a wandering child, to have to play the toady
and to become willy-nilly a rather inefficient Jack-of-all-trades—
engraver, lackey, singing master, lover, tutor, ambassador's
secretary, musician, pamphleteer and polygrapher, until that
afternoon of October 1749 when, while he was on the road to
Vincennes and in the depths of degradation and humiliation,
pride at last restored him to himself and brought about the
reunification of his being. Something which had been sown in
him in childhood, and which had refused to die, eventually,
and in spite of all, saw the light of day.

'The Kingdom of Heaven is like a grain of mustard-seed, which
when it is sown upon the earth, though it be less than all the seeds
that are upon the earth, yet when it is sown, groweth up and
becometh greater than all the herbs and putteth out great
branches, so that the birds of the heaven can lodge under the
shadow thereof.'

Hagiographers tend to diminish saintliness. A kind-hearted
English lady, Mrs. MacDonald, who was a great admirer of
Jean-Jacques, spent many years of her life trying to establish
that he never had any children, which would have been a good
reason for not putting them into a Foundlings' Home. Such an

edifying attempt, prompted by blind devotion, can only serve to destroy Jean-Jacques, to destroy his anguish and, I would even go so far as to say, the principles of his entire work. Thérèse does not appear to have been a loose woman, but of course her virtue cannot be guaranteed. What is certain, however, is that Jean-Jacques himself was absolutely convinced that she had had five children by him, and that the children put into the Foundlings' Home were his. This settles the matter. He believed that he alone was responsible for having abandoned the five children. There is probably no more extraordinary human document than the coded statement which he carried round with him all his life in the notebook into which he had entered all the important documents relating to his case in ordinary writing; it is a copy of a letter which he had written to Mme de Francueil on the 20th April, 1751:

'Oui, Madame, 9:1.9' 12.9.18' 12.5.18' 5.13.6.1.13.18'...'
When deciphered, this gives:

'Oui, Madame, j'ai mis mes enfants aux Enfants Trouvés...'
(Yes, Madame, I put my children into the Foundlings' Home)

The code is of the simplest: a =1, b =2, etc. He imagined it protected him, as if he were an ostrich burying its head in the sand. He imagined that no one else would be capable of interpreting it. He penned the numbers carefully, taking great pains to cover up the truth! This coded copy contained his secret, a secret which was always gnawing at him and that he was to keep all his life. During his lifetime he never admitted the truth, and when questioned, he lied. The admission is to be found only in works which were to be published after his death.

He had committed a sin, light-heartedly and in keeping with the general trend of his century. Once honour had restored him to himself, he pledged himself to virtue through that profession of his own uniqueness, the *Discourse on the Sciences and the Arts*, and he kept his pledge. From then onwards he wrote against the general trend of the century. In many respects his work is simply his rumination on his remorse, his atonement for his sins. This is true not only of *Emile*, in which a father who would nowadays be termed 'unnatural', reminded his contemporaries of the nature of paternal feeling and taught them to love children, and to understand what was owing to children. But he was only able to explain what was right because he knew what it was to have done wrong. He set out to refashion everything—man, love, society, even God himself. He was in this state of 'effervescence' at the point at which the present volume begins. He had just left L'Ermitage which, he considered, had marked his final relapse into society. Mme d'Houdetot had brought the realisation that, for him, 'the time of loving' had passed. His friends had abandoned him. He was alone in his 'tower' at Montmorency; never, however, had he pursued a more grandiose dream.

July 1952

The Greatness and
Wretchedness of
a Human Mind

CHAPTER ONE

In which Jean-Jacques Plays the Part of God (1758)

The *Lettre à d'Alembert*—Voltaire at Ferney and Rousseau at Montmorency—Jean-Jacques quarrels with Tronchin—Jean-Jacques becomes a friend of the Maréchal de Luxembourg and his wife—Jean-Jacques starts on his book about education—The main themes of *Emile*. The century of revolutions. The new man. The *Vicaire savoyard's* profession of faith. Jean-Jacques is an advocate of happiness rather than of truth—Between believers on the one hand and *philosophes* on the other—Jean-Jacques plays the part of God.

HIS HEALTH RETURNED with the fine weather, and the year 1758 was quite a happy one.

In the tenth book of the *Confessions*, where he is still pleading his cause, he falls into self-contradiction. He denounces Grimm's 'system' of slander, which was, he says, to estrange him from everyone, as well as Grimm's 'too rapid advancement and success'. Yet, being anxious to prove that he was not the monster people claimed he was, he makes a point of listing all his friends in the provinces and in Paris. Young Loyseau de Mauléon, Guérin the bookseller, M. Maltor, the Curé de Groslay, the Oratorians at Montmorency, his compatriots, Roguin, Lenieps and Coindet, the entire Dupin household, and

Mme de Créqui, and M. de Margency and even the *Directeur de la librairie* (Controller of publications), M. de Malesherbes. The plot against him, if there was such a thing, had as yet had little effect. The Luxembourg family, who were his neighbours that summer, made very friendly advances to him. But the happenings at L'Ermitage had made him wary and he did not respond to their approaches. He himself is obliged to admit: 'Since I had shaken off my tyrant's yoke, I had led a fairly uneventful and peaceful existence.'

The *Lettre à d'Alembert* was being printed in Amsterdam in great secrecy. When it was ready to appear, Jean-Jacques ceremoniously warned D'Alembert that he had felt 'compelled to reply to his article' on Geneva. 'Had my father himself written such an article,' he explained, 'I would have been unable to remain silent, and it would have been wrong for me to do so.' Moreover 'the poor quality of his work' made up for its boldness. 'Had I thought only of my reputation,' he concluded, 'I would certainly not have allowed the work to appear; in this case, however, it is not a question of what pleases you or does honour to me; in doing my duty, I shall always be fairly satisfied with myself and feel quite justified in your eyes.' D'Alembert must have considered himself highly honoured to have been chosen as an opponent, since he took the initiative of offering his services to Malesherbes as censor, since one was necessary, and announced in advance that the book would meet with his approval. Malesherbes accepted. Things seemed to be going swimmingly; never had Jean-Jacques been shown so much consideration and the road to fame seemed at last to be smooth and easy.

He had specially requested the publisher to send a copy of his book to Saint-Lambert. When Saint-Lambert and Mme d'Houdetot read the extremely malicious note in which Jean-Jacques denounced Diderot, they were appalled. Diderot might reply; the touchiness of literary people could lead to all sorts of indiscretions. Saint-Lambert refused to accept Jean-Jacques' expressions of respect and was on the point of breaking with him once and for all, after making every effort to explain to him that Diderot was not really to blame. He changed his mind, however; with a man like Jean-Jacques, kindness was more effective than wrath.

4

So, towards the end of October, there took place the extraordinary dinner described by Jean-Jacques. Lovers, husbands and mistresses, all the leading characters in the stormy love-affairs that have already been described, were assembled round the same table, as if they were performing the last act of some play. Only Grimm and Mme d'Epinay were absent. M. d'Epinay presided. Francueil, his wife's former lover, was seated right next to him. Mme d'Houdetot sat between her husband, the count, and her lover the marquis. Jean-Jacques graciously entered into the feelings of tolerance and forgiveness of which everyone was trying to set an example. His account is highly amusing: 'My arrival,' he writes, 'created a sensation. Never have I been given a more cordial reception. It seemed as if the entire company felt how much I needed to be reassured. Only French hearts are capable of this sort of refinement.' Usually he was much more critical of 'this sort of refinement', when he himself was not the object of it. We can see here how the fiercest Alceste may sometimes turn into a Philinte.

The *Lettre*, which was published during the first days of October, was, he says, 'a great success'. He experienced a period of true happiness. To the recluse, the echoes of the stir he had caused were infinitely sweet. Once more a battle was being waged around his name. By November, Marmontel was publishing the first instalments of the *Apologie du Théâtre* in the *Mercure de France*. During the course of the year, according to Grimm, there were no fewer than three hundred replies to Rousseau. It is surprising that Jean-Jacques should have completely forgotten these brochures and pamphlets, and should only express worry about the fact that his 'old friends' remained silent. Nor did he notice that only pious people agreed with his ideas. D'Alembert himself replied, with sly irony, but extremely respectfully. He was as fair-minded as Jean-Jacques was eloquent. 'The nature of your philosophy, Sir,' he said, 'is to be firm and inexorable in its progress,' and this was quite a shrewd criticism. He implied that the author of *Le Devin de Village* was perhaps not the person best qualified to attack the theatre, was not as indifferent to fame and public opinion as all that, and that Diogenes himself in his tub would have been most disappointed if the Athenians had passed him by without a glance, and without listening to what he had to say. With great deftness, he

B
5

went to the root of the matter. Jean-Jacques had denounced the theatre as being merely an amusement: 'Life is so short,' he had written, 'and time so precious.' D'Alembert replied: 'Who doubts this, Sir? But at the same time life is so painful and pleasure so rare.' 'Someone,' he added, 'who was acutely bored (most probably a prince) must have been the first to think of this refined amusement, which consists in representing the trials and tribulations of our fellow-creatures on a stage, in order either to console us for, or to cure us of, our own, and turn us into spectators of life, instead of being actors in it, and so make its burden and misfortunes more bearable for us.' Jean-Jacques must have felt an occasional pin-prick, but, all things considered, he had no cause for complaint.

He had presented copies of his book to twenty or so of his Genevan friends, who were ministers or teachers. Most of them sent their congratulations, but the letter which gave him greatest pleasure was one written by a young minster, Paul Moultou, who had just arrived in Geneva from Montpellier. Moultou expressed himself with all the enthusiasm of a beginner:

> Your book is a rallying signal for all good citizens, and spreads shame and terror among the bad; now each individual's love of his country can be measured by the degree of esteem with which he regards your work. In short, if Geneva can succeed in maintaining or returning to its old customs, it will owe this entirely to you, and the Palladium of this Republic will have been created by the article in the *Encyclopédie* which was intended to bring about its ruin . . .

The young man's letter glowed with exactly the kind of fire that Jean-Jacques had sought to kindle. He thought it 'admirable'. He already saw himself as the inspirer and saviour of his distant fatherland. Voltaire, whom he suspected of being the real author of the article *Genève* and to whom he had also arranged for his book to be sent, did not reply. Jean-Jacques was hurt but not 'angry'. Voltaire's silence 'allowed (him) to settle back comfortably' into his hatred and jealousy. An extraordinary process of thought began to take shape in his mind: he saw Geneva as a lost city, corrupted by the master of the *philosophes* who lived in unjustifiable proximity, while he, Jean-Jacques, who might have been its saviour, had to live far away. He convinced himself that there was not room in Geneva for both Voltaire and himself. They were like Good and Evil; if Voltaire was there, it was impossible for Jean-Jacques to be there too. Soon he was to hold Voltaire responsible for his solitude and his being in exile, and to suppose that Voltaire was keeping him away from Geneva in order to carry out his evil work there more effectively. Even before the publication of Jean-Jacques' book, Voltaire had said to Thiériot: 'What is this about Jean-Jacques writing a book against the theatre? Has he become a Father of the Church?' After the book appeared, Voltaire was delighted to see that the people of Geneva still continued 'to pack' the theatres. A kind of necessity was forcing the relationship between the two men to become embittered. From then onwards, Voltaire began to see Jean-Jacques as a 'false friend', a 'Judas'. Jean-Jacques, in his humble little house at Montmorency, was trying to live as exemplary and as publicly noted a life as that led by Voltaire at Les Délices. Fame was now doing to him what it does to the greatest of men—turning him into a personage at once sublime and ridiculous, according to the onlooker's angle of vision. Young men could write and ask his advice about how to conduct their lives. People began to look upon him as a spiritual director. By now he could recognise his own style and tone in the letters sent to him: 'No, great Rousseau, you are not a useless burden on this earth. There still exist mortals whose eyes follow you even to your solitary retreat, and whose courage is quickened when they see the way in which you fight the good fight. May all-compassionate God finally alleviate your sufferings. . . . '

He had set himself up as a model of virtue and could no longer remain unaware of the hold he had over people. He despatched marvellously edifying letters in all directions and issued moral instructions to all and sundry. He declared with false modesty that his time was no longer of much use to the public and that he himself no longer prized it very highly. He could not waste it, however, because he had to earn his daily bread. He wanted everyone to know that his moral principles were those of a craftsman. In February 1759 the Opéra expressed a wish to put on *Le Devin de Village* again, and this gave rise to much discussion. At the same time, he was arguing with his Dutch publisher about the financial arrangements for a complete edition of his works. He deemed it advisable to explain to one of his Genevan friends, Lenieps the banker, what his principles were in such matters.

> If those who accuse me of not being sufficiently disinterested [he wrote], mean to imply that I would not be pleased to be deprived of the little I earn in order to live, they are right, and it is obvious that the only way in which I could convince them of my disinterestedness would be to allow myself to die of starvation. If they mean that one source of income is as good as another to me and that, provided the money is forthcoming, I care but litte about its provenance, I think they are wrong. If I were more easy-going about the means of acquiring money, it would be less painful for me to lose it, and it is well known that nobody is more generous than a thief. But when I am stripped unjustly of what belongs to me, when I am deprived of the modest proceeds of my labour, a wrong is done me which it is not easy for me to redress; it is indeed hard for me not even to enjoy freedom. For a long time now the Parisian public has been creating its own image of Jean-Jacques Rousseau and showering on him gifts of which the Jean-Jacques Rousseau of Montmorency never catches a glimpse. Sick and ailing as I am for three quarters of the year, I must see that I make enough during the remaining quarter to provide for all my needs. Those who earn their daily bread only by honest means know how precious it is, and will not be surprised that I cannot be very lavish with mine.

The whole letter is admirably telling. He was still at this time fully conscious of what he was doing: but why should he take such pains to refer to himself throughout as Jean-Jacques Rousseau of Montmorency? The reason is that he was only too aware of the public interest in him; he was living in seclusion in the tiny village of Montmorency, yet wanted the eyes of the world to be trained upon him.

He was not mad yet; in fact, he was only too lucid. The entire tribe of pen-pushers was now yapping at his heels: Jean-Jacques! Jean-Jacques! He was never referred to by any other name. It was a rather appropriate name for an eccentric, and could be uttered either with pity, affection or scorn, as circumstances required. At that time, there were three Rousseaus in the Republic of Letters. An epigram composed in the year 1758 ran as follows:

Trois auteurs que Rousseau l'on nomme
Sont différents voici par où:
Rousseau de Paris fut grand homme,
Rousseau de Genève est un . . .
Rousseau de Toulouse un atome.

(Three writers called Rousseau are different, and in the following respects: Rousseau of Paris was a great man, Rousseau of Geneva is . . . *fou* (mad), to rhyme with *où*, Rousseau of Toulouse a mere speck.)

The implication was that Rousseau of Geneva was mad. The publicity surrounding his name only served to make him still more convinced of his own peculiarity. He brooded over all this slanderous gossip and, led on by his anguished yearning for purity, his scrupulousness and his passion for self-analysis—the real source of his madness—he imagined himself to be surrounded by a jealous world which was shocked by his solitary existence and eager to slander him and do him harm.

What a fine thing [he wrote in this same letter to Lenieps] is a veneer of courteous behaviour and the tact born of good breeding! Hatred can make such convenient use of both. You satisfy your vengeance and at the same time you display your magnanimity. You discreetly hide the dagger under the cloak of friendship and know the art of slitting someone's throat while feigning compassion for him. Poor citizen! He has no real wickedness in him, but he has an unruly disposition which makes him behave as badly as if he were really wicked. Some ambiguous remark is uttered with an air of mystery, and before long it is taken up, commented upon and circulated by would-be *philosophes;* the poison which they take upon themselves to spread abroad is prepared in obscure and secret assemblies. One person is magnanimous enough to speak very highly of me, after taking pains to see that no one will believe a word of what he says; another proclaims my innocence, while seeing to it that no one can have any doubt about my guilt. This is what is known as cleverness! What can I do about it? I cannot, from my country retreat, hear what is being said in various circles. Even if I could, it would not be like me to base a denial on the revelation of the secrets of friendship even when the friendship itself is dead. No, dear Lenieps, we can repel the blows dealt us by our enemies, but when, among our assassins, we see a friend, with a dagger in his hand, our only course is to veil our eyes.

9

He added a few more lines in which he apologised for his long-winded explanation, and concluded with the following moving remark: 'I feel that my soul is shattered and must lay down my pen.'

In the spring of 1759 he quarrelled with Tronchin. He had had the idea of asking Tronchin to give medical advice to a bourgeois neighbour of his. Tronchin agreed to do so but, having been told by Mme d'Epinay of the happenings at L'Ermitage, he replied somewhat tactlessly: 'How is it, or rather how can it possibly be, that the friend of mankind is now hardly on friendly terms with his fellow-men?' With coarse good humour, he went on to answer his own question: 'I suspect, my dear Sir, that there are two causes of what—using the mildest term—I call your indifference: your geographical location and your bad health. I am happier than you only because I am in good health and because you are not where I am. Why are you not here, my good friend, and why can I not at least provide you with some relief for your ailments, if I cannot cure them?' Jean-Jacques was not at all pleased by Tronchin's admonishments. He wanted to know why he was being brought to book in this way, who his informers were, and of what he was being accused.

> I congratulate you with all my heart [he concluded] on your feeling of well-being, your health and your friends; the fact that I can boast no such blessings is a misfortune rather than a crime. Such as I am, I do not complain either about my lot, or about my abode. I am the friend of the human race and men can be found everywhere. The friend of truth also finds no lack of people who wish him ill . . . and I do not have to look very far afield for them. . . . I prefer to live among the French rather than go off to Geneva in search of them. In a place where intellectual brilliance is so loudly applauded, it is unlikely that Jean-Jacques would be appreciated, and even if he were, he would hardly have cause to boast of it.

Tronchin, as tactless as before, passed Jean-Jacques' letter on to Voltaire, who wrote in the margin: 'Extreme insolence is a form of extreme stupidity, and nothing is more stupid than for a man like Jean-Jacques to say: the human race and I.' This was not quite what Jean-Jacques had said, although it was true that he was the sort of man to consider himself on an equal footing with the entire human race. Voltaire was like that, too, of course. Each of them laid some claim to being the only person who knew how to save humanity. Tronchin and Jean-Jacques exchanged a few more letters which, under the pretence of frankness, became increasingly tart. Tronchin chided Jean-Jacques for having quarrelled with Diderot, and recommended humility and tolerance. Forced back within himself, Jean-Jacques denounced private friendships as being harmful to humanity. Tronchin had the last word. He was a Genevan too, and a skilled and stubborn dialectician. Adopting Jean-Jacques' own system, he brushed aside all compliments. This Jean-Jacques found intolerable, because he was being beaten with his own weapons. The correspondence between the two men, and their friendship, came to an end for ever with this exchange of acerbities.

Yet that same spring, a new acquaintance restored his confidence and pride. The Maréchal de Luxembourg came in person to see him in his humble home at Montmorency. His vanity, which Mme de Warens had developed in the days when he 'played the toady', could not withstand this temptation, and he fell back into the posturings that he always adopted with people of high rank.

His house was in danger of collapsing, and the floor had begun to cave in; repairs were urgently needed. The Maréchal and his wife suggested that Thérèse and he should come and live in the Petit Château while the work was in progress. After some fuss, and an insufferable piece of proud bargaining, he finally accepted:

Having never consented to live with anyone but my friends [he wrote to the Maréchal], I speak but one language, the language of friendship, of intimacy. I am aware to what extent, given the difference between my position and yours, this language will have to be modified; I know that my respect for your person does not dispense me from that respect which is owing to your rank; but I am even more certain that when poverty demeans itself it quickly becomes contemptible; I know that it also has its dignity which the love of virtue forces it to preserve. I am therefore in a constant state of doubt about showing a lack of respect to you or to myself, about being too familiar or too cringing. . . .

And he added the following lines, about which it is difficult to decide whether they are more shocking through their arrogance or their obsequiousness:

11

I will say to myself every day of my life: Remember that if the Maréchal de Luxembourg honoured you with a visit and came and sat on your straw-bottomed chair, among your broken pots and pans, it was not for the sake of your name or your fortune, but because of that reputation for uprightness, slight though it may be, that you have acquired; take care that he never has to blush for the honour he did you. For your part, Monsieur le Maréchal, say to yourself from time to time, I beg of you: on the estate I inherited from my forebears there is a solitary man who is concerned with my actions, who is moved by the reports of my beneficence, who adds the blessing of his heart to those uttered by the unfortunate creatures to whom I give comfort, and who honours me not because I am great, but because I am good.

Poor man! He never managed to find the right tone. Benefactors and beneficiary continued for months to congratulate each other in equally embarrassed terms, on 'the very fine thing' their friendship was. Jean-Jacques and Thérèse took up their abode in the Petit Château on 6th May and stayed there until July, by which time the 'hut' at Montlouis had been repaired. Jean-Jacques wrote to the Maréchal: 'I am fully aware that my stay here, which has but little significance for you, is of the utmost importance to me. I know that, had I only spent one night here, the public, nay posterity, would call upon me to account for that one night. . . .' How naïve he was! For a disciple of nature, he was anything but natural. The Maréchal and his wife agreed to all his 'whims'. They realised that he was difficult to live with, and it was clearly understood that Jean-Jacques would on no account 'sacrifice his seclusion'. He would only see the Maréchal and Mme de Luxembourg from time to time when it suited him, and not in the presence of others, and would never mix with 'the host of people by whom, because of their rank, they were necessarily surrounded'. We know from the *Confessions* that, as things turned out, the moody hermit was somewhat mollified. On occasions, he even dined with 'a few noble lords', but he considered that his dignity was not compromised, since the place of honour was reserved for him next to Mme de Luxembourg, who 'embraced him ten times a day'. He was not absolutely at ease, but he was happy, having at last won recognition and respect. He had clumsy outbursts of affection. He read *Julie* aloud to his hosts and made another copy of the novel, adding in their honour a chapter entitled 'The

Amorous Adventures of Lord Bomston.' . . . 'I have always been everything or nothing,' he writes, 'before long I was everything, and, finding myself made much of and spoiled by people of such importance, I overstepped the limits and conceived for them feelings of friendship which are only permissible between equals.' He agreed on occasions to go to Paris and sup and spend the night at the Hôtel du Luxembourg, but only on condition that he entered the place by way of the garden; he was thus able to keep his word about never again setting foot in the streets of the city. If he happened to dine at the Château in the morning, he would boast that he found more pleasure in supping in the evening with Thérèse, good-natured Pillau, the mason, or with M. Mathas. He deceived himself with this feeble sophistry. He was enjoying his own personality, as it was, and felt so strong and so fully justified in the course he had adopted and in what he had chosen to be, that, as far as the details of day to day living were concerned, it never occurred to him that he might have behaved differently. He was sure that society was adapting itself to him and not he to it. He looked upon himself as a plain man who never stood on ceremony; it was other people who were ceremonious, and who went out of their way to comply with him. Never before had anyone been himself with such intensity. He was therefore convinced of his genuineness. However, he was an easy target for the jibes of his old friends. The professor of virtue cut a rather comic figure as he sat adoringly at the feet of Mme la Maréchale, who had now settled down to a respectable life, but—according to a song written not so long before—had been 'everybody's mistress in turn'.

Yet it must be pointed out that his relations with other people impinged hardly at all on the course of his inner life. Never had he pursued a more grandiose dream, a more splendid illusion. Never had he worked so hard, if work is the right term to use.

An opportunity had occurred to achieve security and dispel the fear of poverty. Margency and Malesherbes had asked him to write for the *Journal des Savants*. This would have involved barely one week's work a month, his task being to produce two short articles for 'a fee of eight hundred *livres*'. He refused, and in the *Confessions* he gives various reasons for doing so. Even at this time, he claims, 'he had decided to abandon literature altogether, and above all the profession of writer,' being resolved to break off all those false relationships which the profession entailed. This may well have been the case. But the truth is that he could only work in his own time; for him, literature had never been, and could never be, a profession.

> I knew [he writes—and on this point we can believe him] that my talent consisted entirely in a certain lively enthusiasm for the subjects I had to treat, and that only the love of the great, the true and the beautiful could stimulate my genius. The subjects of the majority of books from which I would have had to compile extracts, and the books themselves, would have meant nothing to me. My indifference to their contents would have immobilised my pen and deadened my mind. People imagined that I could write professionally, like all other men of letters, whereas I have never been able to write except when moved by passion.

This was the root of the whole matter. Writing for him could not be the sort of light-hearted amusement or diversion or idle tittle-tattle which is, as often as not, the basic activity of the republic of letters. Still less was he capable of writing about the ideas of others. Why should he compile extracts? It was as if he had been asked to write items of gossip. He did not give a rap for security! His one purpose in writing was to say what he had to say. He wrote as Pascal had written. He wrote as a believer believes, and nothing could have turned his thoughts away from the 'passion' which now had him in its grip.

He would go for walks in the woods at Montmorency and day-dream in the open air. His thoughts could be as lofty as the heavens. They grew and spread like the trees around him. . . . His dreams were for himself, and for all men. He dreamed of their happiness. He felt himself to be free, good and happy—he alone. There was only one true man in the whole world and it was he, because he had become once more 'the man of nature'. All men lied and they were slaves, wicked and wretched because society lied, because each one of them, lost within society, debased within society, had become nothing more than 'man made by man'. His own life had led him to define this most supremely important of all problems: 'How can man be remade? How can his lost freedom and happiness be restored?' And his own life perhaps would provide him with the means of solving it, if it were true that he had solved it as far as he himself was concerned. He was going to write a book to end all books.

There could be no more vital problem than education, on which he had already meditated and written. Had he himself not been a tutor? He recalled the memoir he had composed, twenty years before, for M. de Mably. However, he had written it (all to no purpose, as it happened) only in order to keep his job and give proof of his ability. He was young at the time and inexperienced. Later, at intervals throughout his life, he had been questioned by M. Dupin, Mme d'Epinay, and Mme de Créqui as to the best way of bringing up their children, and not so very long before, Mme de Chenonceaux, 'a mother with a gift for reflection', who—in view of her husband's escapades—was afraid of what her son might one day become, had asked his advice. The very anxiety expressed by these women had given him some inkling of the importance of the problem. He had, in reply, merely proferred brief and vague advice appropriate to each situation. To be treated properly, however, the question should be examined independently of individual circum-stances. . . . That was what he now proposed to do. He had not been very successful as a tutor, because both he and his pupil were entangled in the conventions of the century and unable to break free from them. He had done only what he could, what was 'feasible' in the circumstances. That had been a cowardly approach, unworthy of the problem. What he ought to do was imagine an ideal case, an experiment in the absolute, and express the truth without being influenced by preconceived ideas or scruples of any kind. He foresaw what the objections would be. He would perhaps be accused of having written not so much a 'Treatise on Education as the day-dreams of a visionary'. He brushed this objection aside: he would base his work not on other people's ideas but on his own. All he had to do was to express exactly what was in his mind, and it was all the more necessary to be sincere since the ideas in question were of a kind 'which determines the happiness or unhappiness of the human race'. Society and the world at large would have to make what they could of his pronouncements.

He wrote the following lines to be included in the preface of his future work:

I am constantly being enjoined to suggest only what is feasible. This is tantamount to saying: suggest doing what is already being done, or at least suggest a satisfactory course which can be combined with the existing evil. Such a project is, in some connections, much more illusory than my own for, in the combination of good and evil, the good is corrupted and the evil is not cured. . . . Fathers and mothers, the possible is what you have the will to achieve. Am I to be answerable for your determination?

No, he would disregard all external considerations. 'For me it is enough,' he declared, 'that wherever men are born they should be made into the kind of men that I propose and that, having been fashioned according to my proposals, they should be the best men possible, both for themselves and for others.' The world of imaginings was the real world. To give a glimpse of it to an aberrant society could not be a useless task. His book would be a kind of novel which would tell the story of the state and education of man.

In order to bring up a son, 'in order to fashion a man, one should oneself be either a father or more than a man', he declared, and, in fact, what he ought to have described, had he had the courage to do so, was a father's account of his education of his son. He was inhibited by his memories and his remorse, because he was beginning to repent his past actions. Right at the beginning of the book are one or two curious sentences, which were really written with his life's blood, and are a sort of half-confidence that no one could understand:

> When a father begets and feeds his children [he wrote], he is only carrying out a third of his task. He owes it to the human race to create men; he owes it to society to create sociable human beings, and to the State to create citizens. Every man who is capable of paying this triple debt and who fails to do so, is guilty, and perhaps all the more guilty when he only half pays it. He who is incapable of fulfilling his obligations as a father has no right to become one. Neither poverty, nor the claims of work, nor the fear of what the public may think can relieve him of the duty of feeding his children and bringing them up himself. Readers, you may believe me when I warn any man of feeling who fails in such sacred duties that he will long shed bitter tears for the omission, and will never be consoled.[1]

[1] The above lines are all the more remarkable in that Jean-Jacques, prompted once again either by shame or remorse, substituted them for an entirely different passage about the smile of the child and maternal love. Cf. the Favre manuscript of *Emile*, *Annales Jean-Jacques Rousseau*, VIII, p. 275.

Such were the chidings of his conscience. It was inevitable that in undertaking to write about this vast subject he should be brought face to face with himself. But as soon as it happened, he quickly looked away again and, being unable to bring himself to write the story of a father and son, he decided to describe the experiences of an ideal tutor who takes on the task of bringing up a child, Emile, from birth until his marriage at the age of twenty-five. The tutor he describes is a man without peer, a 'sublime soul', 'the like of whom is not to be found'. He has within him all wisdom. Emile is an average child with an 'ordinary mind'. His only peculiarity is that he is an 'orphan', a circumstance which is intended to give clarity and emphasis to the experiment. 'It is not important that he should have a father and a mother,' Jean-Jacques naïvely declared. 'Having assumed their obligations, I can claim all their rights. He should honour his parents but he owes obedience only to me. That is the first, indeed the only, condition I stipulate.' He thus recovered in imagination all those rights which he had neglected or forfeited in real life. Such were the strange effects of the workings of his thought and of his feelings of remorse. Just as *La Nouvelle Héloïse* described the lover he might have been, given a little more luck, so *Emile* was to describe the splendid father he failed to become, and all children as yet unborn would be happier because of him.

He continued to day-dream and to be entirely absorbed in himself. Convinced of his own goodness, he was writing 'in order to be loved by the good, and hated by the wicked'. His heart was, as ever, his sole source of inspiration, and led him, as ever, to the rejection of society as being one vast system of debasement. It forced children, from their very earliest years, and against their natural instincts, to accept its authority and schooled them in its own artificiality and falsehood. It reared them for its own purpose, and original goodness was lost. The whole existing system of education sought to maintain the prejudices connected with social inequality. Schools and convents completed the process of corruption begun in the home. Only too well could he remember the time he had spent in wealthy households, and the number of false children he had met there—little prodigies all of them, 'little French gentlemen', gilded puppets, exquisitely dressed and charmingly loquacious who were being trained, through vanity, to become masters as elegant and shallow as they were insensitive and harsh.

Man appropriates everything [he wrote in one of the first drafts of his book[1]], but what he strives most eagerly to appropriate is man himself. . . . Naturally each individual considers only himself, and social man must always be concerned with others. Such a man is therefore no longer natural man; he is man tamed and domesticated, the kind of man other men have trained for their own purposes. . . . We have reached a point at which we are so bound, oppressed and overwhelmed by social institutions, so completely in the hands of others from the very moment of our birth, that the only freedom left to us is freedom of thought; thought itself is the slave of public opinion; even if it were possible for a man to preserve his original ways of seeing and feeling in the midst of so many prejudices, it would not be safe for him to reveal himself as he really is; prudence would oblige him to be false so that he should not be treated as a madman, to say the very least. . . . Everything we do seems to relate to others at the same time as it relates to ourselves. . . . Our nature is not exactly dual but compound; at times we are swept away by passion and repressed by law, at other times urged on by public opinion and held back by nature; we do not exist properly either for ourselves or for others; we combine the vices of society with the abuses of the natural state, the prejudices of class with the errors of reason; we are peasants, bourgeois, kings, noblemen, commoners; we are neither men nor citizens.

He worked for over three years, building up his ideal portrait of natural man. At the outset, his polemical bias gives an overtone of arrogance to his style; his paragraphs often end with aggressive and provocative remarks. He nags away relentlessly and bad-temperedly. 'Social man is born, lives and dies in slavery; at birth, he is wrapped in swaddling-clothes; when he dies he is wrapped in a shroud; as long as he retains his human shape, he is the prisoner of social institutions.' His pupil is to be rich; in this way 'we shall at least be sure of having made one man more, whereas a poor man can become a man of his own accord'. His pupil is to be sturdy and healthy; for Jean-Jacques 'is incapable of teaching someone to live whose only thought is how to keep from dying'. His pupil is to be brought up in the

[1] Cf. the Favre manuscript of *Emile*, *Annales Jean-Jacques Rousseau*, VIII, p. 271 et seq. The passage was not retained in the final version.

country and not in a town, because 'man's breath is fatal to his fellow-men: this is as true in the figurative sense as it is in the literal'. . . . It is not long however before he is carried away by the grandeur of his theme. He reflects on the tremendous progress that a child, a man, can make if he takes himself as his starting point: 'We are ignorant of the potentialities of our nature; not one amongst us has measured the distance that can separate man from man. Is there any man so base that he has never been fired by this idea, and does not sometimes say to himself, in his pride: how many have I already outstripped! how many more I may yet overtake! Why should my equal go further than myself?' And, from then onwards, his book develops like an epic poem, instinct with warm human feeling:

> Man, be humane, for that is your first duty: be humane towards your fellows of all conditions and all ages. . . . Love little children. . . . Why should you want to prevent these innocent little creatures from enjoying the brief period which will so soon elude them, the precious blessing which they can never misuse? Why should you want to fill the first years of their lives with bitterness and pain when they will be gone so soon and can never return either for them or for you? Fathers, do you know at what moment death will summon away your children? Do not store up sorrow for yourself by depriving them of the few hours that nature grants them; as soon as they become aware of the pleasure of being, see to it that they enjoy it: see to it that, whenever God calls them, they do not die without having enjoyed being alive.

Jean-Jacques, the self-taught man, who had grown up unhampered by any school discipline and who retained nothing but happy memories of his childhood, could not possibly conceive of education as the exercise of discipline and constraint. No, a child growing up into a man possesses a potentiality of happiness, and wicked as well as stupid is the teacher who, in his vanity, tries to make a 'doctor' of his pupil, and, in treating him even at this early age as if he were a man, like himself, destroys both his existing and his potential happiness. Man's happiness is never anything more than the result of a perfect balance between his abilities and his duties. This relationship is never more perfect than in childhood. Education must only consist in maintaining this balance and in arranging everything in the life of the child so carefully that his desires are only awakened as his abilities increase. Such a plan calls for neither strictness, nor leniency. The proper education of a man consists simply in introducing him gently, by means of his own experience and almost without his realising it, into the natural and inevitable order of things. Jean-Jacques hits upon the admirable formula: 'Let us allow childhood to ripen within the child.' Then, his respect for the diversity of human nature and a deep sense of the particular genius of each child led him to invent those methods which have since been referred to as active methods, but which he himself, curiously enough, called on the contrary the inactive method.[1] Emile grows up, learning at each point only what is 'useful at his age', and shielded as far as possible by his tutor from the customs, vices and prejudices of society. The pure, free and joyful forces within him come to maturity. He perhaps knows less than other children of his age, but he has a different and more profound kind of knowledge.

> Always remember [said Jean-Jacques], that the guiding spirit of my educational system is not to teach the child many things but never to leave in his brain anything except right and clear ideas. Even if he knew nothing, I would not worry, provided he had no wrong ideas. . . . Emile has little knowledge but what he has is truly his own, and what he knows thoroughly: among the small number of things he does know well, the most important of all is that there are many things he does not know but that he may know one day, many more that others know, and that he will never know, and an infinite number that no man will ever know.

Emile will become everything he is capable of being according to the laws of his own being. Such was the man Jean-Jacques wanted to create. It was foreseeable that Emile would not be very different from the man he himself had become. He is proud not so much of his learning as of a kind of inner plenitude. He is suspicious of knowledge: *Scientia inflat*. Social competition means nothing to him: the problem is not how to outstrip others but how to advance at one's own pace, in one's own way. To educate a man is to 'prepare the reign of his freedom'.

It is at this point that his solitary thoughts explode with a

---

[1] They are called active methods by present-day educationalists who are concerned with bringing the particular genius of the child into play. Rousseau uses the term 'inactive' because, looking at the situation from the tutor's point of view, he urges him to avoid any kind of tactless interference.

strange new force. He was conscious that he was writing for the future, and that 'the century of revolutions' was at hand. His own life had made him realise that a man's worth cannot be measured by comparison with others, according to their respective stations in life or the privileges they enjoy. Each man's worth is an absolute. 'Each man must live,' he exclaims, and by this he means that he must be able to ensure his livelihood by the exercise of his particular genius and his virtues. This was tantamount to denouncing the society and the times in which he lived, and providing the means of self-knowledge and self-justification for a new kind of man.

With marvellous vehemence he wrote:

> If there exists somewhere in the world some wretched state wherein each individual can only live by doing wrong, and citizens become rogues from sheer necessity, it is not the wrong-doer who should be hanged, but the man who forces him into wrong-doing.
>
> As soon as Emile has discovered what life is like, my chief concern will be to teach him how to preserve life. Up till now, I have not drawn any distinction between class, rank and wealth and will not subsequently do so to any great extent, because man is the same in all classes; since the rich man has no bigger stomach than the poor man and is no better able to digest his food, since the master's arms are no longer or stronger than his slave's, since the great ones of the Earth are in fact no greater than ordinary people; and, lastly, since human needs are everywhere the same, the means of satisfying them ought to be equal everywhere. Adapt the education of man to man and not to what is alien to man. Do you not realise that, in striving to train a man purely for one particular station in life, you render him useless for any other and that, should fate so will it, you will only have succeeded in making him unhappy. . . .

There then follows a prophetic and threatening passage:

> You put your trust in the existing social order without reflecting that this same order is liable to be upset by inevitable revolutions, and that it is impossible for you to predict or prevent the particular revolution which may affect your children. The great become small, the rich become poor, monarchs become subjects; are the blows of fate so rare that you can count on them leaving you unscathed? We are approaching the time of crisis, the century of Revolutions. . . .

He adds in a footnote: 'I consider it impossible for the great monarchies of Europe to last much longer; they have achieved great brilliance and any State which is brilliant is on the brink of decline. I have more particular reasons for holding this view than that expressed in the above maxim. This, however, is not a suitable moment to state them and, in any case, everyone is only too clearly conscious of them.' He remains silent, ostentatiously silent. It is impossible for him to tell the whole truth. The whole truth cannot be told. He knows, however, that for the people who will soon be reading his work, his silence will be far more eloquent than any words. He knows how effective his threats, his appeal to the obvious facts, will be, and that they will only exacerbate the yeasty fermentation of that sense of honour which he feels everywhere around him and is the root cause of the 'crisis'. Not to tell the whole truth was, perhaps, a supremely clever move on his part. His reserves of resentment and anger, the passion which rumbled on beneath his words, corresponding, as they did, to the passionate feelings of all those men doomed to inarticulate silence, would, in the long run, shatter the world. Brevity is more effective than long-windedness. We are reminded of Saint-Just's remark: 'To govern one must be laconic.'

He was being carried away by his passion. This was too good an opportunity not to strike a blow at the rich. Obsessed with his vision of the just society which was to be, he could not resist enunciating its laws, and prescribing work for everyone. Emile was to learn a trade, a manual trade, because 'rich or poor, strong or weak, every idle citizen is a rogue'.

In their eagerness to reduce everything to order, critics have gone to considerable trouble during the past hundred and fifty years to discover some dialectical progression in Jean-Jacques' thought and to work it into a system that they can then approve of or condemn. To me he appears more naïve and simple and his strength lies in his very naïveté. The effort he makes to establish some sort of order in his discourse and his ideas is just another concession to contemporary taste and to the methods of his 'former friends', the *philosophes*. He himself, however, often warns us that he is no great philosopher and that all he claims to be doing is exhibiting in the clearest possible light those obvious truths of the heart that have been revealed to him.

Following, as always, my own method [he writes], I do not infer
these rules from the principles of some lofty philosophy; on the
contrary, I find them in my own heart, where nature has traced
them in characters that cannot be obliterated. I have only to
consult my heart about what I want to do; all that I feel to be
good is good, all that I feel to be evil is evil; conscience is the best
of all casuists and it is only when we bargain with it that we have
recourse to subtleties of reasoning.

He never expresses anything except his own being. He is
Emile's tutor, and he is Emile too. This dualism was to become
one of his characteristic modes of thought. A man who is no
longer young, and who has not had a happy life, fondly teaches
a young man that happiness in which he himself continues to
believe so ardently and, in so doing, he makes it possible for
himself to start afresh. Jean-Jacques was a man of desire, not a
man of truth and his desire is the substance of his teaching. He
justifies himself and approves of himself for being what he is.
What he calls truth is simply the exigency and expectation of his
being.

If philosophy is the determination to recognise the truth of the
world as it exists, independently of men, and however bad that
truth may be, then he is most certainly far from being a
philosopher. He cannot help relating everything to man, in
fact, to himself. 'What is there so ridiculous about believing
that everything is made for me, if I am the only being capable
of relating everything to himself?' Thinking once more of his
former friends, and of Diderot, he writes:

Shun those who, while making a pretence of explaining nature,
sow in the hearts of men disheartening doctrines, whose obvious
scepticism is a hundred times more affirmative and more dogmatic than the resolute tone of their opponents. Under the
arrogant pretext that they alone are enlightened, genuine and
honest, they haughtily force their peremptory decisions upon
us, and present as the true principles of nature what are no more
than the unintelligible systems which they have created in their
imaginations. Moreover, by overthrowing, destroying and
trampling underfoot all that men respect, they deprive the afflic-
ted of the one consolation remaining to them in their wretchedness, and remove the only check on the passions of the rich and
powerful; they root out from men's hearts remorse for crimes
committed as well as the hope of virtue, and yet still boast that

they are the benefactors of the human race. They say that the truth is never harmful to man; I am as convinced of this as they are and, in my view, it is a major proof of the fact that what they are teaching is not the truth.

No doubt the deepest gulf which divides thinking men is that some believe in happiness while others believe in truth. Jean-Jacques believed in happiness. For him, truth could only be comforting and cheerful. Man, and Jean-Jacques himself, must be the 'King of creation', or at least 'the King of the earth'. We must not allow ourselves to be deceived by the lengthy dialectical discussions in his profession of faith. He knew in advance what conclusion he was to arrive at. The truth is not something to be discovered, or invented. He believed that it had always been inscribed in the hearts of men. He remembered two priests he had known in childhood, the Abbé Gaime of Turin, and the Abbé Gâtier of Annecy. Both had been sufficiently buffeted by their passions and their experience of life for Catholic dogmatism to be tempered in them by some degree of freedom. They were the models for the character of *le Vicaire savoyard* whom he used as a mouthpiece for his own faith. Although usually so anxious to prove that he is different, on this occasion he makes no claim to being out of the ordinary and is ready to admit the commonplace nature of his thoughts and feelings. He wants to be no more than 'a man, simple and true'. 'We can be men,' he declared emphatically, 'without being scholars.' Disregarding subtle arguments and vain complications, he believed in God and in the immortality of the soul; he believed that the good would be rewarded and reunited with God. But in that supremely refined and knowledgeable century, greatness and originality (and Jean-Jacques must certainly have sensed this) lay in accepting the commonplace, in being deeply aware of the greatness of the ordinary human soul and in rediscovering the full force of man's eternal yearning. Before Rousseau, natural religion, for the majority of its theorists, had never been anything but a kind of soft, weak, degenerate form of Christian faith. Now, for the first time, it was sufficiently real and deeply enough felt to be perhaps capable one day of restoring spirit and vitality to the faith of Christians. Admittedly, it was common enough to believe, and to affirm, that God existed. But generally accepted thoughts are not the same thing in the minds of the 'haves' as in the minds of the 'have-nots'. For many people, the existence of God is simply a guarantee of social stability and of their own tranquillity. There are others for whom it can be a promise that a certain restless yearning for greatness and purity will remain with us until the end of time.

He did not make any great discoveries; he looked within himself rather than in books, and what he found was that man can be defined as a legitimate love of self (Jean-Jacques was incapable of self-condemnation), enlightened by conscience. Society leads man astray and destroys him; he compares himself with others and self-love degenerates into self-conceit, vanity or pride. 'Self-love, which concerns us, and us alone, is satisfied when our true needs have been fulfilled; self-conceit, on the other hand, which makes comparisons, never is, and never can be, satisfied because, in so doing, it requires that others should prefer us to themselves, which is an impossibility.' But the man who protects himself against society and public opinion preserves his natural state and remains pure and in harmony with God. Diderot had written: 'Only the wicked man is solitary.' The sentence should run: 'Only the good man is solitary.' Man's solitude must be safeguarded, since it allows him to live in the sight of God.

In a passage which he subsequently discarded[1] Jean-Jacques wrote: 'I am convinced that one thing which cramps our souls and helps to make us petty and vicious is that we do not accomplish the important actions of our lives with sufficient solemnity. By a solemn action, I do not mean that which is performed ceremoniously in full view of men, but that which takes place in the infinitely more august presence of the Creator. God must be our witness.' In this case, man feels an admirable sensation of plenitude, an unconquerable pride, and the security and happiness for which God brought him into the world. And like Jean-Jacques himself, he can then murmur quietly:

O conscience, conscience, divine instinct, immortal and celestial voice, the sure guide of a limited and ignorant being who is yet intelligent and free, infallible judge of good and evil who makest man like God, it is thou who ensurest the excellence of his nature, and the morality of his actions; but for thee, I feel nothing

[1] Cf. the Favre manuscript, *Annales Jean-Jacques Rousseau*, VIII, p. 276.

within me to raise me above the level of the beasts, but the sad privilege of drifting from error to error at the promptings of an unregulated understanding and an unprincipled faculty of reasoning.

In the first version Jean-Jacques had written: 'which makes man like the Gods', and this perhaps gave a clear revelation of the purely human pride by which he was inspired. There is no justification for the tendency among modernist Catholic critics, in their eagerness to find support for their views, to transform Jean-Jacques into a sort of Father of the Church. Admittedly, he had a deeply religious nature, but he was the only priest of his religion and he wrote his own Gospel. He allowed neither men nor books to come between himself and God. He alone, through the power bestowed on him by his conscience, was to point the new way to salvation and happiness. If they fully understood his teachings, his followers could not fail to achieve happiness. A note scribbled in the margin of one of his manuscripts enlightens us both as to the plan he intended to follow, and the convictions by which he was inspired. What he wrote was:[1]

> The age of nature, twelve years
> The age of reason, fifteen years
> The age of energy, twenty years
> The age of wisdom, twenty-five years

and below, after leaving a space,

> The age of happiness—the rest of life.

One is reminded of the constitution that Sismondi drafted when he was still a schoolboy: Article I: All Frenchmen will be virtuous. Article II: All Frenchmen will be happy. Jean-Jacques found within himself all he needed to create the world afresh and refashion mankind. Had he been asked to furnish evidence, he would have replied by striking his chest and saying: 'Look at me!' He was convinced that his own life was a constantly renewed proof of the truth of his thoughts. He had excluded from it all artificial needs. He lived according to his own law; it was as if, for him, each moment of life was a new beginning. Society had no hold over him; it was not as difficult as all that to despise and destroy society. Thus, through his

[1] Cf. Favre manuscript, p. 255.

example, the wretched could rediscover freedom, happiness and dignity.

He was a man who walked alone. Between the two parties—since there were two, both equally fanatical and equally misguided, the theologians and the *philosophes*, those who relied on inspiration and those who relied on reason—he formed his own, one-man party. Although he did not always succeed in avoiding terminological contradictions, he knew his own mind and, in the second part of his *Profession de Foi*, he heaped blame and scorn on both parties alike. He turned himself into a *philosophe* again in order to denounce the revelation, with the help of the arguments already used by the *Encyclopédistes* and by Voltaire, and he even went so far as to declare that there was nothing 'more undeniable than the principles of reason'. Yet, immediately afterwards, he showed his opposition to the *philosophes* by confessing that 'the majesty of the Scriptures filled him with amazement', and 'the saintly character of the Gospels moved him', and by declaring: 'Yes, if Socrates lived and died like a sage, then Jesus lived and died like a God.' It is true that he then went on to conclude: 'Even so, the Gospels are full of unbelievable things, things contrary to reason, which no sensible man can conceive of or accept.' However, in spite of these ambiguities, in the concluding pages, he suggested what his final choice was. In order to balance, as it were, the declamatory attack on the *philosophes* that I have already quoted: 'Shun those who, while making a pretence of explaining nature . . . etc.,' he composed another paragraph: 'Shun the pious, nothing is more dangerous than their society . . . ', but in the end he cut it out. As he said in a letter to the Marquise de Créqui, all things considered, if he had to choose, he would prefer 'to be a believer rather than a *philosophe*'. After so many arguments, he had simply come back to what he had learned twenty years before from M. de Chaville's *Traité du vrai mérite*: 'There is no upright man without religion.' He could not stand materialists who were, he said, 'insincere sophists, more willing to grant feeling to stones than to credit man with a soul'.

When the *Vicaire savoyard* gave his final advice to Emile, it was as if Jean-Jacques were talking to himself:

Proud philosophy leads to free-thinking, just as blind piety leads to fanaticism. Avoid both extremes: keep steadfastly to the path

27

of truth, to what, in the simplicity of your heart, seems to you to be the truth, without ever letting yourself be deflected from it by vanity or weakness. Have the courage to profess your belief in God when you are with philosophers; have the courage to preach humanity to the intolerant. You may be alone in adopting this course, but you will be bearing witness in your own person. It matters little whether others love you or hate you, read your writings or despise them. Proclaim the truth and do that which is right; what is important is to carry out our duties on this earth, and by forgetting ourselves we work for our own good. Private interests deceive us, my child: only in seeking what is right are we never deceived. Amen.

'One must be oneself,' was a phrase he often repeated during the last years of his life. He himself had now achieved this. Through years of meditation and introspection he had evolved a number of ideas that he would never thereafter abandon; he was to behave at one and the same time with utter humility and overweening pride. Henceforth, he was pure conscience; he was like God, if not quite God himself, and addressed himself to God on a footing of equality. 'No, God of my soul,' he exclaimed, 'I shall never reproach thee with having made it in thine image so that I might be free, good and happy, like thee.' The end had been achieved: he was free, good and happy like God. Death no longer held any terror for him. To quote again from the words he put into the mouth of the *Vicaire savoyard*: 'I long for that moment when, relieved of the hindrance of the body, I shall be wholly and consistently myself and, to be happy, shall need nothing but my own being.' He was quite confident of not being held up at the Pul-Serrho, the bridge which, according to the Persians, leads into Paradise. He had given no one any cause to tug at his coat, or to denounce him when he came to cross the fearful bridge. Life after death, his life in God, would simply be a continuation of the upright life he was leading, now that he had thrown off all his shackles and was recognised for what he was.

His naïveté lay precisely in imagining that he could behave in this way, like a God among men.

CHAPTER TWO

The Difficult Art of Sincerity (1759–1761)

The posturings of the plebeian—Jean-Jacques' seal: *vitam impendere vero*—The difficult art of sincerity—He plans his final retirement—*Le Contrat Social*—Portrait by Houël—Letter to Voltaire—Publication of *La Nouvelle Héloïse*—Its success—Jean-Jacques becomes a spiritual director—He believes he is going to die and entrusts Thérèse to the care of the Luxembourgs. He tells Mme de Luxembourg the story of his five children.

WE CAN ALWAYS SUMMON up just that amount of pride which is needed to compensate for our latest misfortunes, and it is this which enables us to survive. Jean-Jacques now reached a degree of pride that he had never before attained. He had 'drunk the waters of forgetfulness'. All his past mistakes had been wiped out, and he no longer had anything to hide. Henceforth, he need not even be ashamed of allowing Thérèse to appear, since she was clearly no more than his housekeeper. He had not wanted to 'expose her to the risks of pregnancy', and gradually, in the course of some obscure disagreement the details of which were known only to themselves, they fell out of love with each other. The misery he had endured through his love for Sophie, the insults he had suffered at the hands of Grimm, Mme d'Epinay and Diderot, were now simply an excuse to wax sentimental over his own virtuousness. He had put himself in the position of a man who is just beginning to live. He enjoyed his own being. During these three extraordinarily fruitful years, even his body seems to have left him in peace. He could urinate more freely, had given up taking medicine of any kind, bore his disability with patience whenever it made itself felt, but was firmly determined to enjoy good health the instant he ceased to be in pain. In the spring of 1760, he was almost ashamed of his plumpness. He wrote to Mme de Verdelin: 'Since I became hard-hearted and no longer have any affection for anyone and call everybody my friend, I have grown as fat as a pig.'

No doubt we can sense in this remark, addressed, incidentally, to a woman friend, a twinge of regret for the time when love welled up in his heart as naturally as water gushes from a spring. Yet he was not insincere. Never again would he love as he had loved in the past: easily offended and always wary, he would lend himself to others, without ever giving himself completely, and would stand guard over every aspect of his personality like a watchful gamekeeper. No one would ever get the better of him again; no one would be allowed to penetrate to his soul. His high-born friends, his summer neighbours, were worthy people. Their admiration for him made them patient, while he behaved towards them with a sort of clumsy graciousness. Yet something in the over-zealous attentions they paid each other points to the fact that neither he nor they were absolutely sincere.

None of his friendships followed an easy course. Mme de Verdelin confided all her troubles to him, and told of her love for M. de Margency who was taking to religion and moving away from her. She would have liked 'to be able to confess that she felt as much affection for the man in whom he was kind enough to show an interest', her elderly husband, M. de Verdelin, but 'she was quite powerless to do so'. At least she was certain that she was not the 'monster' she appeared to him to be. . . . On occasions she would write one letter after another to which Jean-Jacques failed to reply. He eventually would answer, but only to protest that he was being made to have a guilty conscience: 'The less you reproach me, the more I reproach myself.' Why did everyone force him to be dissatisfied with himself. . . ? Mme de Créqui was a widow. She was ruining herself in order to help her daughter and her son, a captain in the Dragoons. She was pious, but at the same time blessed with sound common-sense. She had formed a fairly accurate opinion of her century, in which, she declared, women were educated for the harem, while at the same time they were criticised for taking only too readily to the vocation for which they had been intended. She was not put off by Jean-Jacques' bouts of ill-humour, and he was perhaps most natural in the letters he wrote to her. With the Maréchal and Madame de Luxembourg, whose rank impressed him, he indulged in a lavish exchange of absurd compliments. Politeness and affectation were so great on either side that in the end they almost led to misunderstandings and, on one occasion, excessive courtesy nearly caused a quarrel.

With all these people, the major question was whether his dignity allowed him to accept gifts or not. Mme de Créqui was given a good dressing-down for having ventured to send fattened chickens from Le Mans. Jean-Jacques ate the chickens, but she had to accept the fact that she must never do such a thing again. The Comtesse de Boufflers and the Prince de Conti dared to send him young partridges on two occasions. He ate the partridges since His Highness said in a covering letter that 'he had killed the birds with his own hand' and it was quite impossible to reject so flattering a kindness. However, he notified Mme de Boufflers that, 'on two occasions I have considered only what I owed to the Prince; it would only be right, on the third occasion, for me to consider what I owe to myself'. Whereupon he launched into the following sermon, about which it is again difficult to say whether it shows more insolence than servility:

> I am indeed touched by the tokens of respect and kindness with which His Highness has honoured me, who am the last person to expect such attentions. I can respect merit even in Princes and all the more so, since merit, in them, has to be greater than in other men. All that I have seen of him gratifies my heart, except his title; even so, he appeals to me as a person more than I am repelled by his rank. But, Madame, in spite of that, I shall no longer go against my principles, even for him. It is perhaps partly to them that I owe the honour he has done me; this is a further reason why I should always hold them dear. If my thoughts were as other men's, would he have deigned to come and see me? As it is, I prefer his conversation to his gifts. These gifts are only

gifts of game, I agree; but what difference does this make? It only makes them more precious and me more conscious of the obligation imposed upon me to accept them. In my view, we cannot with impunity receive any gift whatsoever. Once one thing has been accepted, it is soon impossible to refuse anything. The habit of acceptance once established, the receiver begins to beg, and once he has stooped to that, it is not long before he is doing everything necessary to get what he wants. In my opinion, this progression is inevitable. But, Madame, in no circumstances would I be willing to go so far.

And all that for a few partridges!

It must be admitted that the givers were amply rewarded by such letters. Who would not have been prepared to present Jean-Jacques with a whole wild boar to enjoy the extraordinary spectacle of such stupidity in a genius? Only the Maréchal de Luxembourg was entitled to bestow whatever gifts he wished. Jean-Jacques would have been ashamed to refuse anything coming from him. 'But,' he explained to Mme de Boufflers, 'I am quite sure that he is too fond of me to exploit his claims on my heart, and to sully the purity of my affection for him. My relationship with the Maréchal de Luxembourg is a thing apart. I belong to him, Madame, he can dispose of his possessions as he wishes.'

What a strange man he was! The reader suffers and feels ashamed for him. Any letter such as this was intended to be seen by at least three people, not to mention all the others to whom Mme de Boufflers would not fail to read it. He himself was careful to keep a copy. To parade one's dignity is not the same thing as being dignified, and in the long run destroys dignity altogether. It was this same vanity which made him devote almost the whole of the tenth book of the *Confessions* to celebrating his association with all the greatest names in France.

It was then, apparently, that he began to make use of his famous motto: *Vitam impendere vero*. He had it inscribed on a seal which he used in his correspondence. I can just imagine him, as a former engraver, evolving the pattern, finding the best lay-out for the words, deciding on the type and choosing the ornaments which would surround it and set it off. In the end he settled for the simplest design, a plain circle with the inscription inside. Perhaps he remembered the medals he had engraved at the age of fifteen 'to be used by himself and his fellow-apprentices as an order of chivalry', and the scolding his master gave him for 'making counterfeit money'. That had been the first occasion on which he had declared war on a world that was incapable of understanding that a child might found an order of chivalry. Now he was without either fellow-workers or friends. Life had taught him that he was the only knight of his own particular order. But no master would ever scold him again. He had rediscovered in his heart the laws governing just relationships between men. And he was conscious of the unity of his innermost life.

We can picture him trying out his seal in molten wax, and reading the gleaming inscription. It was a profession of faith by which he was committed. Somewhere in every man there is something inordinate, a streak of madness which he is at pains to hide through fear of public opinion or through politeness. He avoids those actions which would relate to these traits and might reveal his nature. But Jean-Jacques was not one to avoid such actions. He would no more think of avoiding them as a grown man than he had done as a child. In any case, what was he, if not an elderly child? His inordinate passion, his form of madness, was his honesty; there was no one else now capable of loving truth in the way he did. He was not content to be true. He had to proclaim the fact, and, by so doing, isolate himself and, come what may, set himself apart from the world and its lies. He was secure within his fortress, as the inscription was enclosed within the circle of the seal. The sea of lies raged around him. He was giving a universal warning: anyone approaching him had to be conscious of moving into a different world. Any fine lady and gentleman that he might write to would have to break the seal with polished nail and, before doing so, would read the words which would be tantamount to a punishment, and would arouse remorse. In a little upsurge of emotion, they would be reminded of their lost innocence and their essential duty, and they would know that one just man at least still remained on this earth. Jean-Jacques was on the verge of madness. His motto conveyed an ordinary enough assumption, but normal people turn into madmen. A normal idea can develop a kind of madness through some intensity of vision which is beyond ordinary human experience. The mind may break down in the glare of this vision.

33

As if the seal itself were not enough, from now on he even added the words, which had such an intense significance for him, as an epigraph to his letters, and sometimes to quite unimportant ones. To say that these words expressed an act of will is not enough; they conveyed the obsession which gripped his whole being.

There is no obsession more irritating than an obsession with sincerity, because in fact there is no quality which is more widely claimed. 'I alone am true, all the rest of you are lying,' he seemed to be saying. What kind of a man was this who assumed that it was his own special privilege to be what the common run of men prided themselves on being? He described —as if it called for an heroic effort of which he alone were capable—a way of life in which any individual believes he can achieve his dignity as a human being every day and without any special effort. Sincerity is the final refuge of every man when it has been proved that he is mistaken. Taking advantage of the widespread confusion between sincerity and truth, we claim at least that the mistake was made in all sincerity. Once our lies are exposed, as well as the advantages we derive from them and our complicity, we declare that we did not know. We flaunt our naïveté. We are sincere only when all has been consummated, after happiness has been achieved and wealth amassed. Ours is a sincerity born of self-justification, still stubbornly trying to save as much of the old lie as can be salvaged. Any genuinely true man offends us, and all the more so in proportion as we find falsehood more profitable. His utter nakedness seems to strip the clothes from our own backs. We struggle into our old clothes again and draw them around us. If his sincerity really springs from the heart, if he is committed to it whatever the risks entailed, if he declares his truth to be *the* truth, and sets up as an exponent of truth, then we are humiliated by a feeling of hypocrisy of which he forces us to become conscious and we label him a charlatan. This is what happened to Jean-Jacques. All those who were naïvely benefiting from the established order of things tried to overwhelm him with ridicule. But he aroused both astonishment and love in those who still hoped for truth.

Dear Jean-Jacques! You and I have now been living together for many years and the time has come for me to express an opinion about your obsession. Does this mean that I too must

34

sit in judgement on you? You had faith in posterity and in your last works you were constantly calling upon people to judge you. And judges have certainly not been lacking. Perhaps they should be called avengers rather. In your naïveté, you put weapons into their hands and, by your pride and self-assurance, even by your choice of motto, authorised them to exercise the greatest possible severity. Dear Jean-Jacques! I now feel that I know you fairly well. I have studied everything that happened to you during fifty years of your life with unrelenting attention. I too have totted up all your petty falsehoods; I found no major ones and I do not intend to gloat over the others.

When I decided to live in such close proximity with you that now I think I am better acquainted with your life than I am with my own (since my own life slips from me with every passing day, whereas I learn more and more about yours as I relive it day by day, with the help of thousands of documents which remind me of events in it that you yourself could not possibly remember) the reason was that I felt you to be a true man, and had a passionate desire to find out what exactly such a man was like. It was a strange undertaking to embark upon in this day and age. Love of truth is even less fashionable now than it was in your time. It has become suspect. You and your 'former friends', the *philosophes*, were unable to agree as to what truth was, but at least you were at one in believing truth, or the search for truth, to be useful. It never occurred to you or them that some base idea might be necessary for the salvation of the world. The progress of truth, however truth might be defined, seemed to you to lead inevitably to the enhancement of human dignity. All that has been altered. Today, people who profess to be thinkers will tell you that everything can be explained in terms of forces, and that what counts is to be more adept at lying than your opponent. What you called 'virtue' has become ridiculous. It seems that the age of the individual is over, and this is no doubt the most revolutionary occurrence that has taken place. Man's whole mode of being is changing. He no longer believes himself to be an indivisible unit, assured of his own peculiar destiny which he can modify by an exercise of will; this involved a tremendous effort, and the inscription on tombstones: *Hic iacet* ... was evidence of man's passionate desire to be himself, distinguishable among the millions of the dead. Now, each

35

THE DIFFICULT ART OF SINCERITY 1759–1761

individual seeks only to be a member of a herd; he is lost or saved along with the rest and leaves to others the responsibility for his vices or virtues, so that soon a communal grave will become the most fitting and legitimate charnel-house for such hordes. Slaves claim that they have adopted the manners and morals of the masters in order not to be exploited by them. Both parties raise their voices with equal force and have recourse to the same devices in order to scream out their lies. Even hypocrisy is no longer a current practice. If you are not a cynic, you are no better than a simpleton, and you must be positively antediluvian if you consider all this to be nothing but a vast aberration, and if you still believe that man is made for truth and, without truth, can never hope to be at peace. The long, fervent evenings I have spent with you, trying to capture the essential quality of your anguish, will strike people as a stupid waste of time. Why keep alive such a pointless anguish? Some people, for whom I have regard, may consider that what I am doing is an act of betrayal, when so many of our fellow-creatures are in a state of desperate wretchedness. I can hear them crying: 'Action is what is needed!' I shall probably leave them unconvinced if I say that to cultivate a certain kind of anguish is also to nourish hope, but they, for their part, will never persuade me that truthfulness must be abandoned.

As I look at your seal, I cannot but admire you for having had the courage to make use of it. I would never have dared to do so. I might have kept the words in front of me on my table as a recommendation and a warning. They are acceptable as a promise, but to use them as one's motto is more questionable. I have, in fact, learned from my close study of your life that no one is ever truthful, no matter how hard he tries; no one is ever absolutely truthful, either with others, or with himself. Whoever considers our lives in the way I have considered yours would have no difficulty in discovering inconsistencies. We are capable only of one kind of sincerity—the sincerity of the moment, and what is the value of that? A man's life, even your life, has neither the unity, the coherence nor the density to be like a solid mass of virtue, capable of steadying the drifting soul. We shift our ground, and constantly betray ourselves. What we are today belies what we were yesterday. And you yourself, poor 'Protean character with a soul that differs from week to week', how often you prided yourself on being . . .; no, every statement you made was not corroborated by your life as a whole, or would sometimes have received but poor corroboration. You can hardly be blamed for having put on airs and graces with your high-born friends. This meant nothing—you attitudinised and played the social game in spite of yourself, as we all do. But come now, forget your pride, and let us be frank with each other, as we sit together under my reading lamp: are you so sure that you were uncorrupted, and incorruptible? Are you as satisfied as all that with yourself? Are you sure that all the wrongs were on Diderot's side? Did fifteen years of friendship not place some obligation on you? Was he not entitled to expect something in return? Can you really be proud of the *Letter* you kept so secret until you suddenly released it like a bombshell on the literary world? And what about your sentimental attachments? What about Sophie and Saint-Lambert? And the novel you are about to publish? Are you sincere when you refer to it, in writing to your fellow-countrymen, the Protestant ministers, as being nothing but 'a flat and lamentable' rhapsody? You are lying, Jean-Jacques. And why do you leave the public in doubt as to whether you are the author or simply the editor? Why do you display such contempt for the literary world, if you yourself obey its rules? Admittedly you dare not stamp the novel with your motto, and that is tantamount to a confession. Moreover, you know perfectly well that you too are hiding something, and very often you are longing to blurt it out. You, too, have twinges of remorse; there are things about which you never talk, even to Thérèse. There is something you both sometimes think about when a child goes past your window and the pair of you exchange a baleful look. No, even you could not tell the whole truth or proclaim the whole truth to the world at large. *Vitam impendere vero.* But our past is a prison from which we cannot escape. Changing times change us too, and compel us to go on; circumstances make our decisions for us. At what particular moment can we be said to be truthful? You are afraid, and there are a few people in Paris and Geneva who know this. Suppose they were to talk? Suppose they, instead of you, revealed your heart's secret? What a fine sensation that would be! Why do not you yourself speak up and unburden your soul . . . explain what happened . . . ? Your courage fails you? The truth chokes you. Yet in order to soothe your conscience, you slipped in, between two lines of *Emile*, a mysterious remark, a sort of confession which the reader could not possibly understand. Forgive me, Jean-Jacques, my old friend. I must stop harrying you. Life is not yet over. You still have time in which to prove yourself.

What we learn from his life and his work is that sincerity cannot be achieved without a struggle. He may sometimes have been defeated in this struggle, but he never abandoned it. Human thought, either in literature or in art, is probably never more effective, never achieves greater nobility and dignity, than when some artist who is marvellously gifted for all forms of literary artifice and entertainment openly renounces them and chooses to measure the validity of his thoughts by their closeness and strict equivalence to his life. Then and only then we hear the voice of a man, but a man through whom, in whom, all men are able to recognise their own anguish. This is a rare occurrence in the history of world literature. Like Socrates, Jesus, Montaigne or Pascal, Jean-Jacques shows us the way back to our inner life. But he was still too proud, too ready to confuse truth with the impulses of his own heart. There is always a danger in believing that the truth lies within us. He himself had, indeed, some inkling that it is only to be found by reference to something greater than the self; his God was his point of reference. He was, however, too ready to plead that he had an inadequate knowledge of truth and to make God responsible for his ignorance. But at the same time he expected no help from God, no special 'grace', and through yet another upsurge of pride, he claimed that he alone was responsible for any wrong he might have done. Blind egotist that he was, he was too eager to declare: 'I have done what I could to reach the truth; but since the source of truth is beyond my grasp, can I in any way feel guilty if I lack the necessary strength to approach it more nearly? Let truth move closer to me.'

Sincerity involves us in an initial struggle, but the search for truth is another struggle again. Perhaps only those sincere and upright men who have triumphed in the first can embark on the second. But truth is outside us; it is as much in others, in other beings and other things, as in ourselves, and the final victory of the wise is to reconcile within themselves truth and sincerity, the

38

self and the world. They approach this task with humility, and never forget that the truth does not belong to them.[1]

In the autumn, his aristocratic friends would go back to Paris, leaving him in the company of a few neighbours—M. Mathas, the Oratorian Fathers of Soisy, and Coindet, a young Swiss who was something of a schemer and who, not entirely disinterestedly, eventually became a regular visitor to his house and brought him news from Paris almost every week. In summer, he would often bring with him 'carriage-loads of people', which rather displeased Jean-Jacques. In winter, however, his visits were much appreciated. More often than not, Jean-Jacques was alone with Thérèse. He was working. There is no indication that he devoted much time to copying during these years, apart from the elegant copies he made of *Julie* and *Emile* for Mme d'Houdetot and the Maréchal de Luxembourg. He was feverishly absorbed in composition. We must remember that *La Nouvelle Héloïse*, *Emile* and *Le Contrat Social* were written in less than five years. His plan was to finish these books, prepare an edition of his complete works which he would then sell to the bookseller–publishers in order to amass a small amount of capital, and then throw away his pen. He would publish nothing more. He would live on the modest interest from his capital and from the proceeds of copying, and find satisfaction within himself. This was the kind of happiness he set himself to achieve. For two years he corrected proofs almost without a break. After prolonged and difficult negotiations, Rey of Amsterdam was entrusted with the printing of *L'Héloïse*. No

---

[1] Cf. André Ravier, *L'Education de l'homme nouveau*, an historical and critical essay on Jean-Jacques' *Emile*. His prayer, as Father Ravier so appositely points out, is a 'low' prayer (*une prière 'close'*) and he quotes passages to prove this fact: 'I converse with him (God), I allow his divine essence to permeate all my faculties; I am moved by his kindness, I bless him for all his gifts, but I do not pray to him.' . . . 'Nor do I ask him to grant me the power to do what is right: why should I ask him for what he has given me? Has he not granted me a conscience in order that I should love what is right, powers of reasoning whereby I may learn to recognise what is right, and freedom which allows me to choose what is right? If I do wrong, I have no excuse: I do wrong because I want to do wrong. . . .' 'To ask God to change my will, is tantamount to asking of him what he asks of me: it is tantamount to wanting him to do the work while I collect the wages; not to be satisfied with my state is to cease to want to be a man, it is to want something other than what exists, it is to want confusion and evil.'

doubt he would have got money in Paris, but he wanted to remain independent of the French authorities. He lived in France, but he was a foreigner, whose works were published abroad. In these circumstances he believed that Paris could have no criticism to make. On 31st October 1758, Rey and Jean-Jacques came to some sort of an agreement. Jean-Jacques was to send *Julie* in instalments, and Rey would pay him on receipt of each batch of manuscript. He was to be paid in all ninety *louis*, i.e. two thousand six hundred *livres*. But Rey could not commit himself to finishing the whole operation by the following September, and the publication of the complete works was postponed. A disagreement arose when Rey declared that the plan was beyond 'his present powers'. Jean-Jacques finally allowed Rey a further three months in which to print the novel. Another of his demands was that Rey should not send a single copy of his book to Geneva. Through some strange scruple, he did not want his compatriots to be contaminated. Rey, however, stood firm and Jean-Jacques gave in. During the course of the year he sent off the six instalments of *Julie* at intervals. He was to be paid at once, in cash, but in August the whole project nearly fell through because Rey was slow in sending the money. Jean-Jacques was on the point of returning the amounts he had so far received. Such behaviour was not prompted by meanness, but by his artisan-like insistence on the strict keeping of accounts. After all, he had staked his freedom on the success of this minor business deal. Rey started to print the work in February 1760. The proofs were sent first to Malesherbes who had offered to act as intermediary as a precautionary measure and in order to eliminate postal charges. Author and publisher continued to squabble, but only about such details as the lettering to be used and the typographical ornaments. Jean-Jacques was not easy to please. Rey would have liked the book to bear the motto, *Vitam impendere vero*, but Jean-Jacques took the 'jest' rather badly and replied with the following note, falsely light-hearted in tone: 'I do not agree that my motto should adorn the title-page of the novel. I do not think it would serve much purpose, and in any case it seems to me to be in bad taste for the title-page of a book of this kind to be a medley of Latin, French and Italian. Apart from this, I appreciate the jest, so much so, indeed, that I will make a point of congratulating you on it in public at a fit and proper time.' He was not at all happy about having written a novel.

He wanted to wind up the whole of his literary career. He wanted to take advantage of all the work into which fate had inveigled him during the past ten years, all the sheets of paper he had covered, in order to enjoy peace and security during his few remaining years. While he was finishing *Emile*, he also went through the rough drafts of his *Institutions politiques* and, abandoning the vast work he had originally planned, completed one fragment as *Le Contrat Social*. Once he had entrusted all the manuscripts to the publishers, he would be able to go away for good, leaving his life's work to the world, as an eternal monument of his sincerity and virtue, for the world to do as it pleased with it. *Le Contrat Social* was intended to complete the major critical operation he had first embarked upon in the *Discours sur les Sciences et les Arts*. He had begun his literary career by exposing society and its attendant evils, and the debasement of man by man. He was to end it by stating in what conditions man could be restored to his natural dignity, and society be made 'lawful'. This was to be his final 'vision'. He was moving on from factual considerations to considerations of right, and thus felt certain that he was composing 'a book for all times'.

All the political writers he had studied—Grotius, Puffendorf, Hobbes, Locke, even Montesquieu too—had the same fault, which was that they could only argue about facts, about established governments and the errors of history. He himself did not always succeed in avoiding this same fault; willy-nilly, he sometimes confused the ideal with the real; at times he followed in the steps of those who had studied the principles of political law before him, which meant that his arguments were somewhat confused. But whenever he succeeded in being truly himself, he listened only to his own conscience; he then behaved as if he were God, and dismissed all facts as being merely the deviations from right which had occurred during the long and confused course of history. 'What I am searching for is right and reason,' he had noted in his initial manuscript, 'and I am not concerned with disputations about fact.' Usually, he was guided only by his passion and the fulness of his heart; hence the inordinate length of *La Nouvelle Héloïse* and *Emile*. This time, however, he chose deliberately to write only a 'short treatise',

41

which was to be brief and compact and governed by a single idea which he bore in his mind; it would be a kind of code to which men would always have to refer, as they did to the Ten Commandments or the Sermon on the Mount.

'People will ask me,' he wrote with a certain amount of false modesty, 'if I am a prince or a legislator, since I write about political matters in this way. I would reply that I am neither, and that this is precisely the reason why I am writing about political matters. Were I a prince or a legislator, I would not waste my time saying what had to be done; I would either do what was necessary or hold my peace.'

This latter-day Moses was somewhat heavy-handed. He felt he was entitled, as a man, to set the world to rights, and this produced in him such an extraordinary state of exaltation that he sought no other justification. His own memories fed his passion. As a citizen of Geneva, he could restore order to the world and instruct all slaves. He therefore added: 'Since I was born a citizen of a free State, and a member of the Sovereign Council, however weak an influence my voice may have in public affairs, the fact that I have the right to vote imposes upon me the duty of acquiring knowledge of them, and I am fortunate in that each time I reflect on the governments of the world, I always find fresh reasons for liking the government of my own country!' And it seems likely that he was still thinking of himself, although perhaps only half-consciously, when he wrote, in the chapter on the Law-giver:

Only Gods could dictate laws to men. . . . He who dares to undertake to draw up the institutions of a nation must feel able, as it were, to change human nature, to change each individual, who is in himself a perfect and separate whole, into a part of a greater whole from which, in a sense, this individual receives both his life and his being: to modify the human make-up in order to strengthen it: to substitute a partial and moral existence for the physical and independent existence bestowed on all of us by nature. In short, he must deprive man of the strength which is proper to him in order to give him a kind of strength which is foreign to him and of which he cannot avail himself without the help of others. The more natural strength is suppressed and stifled the greater and more lasting the acquired strength becomes, and the more firmly established and perfect the institution becomes: with the result that if each citizen is nothing,

and can do nothing except through others, and if the strength
acquired by the whole becomes equal or superior to the sum of
the strength of all individuals, we can say that legislation has
reached the highest degree of perfection to which it can attain.

Jean-Jacques felt that he was that 'exceptional man', capable
of drawing up institutions, not only for one nation but for all
nations, in justice and dignity. How defiantly he begins!

'Man is born free and everywhere he is in chains. . . . How
has such a change occurred? I do not know. What can render
it legitimate? I think I am in a position to solve that problem.'
Social life, such as it is, is nothing more than universal slavery.
He knows what conditions are required for the state of depend-
ence in which men are living to be changed back into freedom.

Justice is engraved indelibly in our innermost being. In order
to rediscover natural right, man had only to hearken to the
voice of his conscience. Just as the laws of nature ensure the
harmony of nature, there must exist some civil law, some ideal
contract, which would guarantee the same underlying order and
the same harmony within society. The source of law could be
only within man himself. But man had become corrupt. The
entire history of States and governments was nothing but the
story of the innumerable infringements of the ideal contract.
To go back to the contract would be to restore the rights of
nature and of justice. But how exactly was the contract to be
defined?

It was the common demand of all consciences; it was
absolute; in nations, it had the same ideal and universal reality
as, in the individual, the sense of what was right and just.
Although it had so often been disregarded or betrayed, it
nevertheless remained the ultimate hope of men in society, and
the basic assumption of any true community. It was all that
went to the making of a people.

A people! Never before perhaps had the word been infused
with such faith, and such love. It was Jean-Jacques who gave it
that mystic quality which it has in the works of so many French
writers of the nineteenth century, and of the present day too—
Hugo, Michelet, Vallès, Zola and Jaurès. Because he had lived
among 'slaves', as he said, the nation in which he had grown up
inspired in him an especially tender feeling of nostalgia. His
own nation seemed to him to be truly worthy of the noble

43

appellation of 'a people', and what he described in the *Contrat* was none other than the constitution of an ideal Geneva, his lost fatherland. He had only to call upon his own memories to give an entirely new interpretation to the idea of the contract that he had found in the works of earlier political theorists. In Grotius, the contract presupposed the existence of subjects and leaders, of a nation on the one hand and authority on the other. Jean-Jacques, as a 'member of the Sovereign Council', found within himself, in his earliest and proudest recollections, the necessary conviction with which to repudiate such a duality. The People and the concept of Sovereignty were indivisible. 'The first contract did not consist in the establishment of a government, but precisely in the establishment of the sovereignty of the people.' A nation was a nation, even before it chose a prince as its ruler and irrespective of the kind of prince he might be; it could not, without falling into absurdity, submit to any other prince but itself. A nation is the product of man's virtue and reason. There is no law according to which might is right. Might exists in fact, but fact does not constitute a right. 'To renounce freedom is to renounce one's status as a man.' Thus, 'to say that a man surrenders himself of his own free will is to say something absurd and inconceivable; such an act is unlawful and void, through the mere fact that he who commits it is not in his right mind. To say the same thing about a whole nation, is to assume that it is a nation of madmen; madness does not constitute a right.'

The world is full of conglomerations of men but not, as yet, of nations. A nation is necessarily sovereign. The social contract, being a covenant of association, 'creates a moral and collective body composed of as many members as the assembly contains voters, and receives from this same act its unity, its common identity, its life and its will'. This new personality has been created through the exercise of the freedom of all the contracting parties. Each individual surrenders to the whole, yet surrenders to no one. A nation is a kind of huge living creature, a public organism in which everyone both finds and loses his identity. Enjoying equal rights, transformed and renewed by the surrender of self, each individual derives greater strength from the general will with which he is imbued. Through the acceptance of this fundamental pact, man loses the freedom of his

44

instincts, but to be prompted by appetite alone is slavery: by the same token, he achieves civil liberty. The contract 'substitutes a lawful, moral, equality for all those physical inequalities which nature has decreed should exist among men, and although they may be unequal in strength and genius, they become equal through convention and by right'. And, since 'force of circumstance is always tending to destroy equality', the task of any government, and the object of all legislation, should be to aim at maintaining it.

We are often misled by philosophical terms. The *optimistic* Jean-Jacques, who proclaimed his belief in the goodness of human nature, mistrusted it, in fact, more perhaps than the *pessimistic* Voltaire did. He did not agree that it should be left entirely to its own impulses: this was something he dreaded. His was a 'restrictive Christianity', to use the expression Jaurès applied to Robespierre. His whole system tended to imprison man in a small virtuous city, theocratic, poor and with plain, simple needs. He arrested revolution at the same time as he unleashed it. He had faith in man, but not in the human mind. But if you want man to try to live a complete life, you must have faith in the human mind. Thus, the conservative Voltaire was constantly unleashing the revolution he dreaded, because of his passionate determination to go as far as it was possible to go, to carry his thought to its ultimate conclusions. Jean-Jacques' thought, on the other hand, was constantly inhibited by his conviction that only the poor could enter the Kingdom of Heaven.

It was in this manner that he uttered his oracular pronouncements and laid down laws for the future. It is not certain whether he himself realised what a strange character he was. Whenever he walked down the village streets or through the countryside, whenever he went beyond the confines of his '*petit château*', he inevitably came face to face with a social reality which was in harsh contrast to his own 'visions'. But he was entirely absorbed in his visions, whether he was contemplating the woods and lakes of the vicinity, the 'deep and delightful solitude' which held him in its spell, from the colonnaded porch of the castle that had been lent to him, or was dreaming his dreams in the small house he rented from M. Mathas, or in his 'tower'. An engraver called Jean Houël, who came to see him with young Coindet during these years, made a drawing

45

which gives a glimpse of him as he was in every-day life: he is sitting at the fireside with a nightcap on his head and is wearing a long dressing-gown with pleated sleeves, and buckled shoes. At his feet is Duke, his dog, whom he called Turk in order not to offend his aristocratic acquaintances, in particular, the Maréchal de Luxembourg. Balanced on his knee and stretched out towards the fire in a position she alone feels to be secure, is his beloved cat, Minette, or 'la Doyenne'. Behind him are books, but also jugs, dishes and a frying pan. A visitor from Geneva, whose letter is still extant, was to find him in this same setting. Thinking to please him, the visitor called him 'a philosopher'.[1]

'I am not a philosopher,' Jean-Jacques replied, somewhat piqued. 'I am just a decent fellow, and that is all I want to be. My only skill consists in knowing how to prepare my own broth: look, here's my soup; will you help me to prepare it and eat it?'

Such was the 'Law-giver', all ready to be enshrined in edifying *images d'Epinal*. Rome had come to life again, since there was at least one Roman, a kind of Cincinnatus, among the living. Being intoxicated by his own virtue, he felt he was associated with everything noble in the world. When M. de Silhouette, the Comptroller General of Finance, after forcing the financiers to make restitution, was obliged to relinquish his post, Jean-Jacques felt in duty bound to write and congratulate him for having 'braved the cries of the money-makers' and, more especially, for having straightway relinquished his post, and 'remained true to himself'. Jean-Jacques, as a 'just' man, had perforce to pay tribute to another 'just' man.

While he was busy determining what men should be, his 'former friends', the *philosophes*, continued to consider men as they actually were, being convinced that this was a more effective way of changing them. Voltaire had published *Candide* in 1759. Jean-Jacques, who viewed everything in terms of himself, regarded it as a reply to his own Letter on Providence of three years before. In point of fact, he was misled by his pride. He was, however, right to consider Voltaire as his most relentless opponent. He himself would never be capable of Voltaire's ironical and prudent wisdom, nor were his courage or his 'virtue' as discreet as Voltaire's. The two men did not belong

[1] Translator's note: *philosophe* = 'philosopher' in the general sense, or eighteenth-century writer and thinker in the style of Diderot and Voltaire.

46

to the same human family. In his present position of supremacy in which he felt himself to be 'happy and free', in the 'earthly paradise' which he had won for himself by adhering to the simple life, Jean-Jacques had no difficulty in behaving generously towards the *philosophes*. Nor does he fail to pride himself on the fact in the *Confessions*. He had a certain generosity, but he is too keen to let us know about it. When Duchesne, the bookseller, made him a present of Palissot's play, *Les Philosophes*, he sent it back with a letter which was only too obviously intended to be passed around. He could not accept the 'horrible present' of a book in which Diderot, his 'former friend' and a 'respectable man', was shamefully 'slandered'. He went even further: through the Maréchal de Luxembourg and his wife, he obtained the release of the Abbé Morellet, who had been put in the Bastille for having published a comment on this same play and having tried to defend Diderot. Jean-Jacques saw himself as a kind of arbitrator. Having climbed to a peak of certainty and being surrounded by general acclaim, he no longer felt any diffidence in his dealings with his fellow-writers, even the most famous, including Voltaire himself. He heard from Abbé Trublet that his long letter on the Lisbon disaster had been published in Germany, the manuscript having been sent there in all probability by Grimm. Now that the text had been made public, Jean-Jacques considered the possibility of publishing it in France, and was prepared to include a reply from Voltaire, if the latter were agreeable. He made the proposal to Voltaire 'in all truth and simplicity'. However, impelled by pride and an urge towards plain speaking, he could not resist adding a final paragraph:

I do not like you, Sir: you have inflicted on me, your disciple and ardent admirer, wrongs which could be most grievous to me. You have destroyed Geneva in return for the asylum you have been given there; you have estranged me from my fellow-countrymen in return for the high praise with which I spoke to them of you; it is because of you that I find it impossible to live in my own country; it is because of you that I shall die in a foreign land, deprived of all the comforts by which the dying are normally surrounded, and the only token of esteem I shall receive will be to be cast on to some garbage-heap, whereas you, in my country, will be attended by all the honours a man can expect.

47

In short, I hate you, since you willed it thus; I hate you, however, as a man who would have been worthy rather of loving you, had you so willed it. Of all the feelings which I had for you, there remains only the admiration which your splendid genius cannot fail to arouse, and love of your writings. If I can respect you only for your gifts, the fault lies not with me. I shall never fail to respect them, as I ought to, nor shall I ever fail in the duties demanded by such respect. Farewell, Sir.

Voltaire never replied. The letter was written during those years when he had resolved 'to love only what was gay', and 'to spend the rest of his life reading and laughing'. This sort of gaiety seemed to him the greatest victory that man can win over fate. He made his only comment in writing to Thiériot: 'I have received a long letter from Jean-Jacques Rousseau: he has become completely mad; it is a pity.'

At the end of October, *La Nouvelle Héloïse* was at last ready to appear. But in the eighteenth century, the publication of a book was always a very hazardous undertaking. It would take a long time to relate the various ups and downs which attended the publication of *La Nouvelle Héloïse*. Jean-Jacques was obliged to wait a further three months. Rey was afraid of pirated editions. He negotiated with Robin, a bookseller–publisher in Paris, to whom he agreed to send half of the edition, that is, two thousand copies. Malesherbes would not agree to protect Rey's copyright since it was not considered illegal to bring out pirated editions of a work published in a foreign country. Jean-Jacques, for his part, tried to defend the interests of his Dutch publisher. It was winter-time and the packages took a long time to come by sea, by way of Zealand and Brussels, and Jean-Jacques imagined the boat being captured by the English. They finally reached Paris about the middle of January. Even then the books were not yet put on sale. Robin himself had to be protected. With the authorisation of Malesherbes, but without informing Jean-Jacques, Robin printed one thousand new copies, thus himself becoming the first publisher to infringe Rey's copyright. Malesherbes merely stipulated that he should pay Jean-Jacques a hundred *pistoles*; the latter, when he was told of this development, wanted to share the sum with Rey. Rey, however, nobly refused. As compensation, Jean-Jacques entrusted to him the printing of *Le Contrat Social*. Robin's edition, being printed in

France, was naturally subject to censorship. Eventually, at the beginning of February 1761, the Dutch edition began to appear in the bookshops.

At first Robin's censored edition made Jean-Jacques so angry that he considered disclaiming authorship of the work. Then he was consoled by the pleasure he experienced at the appearance of the other edition.

Malesherbes would have liked the Paris edition to be revised, under Jean-Jacques' supervision. We have the report drawn up by the censors and Jean-Jacques' reply and both documents would be worthy of long and careful study. The censors' report was written in an extremely polite tone; nevertheless the theologians who had done the censoring had combed through the whole novel, more especially the last two sections, and had picked out all those expressions in which Jean-Jacques' disrespectful and irrepressible wit was most clearly revealed. The following sentence, which occurred on page 304 of Volume V, must be cut at all costs: 'A charcoal-burner's wife is more respectable than a prince's mistress'; also the whole of page 135 in Volume VI, particularly the following blasphemous remarks: 'However much respect I may owe to Holy Writ, I owe its Author even more, and I would rather believe that the Bible has been falsified and made unintelligible than that God is unjust and evil'; and on page 162 of the same volume, the following passage in which the King himself was attacked: 'If, in any kingdom in the world, you are looking for the man who suffers most from boredom, always go straight to the sovereign, especially if he is an absolute monarch. What is the use of making so many people wretched? Could he not find some less costly way of being bored?' etc. . . . .

Jean-Jacques was familiar with Malesherbes' enlightened kindliness, and admitted that the censors had been polite and tactful. Somewhat embarrassed, he wrote to Malesherbes saying, with all the humour he could muster, that Héloïses had always been unfortunate in their relationships with theologians. As far as the new Héloïse was concerned, 'I see,' he wrote, 'that they have worked most zealously to bring about her conversion, and I have no doubt but that their pious efforts have turned her into a very orthodox person, but I feel that they have treated her rather roughly: they have blighted her charms, and I confess I liked her better when she was lovable, although a heretic, than now, when she has been made narrow-minded and sour.' After this polite introduction, he stuck firmly to his guns, adding to his letter a note intended for the censors. He could not 'abjure his faith'. 'Even were he faced with instruments of torture, he would not withdraw one word of this speech.' 'To him it was inconceivable that a novel by a Genevan, printed in Holland, should need to be approved of by the Sorbonne'. 'He neither knew nor wanted to know how a book should be adapted so as to make it suitable for printing in Paris.' Malesherbes gently pointed out that 'not to allow a writer to say everything he thinks is certainly not the same thing as demanding that he should express views he does not hold,' and that 'it would not be reasonable on M. Rousseau's part to reply to the proposal made to him simply by a short and categorical refusal to make any compromise'. Jean-Jacques, under duress, went through the censors' report point by point, but held his ground. He might 'be wrong' but, he concluded, 'I can only reason with the help of my own mind'.

While this exchange of notes was in progress, the success of the book made them at once pointless and ridiculous. Robin abandoned the idea of bringing out his edition. As early as the month of March, pirated editions using the text of the Dutch edition began to appear on all sides. Copies were printed in Lyons, Rouen and Bordeaux. . . . Soon each one was boasting that it had been 'revised, corrected, and enlarged', the implication being that it kept ever more closely to Jean-Jacques' thought, against the will and authority of the official powers. Every word Jean-Jacques uttered seemed to be as precious as gold.

The book benefited from what present-day publishers would call, in their jargon, a major publicity campaign, and it was such as to make all Jean-Jacques' fellow-writers turn pale with jealousy. Even before the novel came out the public had heard about it from the privileged few, such as the Luxembourgs and Duclos, to whom Jean-Jacques had either read or shown his book. Rey had published an announcement in December. The entire European literary world was awaiting the event and curiosity was not allowed to flag. The novel itself was followed a few days later by the publication of twelve engravings by

Gravelot, edited by Coindet, and intended as illustrations to the work, and then by a 'second preface' published by Duchesne on Jean-Jacques' behalf. Country bumpkin he might be, but he was as clever as anyone at attending to his own publicity. In this second preface, he pretended to despise Paris and to have a high regard for the provinces; this was a way of provoking the Parisian public and pleasing his provincial readers. One preface took the form of an extremely clever dialogue between the publisher and Jean-Jacques himself, the general purpose being to justify his choice of subject, his manner and his style. Its main feature, however, was that it shrouded the whole novel in the sort of mystery best calculated to encourage speculation and gossip. Who, for instance, was Julie?

> Non la conobbe il mondo, mentre l'ebbe:
> Connobil' io ch'a pianger qui rimasi.[1]

This much was disclosed in the epigraph, borrowed from Petrarch. Poets have constantly had recourse to such pathetic ruses in order to keep the attention, affection and pity of the mass of humanity.

Nor was the nature of the letters clear. The characters could be drawn from live originals or the whole story might be purely fictitious, just as Jean-Jacques could be the editor, or the author, or perhaps even the hero. Jean-Jacques insinuated that all these possibilities might be true, now that he had moved, as he said, from the age of experience to the age of recollection. He refused, however, to divulge his secret. At the same time, with typical false modesty, he pretended to believe that his book would be a failure, and gloried in the fact that his name would appear on the title-page as editor.

'You will actually state your name?' he asked himself, in the guise of an interviewer.

'Yes, I will.'

'You mean you will actually allow your name to appear?'

'Yes, Sir.'

'Your real name? Jean-Jacques Rousseau, in full?'

'Jean-Jacques Rousseau in full.'

'You don't mean it! What will people say?'

[1] 'The world did not recognise her while she was in the world: I however knew her and am left here below to mourn her.'

'They can say what they like. I will put my name on the title-page of this work, not in order to claim authorship, but so that I can be answerable for it. If there is anything bad in it, let the blame be laid at my door; if there is anything good, I do not intend to take the credit for it. If the book is found to be bad in itself, that is an additional reason for stating my name. I have no desire to be considered a better man than I am.'

He was play-acting and it is in moments such as this that we get the truest picture of him. He added that, on this occasion, he would not, however, put his title of citizen of Geneva after his name, and went on to make a further boast: 'I do not desecrate the name of my fatherland; I put it only on those writings which, I believe, may do it honour.' And the fact that he had not put his motto on the novel in no way meant that he was abandoning it: 'I have already accused myself more fiercely perhaps than anyone will accuse me,' he declared. 'He who prefers truth to fame, can look forward to holding truth dearer than life. You want men to be always consistent, but I doubt whether that is a human possibility; however, it is possible to be always truthful, and that is what I want to try to be.'

This is a piece of bombast, because neither his reputation nor his life were threatened. He returned once more in the dialogue to the question of whether or not he was the author of the novel, and again side-stepped by means of the following remark: 'One can still render homage to the truth by declaring that it is one's intention to withhold it.' In spite of his profession of sincerity, he was too wily by half; such debating skill verged on dishonesty.

The book had a stupendous success, the like of which had been achieved by no other novel of the century. We possess a mass of evidence testifying to this fact. It turned out that the avowed opponent of romantic literature had written exactly the sort of novel to charm an age which, after enjoying itself a great deal, had now grown tired of its amusements and, having failed to find complete happiness, once more developed a taste for serious things. Yet the morality and tone of the book were not entirely new. In that year, 1760, the public found in it exactly the required mixture of the novel and the old. The pious Mme de Créqui was struck by what she referred to rather quaintly as 'learned disquisitions on the art of getting into bed'; they caused her some uneasiness, but cannot have displeased other readers.

They were led, by gentle transitions, from the pleasures of love to the delights of sentiment and virtue, and this eased their consciences. Professional critics, who on the whole took rather a harsh view and condemned the forced, not to say absurd, situations in the novel, failed to produce any effect whatever. People went on reading the book, as Jean-Jacques wanted them to do, with their hearts. Women, especially, who were beginning to realise that they had perhaps been the losers in the round of gaiety offered them by innumerable gallants, and were beginning to weary of falsehood, felt at once justified and avenged by a novel in which a sinner like themselves was shown dying a saintly death through having loved too well. Meister said of them, in the style of the age, that they 'would spend the nights they could not put to better employment reading it and weeping over it'. Not that they were always accorded gentle treatment in it; occasionally the author, ill-mannered fellow that he was, inveighed against them. He had days or moments when he wanted to behave with Spartan austerity, and at such times he assumed a masculine severity and expressed contempt for womankind as a whole. But they could all guess that in spite of himself, in his heart of hearts, he loved each one of them, and exactly in the way they wanted to be loved. They felt reassured by the very fact that he had drawn this portrait of themselves. They recognised themselves, and admired themselves, in Julie. At last they had been understood by a man. Because of him, all their sins were forgiven them. Julie was all they had ever dreamed of being. If they had not always succeeded in emulating her, it was because they lived in an age when, as Mme d'Epinay remarked, 'it was no easy task to be a woman'.[1]

Jean-Jacques received innumerable letters. The following is an extract from one of them. Actually it was not addressed directly to him, but passed on by Mme de Verdelin, to whom it had been written by Mme de Polignac:

3rd February 1761.
. . . I have finished M. Rousseau's book. What a book, my

[1] Sainte-Beuve was right when he said (*Lundis*, II, p. 65): 'It was Rousseau who started this major revolution in France and, as far as literature was concerned, brought women into the forefront. He won the support of half of the human race which up till then had remained fairly discreetly in the background; the enthusiasm shown him by the fair sex was unparalleled.'

dear! And what a soul must be his for him to have been able to write it! Think what our opinion must be of its hero. Everyone is convinced that it must be the *citizen* himself, and I for one prefer to believe this. So sensitive, refined and virtuous a soul does honour to humanity. The first five volumes drew tears from my eyes, but the sixth! Oh my dear, I dare not describe to you the effect it had upon me: no, I was beyond tears, an acute feeling of sadness took possession of me and wrung my heart. Julie on her death-bed was no longer like some unknown person: I felt I was her sister, her friend, her confidant: my emotion rose to such a pitch that had I not put down the book I would have felt as faint as those who were actually present at the last moments of the virtuous woman. I must have absolute confidence in you, my dear, as indeed I have, to confess my weakness to you. I must admit my madness. You know that as long as I thought of the *citizen* as a philosopher and a man of ability, it never occurred to me to cultivate his acquaintance; but Julie's lover, the man who loved her as she deserved to be loved, oh! that is quite another matter; my first impulse was to order a carriage and drive over to Montmorency. I felt I had to see him at all costs, to tell him how his tender emotion seemed to me to put him far above other men, to ask him to let me see Julie's portrait, to let me kiss it and kneel before the image of that divine woman, who, even though she ceased to be virtuous was ever a model of all the virtues; in short, to adore her and on leaving, to say, like Saint Simeon: *Nunc dimittis*. . . . There, my dear, you have a full account of my folly. You must admit that your friend is indeed mad. Even I can laugh about it, now that the frenzy has subsided. However, I should like you, who are a friend of the *citizen*, to see the portrait I longed to look at, and to offer it my respect and adoration. Do not tell me that all I have read is only fiction: I would like to believe, for the sake of men's honour, that one of them has a tender, refined and sensitive soul. . . .

Letters such as these testify to the impact the book made on public opinion. For a few weeks, Jean-Jacques was happy. The eyes of the world were fixed upon him. He got rid of the inter-lopers, schemers and cranks who are attracted by fame and who hope, by attaching themselves to a fashionable writer, to share the limelight and the radiance, and to advance their own careers. But there was no lack of genuine and disinterested manifestations of enthusiasm, and by these Jean-Jacques was touched. He took a 'childlike' interest in his success. Who can say to what extent the success of a great book is a matter of cause or effect, whether it records or creates new manners and morals. It is, at any rate, a sign. Just as the earth is thirsty after the long summer months, so an entire society, desiccated through the abuse of the intelligence, needed to start again to believe in love, and it was a recluse who, up till then, had been famous only for his paradoxes and freakish behaviour, a man past his prime and who had never known love, an invalid constantly preoccupied with his bladder and his catheters, who benefited from the ambiguity he himself had created and became the hero of the return to fidelity and love. Societies feed on such fictions, and through them manners and morals undergo gradual change. No writer, perhaps, had ever experienced the kind of fame which he enjoyed from then on. Already, the nature of his previous works had compelled the public to consider him as a 'citizen' and a man, rather than as a writer. But never before had he succeeded in establishing such profound and close understanding between his readers and himself. It was what he implied and left unsaid, rather than the secrets he disclosed, which now won him the pity, admiration and affection of the public.

Art and literature hardly came into the matter. The question at issue was the problem of living. Jean-Jacques knew how people ought to live, just as well as the priests did, and even better than they. In the new world which was beginning to dawn and where doubt hovered in the air like a cloud of dust and it was no longer possible to be a whole-hearted believer, and yet where life had to go on, he appeared as a kind of mentor of souls. He was the first of the non-religious writers in Europe to whom men turned for guidance, now that religion was in decline, as they had turned in the past to their spiritual directors. Literature has since reasserted itself, and there has been more than one instance of a writer imitating Jean-Jacques' attitudes, and even his tone, in order to win the same kind of fame as he did. Everything can become an affectation, and sincerity is no exception. But it was only right that on the first occasion when supreme literary art adopted this sincere and moving tone, the whole of Europe should have experienced a thrill of joy. It was as if the novel had served only one purpose—to allow Jean-Jacques to gain a hold over the souls of his readers. Once he had charmed them, he proceeded to offer them more serious instruction, such as was to be found in *Emile* and *Le Contrat Social*. Saint-Preux-Jean-Jacques recruited readers for Rousseau the ideologist and political writer.

Perhaps he was at last harvesting the fruits of his genius. All the work he had done in solitude during the past five years came to maturity at the same time. In March, Bastide the bookseller published the extracts Rousseau had made from the Abbé de Saint-Pierre's *Projet de Paix Perpétuelle*, and this provided a further opportunity of talking about him. A few weeks later, there appeared in the *Journal Encyclopédique* a 'Rescript issued by the Emperor of China on the occasion of the *Projet de Paix Perpétuelle*'! The Emperor expressed his astonishment that Jean-Jacques should have forgotten him and, while granting peace to Europe, should have neglected the rest of the world. This was only Voltaire having his little joke. Nevertheless, at that moment, there was no more famous writer in the world than Jean-Jacques.

Had Voltaire been better informed, however, he would not have failed to remark that the fate now being meted out to Jean-Jacques provided another example of the quirks of Providence. Jean-Jacques, at the very moment when his praises were being sung by the whole world, was almost at death's door. During the early days of May, his disability suddenly took a turn for the worse. In accordance with his principles, he stubbornly refused to see a doctor, 'not wishing to be at the mercy of the medical profession as well as in the grip of necessity'. Then, for a day or two, he imagined he was feeling 'some slight respite'. He had a further attack, however, and at the end of May he felt he should lose no time in making his last will and testament. If he was going to die, the first thing was to see that his works were left in safe hands. He wrote to Moultou, his friend in Geneva, asking him, in great secrecy, if he would agree to go through his papers and documents, take responsibility for them, and publish the general edition of his works that he himself had not had time to undertake. Then he thought of Thérèse . . . and his children. On the 12th June he wrote to Mme de Luxembourg. At the time, the Luxembourg family, too, had been stricken by disaster. The Maréchal's son had died on the 22nd May, and his grandson was to die on 17th June. Jean-Jacques, in all sincerity, had shared his friends' grief. Never had the plebeian and the aristocrats been closer to each other than they were at this time, when they were being buffeted by the same fate and face to face with death, which obliterated falsehood and made truth obligatory. It was then that Jean-Jacques found the courage to reveal what he had hitherto concealed. On this point his *Confessions* are not absolutely accurate. He explains that as soon as he had become aware of Mme de Luxembourg's friendship for him, 'I had straightway relieved my feelings by confessing all my sins to her, since it is an inviolable principle with me to show myself to my friends exactly as I am, neither better nor worse'. This is untrue. During the three years when he had been a regular visitor to the château, and playing the part of the man of virtue, he had been careful to reveal nothing. But now that he believed he was going to die, he felt remorse at having remained silent and was compelled to speak out so as to die in a state of truthfulness. He was so weak that he was no longer capable of any display of eloquence: 'How much I would have to tell you, before taking my final leave of you!' he began. 'But time presses: I must cut my confession short, and commit my last secret to your charitable heart.' And very briefly he told her everything, plainly and simply, like a man muttering in the confessional-box: 'I must say, then, that for sixteen years I have lived with this poor girl who shares my abode, in the greatest possible intimacy, except since my retirement to Montmorency, from which time my state of health has obliged me to live with her as if she were my sister; my affection for her has not diminished, however, and but for you, the thought of leaving her unprovided for would poison my final moments.'

At this point in the letter, he started a new paragraph. In all probability Thérèse was watching him write, and full of apprehension about what life would hold in store for her if he died. It was for her sake that he was writing even more perhaps than for the sake of settling his account with truth. He had to find someone who would look after Thérèse and, in order to do so, he had to tell the whole truth, since she herself would not fail to do so. He had to make it clear what claims she had on him. Who could tell, perhaps his children might even be found? The eldest was nearly fifteen, almost a man. He went back to his letter.

Five children were born of this liaison, and all were placed in the Foundlings' Hospital, and with so little thought of the possibility

57

of their later identification that I did not even keep a record of their dates of birth. For several years now, the self-reproach which my neglectful behaviour has aroused in me has disturbed my peace of mind and I am about to die without being able to remedy it, much to the mother's and my own regret. All I did was to have a mark put on the clothes of the eldest child, and I have kept a duplicate of it; he must have been born, I think, during the winter of 1746-1747, or thereabouts. That is all I remember. If there were some means of tracing the child, it would give great happiness to his loving mother; I, however, have no hope of this, and shall not take this consolation with me when I die. The ideas with which my mind was filled as a result of my error were to a large extent responsible for my writing the *Traité de l'Education*, and in the first book you will find a passage which shows my attitude in this respect. I did not marry the mother, nor was I in any way obliged to do so, since before we lived together I told her that I would not marry her; in any case, a public marriage would have been impossible because of the difference of religion; I have, nevertheless, always loved and respected her as my wife, because of her kindness of heart, her unparalleled unselfishness, and her absolute fidelity—in respect of which, indeed, she has never given me the slightest cause for suspicion.

He was falsifying the facts a little. It was not true that Thérèse and he were of different religions in 1743. But he had to give some sort of justification for what Thérèse and he had done.

Herein, Madame [he concluded], lies the only too well-founded reason for my concern as to what will happen to the poor girl after I am gone. My concern is such that had I less faith in your friendship for me and Monsieur le Maréchal's, I would depart this life grieving at the fact that I must abandon her to her fate; however, I entrust her to you, and in this respect I can die in peace. It only remains for me to tell you what I think would be most suitable to her situation and character, and allow her defects less scope.

He dismissed the idea that she should be given refuge in Mme de Luxembourg's own house, 'alongside the child on whom the hopes of the household rest'—the young child who was to die five days later—because she would be at a loss among the wiles and intrigues of the other servants. Nor did he want her to stay in Paris, because, being easily influenced, she would once again be exploited by her family. Still less did he want her to be near her mother, who had taken sides against him in every plot. What he would have liked was that someone should help her to live 'both on the proceeds of my writings and of her own work, because she is a very good sempstress'; he would also like her either to remain in her present lodging at Montmorency, or go and live in some provincial community. The essential thing was 'that she should be provided for until the end of her days'.

This, then, was the style in which he spoke on this occasion when, face to face with death, he abandoned all pride. He had confessed everything. He could now believe that everything was settled. He was free to die.

> You see, Madame, how simply and how trustingly I open up my heart to you. The rest of the world no longer means anything to me. My heart, which loves you sincerely, lives now only for you, for the Maréchal de Luxembourg, and for this poor girl. Farewell, dear and loving friends, remember me with some affection when I am gone. I, for my part, hope to go on loving you in the after life; but whatever the truth about that dark and fearsome mystery, death can surprise me at any moment and I am sure it will find me thinking of you.

CHAPTER THREE

The Ordeal (1761–1762)

Fruitless searches carried out by Mme de Luxembourg—The first letters from Mme de La Tour-Franqueville—Mme de Luxembourg herself makes arrangements with the bookseller Duchesne for the printing of *Emile*. The printing is delayed. December 1761; Jean-Jacques is literally mad—Jean-Jacques finally receives the page-proofs of his book and is ashamed of all his imaginings—Rey and Moultou urge him to write his Memoirs —Letters to M. de Malesherbes—Jean-Jacques' laziness, solitude and uniqueness—Rey grants Thérèse a pension—*Emile* is printed —Jean-Jacques insists on signing his works with his own name— *Le Contrat Social* is banned—*Emile* is seized—Jean-Jacques is forced to flee.

HE WAS MISTAKEN: he did not die. We rehearse death several times before we are finally laid to rest in our shroud. He had not finished with life: he still had a long way to go. The urea which was poisoning his bloodstream still further, merely brought him a little closer to madness. Twice the Maréchal sent for the best healer in the country to visit him; this was Brother Côme, a Bernardine monk, who succeeded in draining off urine and in setting his mind at rest. Contrary to what he had believed, there was no stone. Brother Côme explained that he would suffer a great deal, but would live for a long time; his complaint was incurable but not fatal, and he would take it with him to the grave. Thus reassured, Jean-Jacques began to bear his afflictions

60

with patience. Moultou had felt it an honour to be entrusted
with his documents and his works. Mme de Luxembourg had
embarked on her search in connection with the Foundlings'
Hospital. Life went on. He spent weeks in a state of utter
weariness. He took up copying music again and did some work
for the Prince de Conti. He was sad and pitiful.

His dog, Turk, the most faithful of all his friends, was sick too,
and had to be put down on the 15th July. Jean-Jacques was in
despair: 'Poor Turk was only a dog,' he wrote to Mme de
Luxembourg, 'but he loved me: he was sensitive, unselfish and
good-natured. Alas! as you say, how much better he was than a
great many of our so-called friends! How happy I would be if
qualities such as these were found as a result of the inquiry you
have so kindly undertaken. . . .' Everybody sent him expressions
of sympathy—the Maréchal and his wife, the Comtesse de
Boufflers, the Prince de Conti, the Duchess of Montmorency.
He eventually convinced all those who came to see him that no
creature was more wretched than he. They treated him like a
child. In August, Mme de Luxembourg informed him that her
inquiries were proving difficult and had yielded nothing at all.
He was not particularly upset. It was 'too late'. 'In my present
state,' he replied, 'I was interested in this inquiry for someone
else's sake rather than my own, and given the very weak character of the person in question (Thérèse), it is not impossible that
what she might have found fully formed for good or evil might
have proved a disastrous gift.' Nobody gave the matter another
thought.

Concern for his work brought him back to life. Mme de
Luxembourg had wanted to see to the publication of *Emile*
herself, since she considered that Rey had not treated Jean-
Jacques fairly. She thought it should not be difficult to discover
a bookseller in France who would allow him a greater margin
of profit. Jean-Jacques could not help feeling rather anxious.
What he set most store by in his book was his Profession of Faith,
and, as he had said to the bookseller Guérin, he could not
conceive of it 'being published in France, at least for the first
time, without it being subjected to cuts to which he would never
agree, given the fact that the parts which would have to be
removed were precisely the most worth-while in the book'.
However, he allowed things to take their course, arguing that,

since the people who had undertaken to patronise and publish his work were themselves high-ranking courtiers, he would not be running any risks. What had he to fear when Malesherbes, the Director of Publications, was conducting the negotiations? The contract was signed at the end of August. It was brought to him by his neighbour, Guérin. Jean-Jacques sold his book to Duchesne, the bookseller–publisher, for the sum of six thousand *livres*. At the same time he himself arranged with Rey for the printing of *Le Contrat Social*. He had visions of himself being quite comfortably off. He was anxious to be able to retire completely. He would 'never write another word', and he conceived a vague intention of settling in Touraine.

On the 29th September he received a strange letter. It was unsigned, but gave details which made a reply possible.

> You will not know, Sir, who I am [the correspondent wrote], but I must inform you that Julie is not dead and that she lives in order to love you. I am not Julie, as you can well see from my style of writing; at best I can only claim to be her cousin, or rather her friend, just in the way Claire was. . . . You must believe a woman when she praises another woman. . . . Julie exists, Sir, of that you can be sure; and why should you doubt her existence? M. Rousseau exists so why should not she? The Julie to whom I am referring, who has a positive dislike of making new acquaintances, would give anything in the world to make yours. She dare not count on it but at least she hopes that I shall be able to show her a reply from you: it is only because of her confidence on this score that she has allowed me to talk to you about her.

This air of mystery and romance could not fail to charm the inveterate dreamer. He replied the very same day, and this was the beginning of a correspondence which was to go on all his life. He played the ladies' man, but at the same time referred somewhat ponderously to his 'cruel and incurable' complaint. He both wanted and did not want to make Julie's acquaintance: 'In spite of age, disabilities, reason and experience, a recluse should not expose himself to the risk of meeting Julies and Claires, if he wants to retain his peace of mind.' Then it was Julie's turn to reply, but this was as far as she had the courage to go. Now she was unwilling to make his acquaintance. 'You would gain nothing from knowing me,' she wrote coyly. 'The man who invented the speech of Saint-Preux would be too dangerous for a Julie bound by the ties of marriage. . . .' And she went on: 'If Julie really existed, you are certainly Saint-Preux, and in this case, the memory of her must fill your thoughts entirely.' For a moment, Jean-Jacques was afraid he had been taken in and that Julie might be a man. But the two friends eventually convinced him that they were not deceiving him. They expressed concern for his wretched state of health, and urged him to take care of himself and to see a doctor. These banal expressions of sympathy warmed his heart. Such tender exchanges with an unknown woman were somewhat reminiscent of the love he had felt for the Sylphides. It was a way of talking about love without practising it. Soon Claire grew tired of the game they were playing, and only Julie continued to write, still on the purest, platonic level. 'Ought the trifling difference between the sexes be considered in a relationship involving only the soul?' she wrote. Claire, who was more commonsensical, had decided that Jean-Jacques was 'a man like other men'. It was three months before Julie finally revealed her name. It was Marianne de la Tour-Franqueville; she was thirty years of age and like so many other women of her age she was unhappily married and starved of love. She lived in Paris in the Rue Richelieu, and it would not have been at all difficult to visit her. Jean-Jacques explained, however, that as 'his situation had worsened' it was impossible for him even to keep up a regular correspondence. He imagined that the romantic episode was over, but Marianne, who was as faithful as Julie, was to go on writing to him for the rest of his life.

It is true that, after a fairly peaceful September—he had even been able to go to Paris one day—he was once more in a most lamentable state. He wrote to Moultou, 'A piece of the soft end of the catheter, without which I would find it impossible to urinate, has remained in the urethral canal, and makes it considerably more difficult for me to pass water. You know that in this area, foreign bodies do not remain in a constant state, but go on growing by becoming the nuclei of so many stones.' This had happened in November. The secrecy with which the printing of his book was naturally surrounded would have been enough to throw him into a state of appalling panic. But at no time in his life can we see more clearly than during those winter months of 1761 to what extent he really was the victim of his body, and how far his eccentric behaviour was bound up with the poisoning of his bloodstream. In January, once the urethral passage had been freed and he was suffering less pain, he would feel deeply ashamed at all the dreadful possibilities he had imagined. Duchesne was busy printing one edition in Paris, and had arranged with Néaulme to print another in Holland. To begin with, Jean-Jacques, like all writers, felt that his publisher was slow in sending him proofs. When they finally arrived, it seemed to him that they were being despatched at irregular intervals, that the whole operation was being delayed, and that Duchesne was making a pretence of printing his work, when in actual fact he did not want to do so. Suddenly, Jean-Jacques saw the whole situation with blinding clarity. On the 18th November he wrote to M. de Malesherbes. He was sure that Guérin had handed over his manuscripts to the Jesuits and they were only waiting for him to die to publish their own abbreviated and garbled edition of his work. 'That, Sir', he wrote, 'would be the disaster I dread most of all, since I would infinitely prefer my book to be destroyed, rather than mutilated in such a way as to bring disgrace on my memory'.

Poor Jean-Jacques! We can see only too clearly, in this one instance, what the theme of all his hysterical outbursts would be. He had heard that a certain Abbé de Graves, a Jesuit and a schemer into the bargain, was on friendly terms with Grimm. Duchesne, however, finally sent some of the proofs. At this point he began to have doubts about his wild suppositions. On the 20th he wrote to Malesherbes: 'Ah, Sir, I have done a dreadful thing', and asked that his previous letter in which he accused everybody should not be divulged. Then his madness got the upper hand again. On the 29th and the 30th, he wrote once more to Malesherbes:

I am convinced, Sir, that you will be able to verify at a glance what I can only deduce here from a list of indications slight enough in themselves but clear in their general implication— namely that my work has been ruined. For although I do not know who is withholding it, I cannot help presuming that it is being withheld, and although I am aware of the weight of your authority and can imagine with what indignation you will exercise justice, I also know that *nescit Orcus reddere praedam*.

It would have been a simple matter to go to Paris, see Duchesne and clear the whole thing up. Jean-Jacques, however, did not go, either because of his usual indolence, or because he was not at all anxious to discover exactly how and where the highly illegal edition of his book was being printed, so that, should the occasion arise, he could profess both his ignorance and his innocence. His friends undertook all the necessary negotiations. The good-natured Malesherbes would have preferred less hullabaloo about a matter that he himself had arranged but of which he had to appear ignorant; he showed inexhaustible patience. He went to see Duchesne, whose integrity seemed to him to be above question, and suggested that one of his own men should supervise the printing. Nothing would convince Jean-Jacques: he devoted a few days to rewriting the *Profession of Faith*—the part of his book which seemed to him to be the most important, and the most open to attack—from the first drafts. He then sent it to Moultou so that he would eventually be in a position to reassert the truth against the falsifications made by the Jesuits. On the 13th December, 'the affair' appeared in Jean-Jacques' eyes 'to be clearer than ever'. Malesherbes and Mme de Luxembourg, intervened once more and again went to see Duchesne. Casting all prudence aside, Malesherbes even went so far as to write to Jean-Jacques himself: 'I have known for a long time that the work was being printed in France; I thought that you knew this too: that is why I failed to inform you of the matter. If part of your anxiety springs from the fact that you were unaware of this, then your mind can be at rest on this score. There was never any intention of doing anything without your knowledge.' This merely added to Jean-Jacques' worries. To tell the truth, he would have preferred not to know too much about what was going on, so that he could continue to keep his conscience clear. Malesherbes explained to him in full what had happened.

> Duchesne signed his first contract on the assumption that the work was being printed in Holland. Since then, it has been decided that it would facilitate matters to print it in France. I knew this, although I pretended not to for reasons which are too involved to enumerate in a letter. . . . You remember, Sir, that you yourself did not think that your book could be openly printed in France. You did not even want it to be, because you would have had to submit it to censorship which you were extremely loath to do. This explains why it has been necessary to maintain a

certain degree of secrecy about the edition which is being printed in France, and why all these misunderstandings have arisen. The deplorable state you are in has forced me to reveal far more about the French edition than I would have wished, since it has been necessary to discuss it with Duchesne in order to set your mind at rest. That is the sum total of the plot.

Malesherbes added a further four pages to convince him of Duchesne's integrity and of the Jesuits' inability to harm him: he advised him, for his own peace of mind, to come and stay in Paris 'until the printing of the edition is completed'. 'I came to the conclusion,' he wrote, 'after reading half your letters that you were the most upright of men, and on reading the other half that you were the unhappiest.' Jean-Jacques still refused to be convinced.

On 22nd December, however, he received six sheets of page-proofs of his book. At this point he was plunged into a different kind of despair. He was in pain once again and believed he was about to die. Overcome with remorse, he wrote to all those he loved, to Moultou, Malesherbes and Mme de Luxembourg, and admitted that he had behaved shamefully:

> What humiliates and distresses me is that I should come to an end so unworthy, if I may say so, of my life, or at any rate of my feelings. For six weeks I have done nothing but perpetrate a series of gross injustices and devise slanderous accusations against two honest booksellers. . . . I know not what blindness or attack of melancholia, brought on by solitude and a dreadful malady, made me invent this tissue of horrors to cast a slur on my own life and on the honour of others. . . . The frenzy of grief has deprived me of my reason before it had deprived me of life: If I behaved wickedly, it was because I was distraught.

And recalling the words of Lord Edward on suicide, he implied that, when the time came, 'rather than cease to be a man before he died', he would know how to follow 'the advice of virtue itself'.

The appalling crisis through which he had just passed restored him to himself. Admittedly he had succeeded, in accordance with his own principles, in 'being himself'. But what was this 'self'? As it happened, Moultou was asking him to write his *Memoirs* and to send them to him, so that he could, later, write Jean-Jacques' 'eulogy'; and Rey, who, like the good publisher he was, had a flair for what would appeal to public curiosity, wrote to him: 'There is one thing that I have been eager to have for a long time, and that is your life-story, which I would bring out as an introduction to your works. . . .' Jean-Jacques reflected on this possibility. In January his health improved, and he suffered less pain. He was, however, a prey to remorse after his recent frenzied outburst. He had implicated everybody, and felt the need to justify his behaviour. He was afraid, too, that he might have lost the confidence of his friends. To Malesherbes, in particular, who had shown him such kindness and forbearance, he owed some sort of explanation. As early as the 23rd December he had written to him: 'You have done everything you could to calm my agitation. I look upon myself shudderingly and realise how contemptible I have become. Become? No. He who, for fifty years, bore the heart that I now feel stirring once more within me is not the man who forgot himself to the extent to which I have just done.'

It is a remarkable fact that, at this stage, Jean-Jacques should have supplied himself with excellent reasons for never writing 'Memoirs'. He replied to Moultou:

It is enough for me to be respected and mourned by men such as you and I need no further praise. . . . Since my most estimable feature has been a very loving heart, everything in the actions of my life that is to my credit is hidden away in very intimate relationships, and cannot be divulged without the revelation of secrets of friendship which ought to be respected even when friendship has faded, and without the disclosure of facts which the general public ought never to know.

It was his madness, his morbid need for self-justification, which, in the end, was to make him write the *Confessions*. However, without appealing to his memories, but under the impetus of the self-examination on which he was already engaged, he embarked on a series of letters to Malesherbes, at first, apparently, without any precise intention, apart from that of drawing a portrait of himself for Malesherbes' sole benefit, in order to justify the solitude in which he lived and which Malesherbes attributed to his melancholia and his sufferings. He wrote one letter after another, at a leisurely pace, and allowing 'his heart to unburden itself', as he says; but the fact that he says this should put us on our guard.

67

Are we at last about to grasp the essential Jean-Jacques, discover the exact measure of his sincerity and estimate just how much pretence there was in everything he did? Saint-Marc Girardin would have us believe that Jean-Jacques wrote these letters rather in the spirit of a priest who, knowing how fond his parishioners are of him, paints his own portrait to be placed in a niche between two candles. The situation was not quite as simple. He was writing as a man who thought he was about to die. But even in this case it is perhaps impossible for a writer to be absolutely sincere. His initial cry comes straight from the heart, but he has no sooner written a dozen lines than he falls under the spell of his ego, particularly when, like Jean-Jacques, he is a musician who responds to the sound of his own voice; from then on, he ceases to be himself and becomes his persona, the man he wants people to think he is.

Here, then, is what he believed he was, or rather how he wanted people to see him, how he wanted Malesherbes, the Director of Publications, to see him at this particular moment in his life, when he believed he was about to engage in the final and decisive battle. Chance had made him a writer; he had not wanted to become one. His whole career had developed in the space of ten years. Before that, he had been only an unknown and solitary figure, which was precisely what he aspired once more to become. He was grateful to Malesherbes for not having attributed the decisions he had taken to *vanity*, like all 'those Men of Letters, who, being concerned only for their reputations, judge feelings by their own'. If he had chosen to live in retirement during these ten years, it was only through fidelity to himself. 'It is not at all credible,' he writes, 'that a man who feels he has certain gifts, and who has waited until the age of forty before making himself known, should be so stupid as to spend the rest of his days in solitary boredom, simply in order to acquire the reputation of being a misanthropist.'

It is true enough that he had waited until the age of forty before becoming known, but the least we can say is that the delay had not been intentional. He had forgotten this, now that he had achieved great fame. As he himself, in a recent boastful mood, had felt impelled to write, there was 'not a man of letters living, not even Voltaire, who had achieved more brilliant moments of fame', but he pretended to despise his own success.

He was not the sort of man to be impressed by the 'vanity' of fame. What he did find, deep within himself, was a 'natural love of solitude which became even more pronounced as he got to know men better', and 'an indomitable spirit of freedom which has remained unconquered', and above all a kind of 'laziness', 'an incredible laziness' which 'shrinks from all the most ordinary obligations of social life, such as making conversation, writing letters, or rendering an account'. These three things were, in fact, one and the same. Solitude came naturally to him. Although, in the past, he had made certain efforts to achieve success, he had always done so with the sole purpose of providing for his retirement and old age: moreover, these efforts had been spasmodic and short-lived, and his misfortunes, when they occurred, had provided him with an excuse for giving in to his passion. 'Lazy!' Yes, he revelled in his laziness. That was the sum total of his crimes.

This is the beginning of the litany; it is a kind of lyrical portrait, above and beyond fact. He was prepared to continue it, if it were pleasing to his influential protector.

I am writing to you in the fulness of my heart, and I am incapable of adopting any other tone. I shall portray myself without pretence and without modesty; I shall reveal myself to you as I see myself and such as I am; for since I spend my life with myself, I must perforce know what I am, and I can see from the way in which those people who think they know me interpret my actions and my behaviour that they know nothing whatever about me; no one in the whole world knows me except myself; you can pass judgement on me when I have told you everything. . . . Whether the evidence exonerates me or not, I am not afraid of appearing as I am: I know my great defects, and am acutely conscious of all my vices: in spite of this, I shall die full of hope in the Supreme God, and absolutely convinced, that of all the men I have known in my life, none was better than I.

In respect of his 'laziness', he was not mistaken. It was, indeed, his essential characteristic, if action of any kind presupposes that we are prepared, to however slight an extent, to fit in with other people, and if laziness consists in being temperamentally unsuited to any sort of social task, and totally incapable of working in the service, or under the orders, of other people, according to their methods and their rules, and at their behest. The only thing that gave him pleasure was self-fulfilment in independence and freedom. In his youth he had known Paradise, a happiness from which he never recovered. How nostalgically he recalled Les Charmettes, the delightful and lazy existence he had led wandering through the countryside, browsing through books and exploring his own soul! The boy from Saint-Gervais, the engraver's apprentice, the youth who had been a valet at Turin and a musician at Chambéry, the man who had been the lover in the idyll at Les Charmettes, a secretary in Venice and a Parisian bohemian—these had all been the same 'lazy' person, if we except society's definition of words, and if society restricts the meaning of work to effort made on its behalf. He had worked, and with remarkable zeal, but always for himself, for the pleasure of feeling his heart expand and grow. His self-deception began, no doubt, only when he imagined that he was in fact the inoffensive creature he made himself out to be. For this to be the case, he would have had to be even lazier still, and to have kept his day-dreams to himself.

After his laziness, he also discovered in himself, however contradictory the discovery might appear to be, a kind of feverish zeal, a fiery, irascible temperament which was easily upset and unduly sensitive to everything which upset it. He felt compelled to confess this aspect of himself, which had involved him in all manner of difficult situations. He had been an exceptionally sensitive child and, at a very early age, had acquired from Plutarch and the reading of novels 'a taste for the heroic and the romantic', which had made him the victim of every kind of disillusionment. He would first be 'deceived', then 'undeceived', and then very quickly 'embittered'. This had been the pattern of his reactions during forty years of his life.

However, he glides over all this rather quickly. He cannot be accused of not telling the whole truth. He even slips in a reference to his misbehaviour between other remarks more expressive of his noble sentiments: 'Embittered by the injustices I had suffered and by those I had witnessed, often distressed by the misdeeds which I myself, either through the example of others or through force of circumstance, had been induced to commit, I began to despise both the age in which I lived and my contemporaries.' One feels tempted to quibble a little over his brief and mysterious reference to his 'misbehaviour'. A statement of

70

the facts would presumably have destroyed the rhythmic flow of his prose. But ought he not to have 'confessed them in the fulness of his heart', however disgraceful they were? He is careful not to do so. And if the example of others and force of circumstance excused his behaviour, surely they excused that of his contemporaries too?

But he believed that he was unique and for this reason answerable only to his own jurisdiction. Sincerity is a closed system which it is impossible to enter. A sincere man is invincible. You can never succeed in proving to him that he is not. He is fundamentally a man who has his own rules, and for whom the rules of others are not valid. All things considered, his sincerity is perhaps no more than the certainty and vindication of his uniqueness.

He had been born an artist, in so far as this is possible. He had created a world of his own which belonged only to him. If he loved solitude as much as he did, it was because solitude was, so to speak, essential to him. The pleasure he found in being with himself had, consciously or unconsciously, determined the pattern of his life. It is true that the root of the matter was his invincible uniqueness; it was not life which had doomed him to solitude, but rather his solitariness which made it impossible for him to live with other people. His only mistake was to accuse other people. He was *alone;* never before had anyone succeeded in being alone in this way. And so there began with him a new manner of writing, a new form of literature, and a new form of art. The arts and the sciences had always been founded on a kind of false agreement, regrettably peculiar to men or the societies to which they belonged. It was as if all men had conspired together to live a lie *en masse.* One man now rejected this generally accepted world, denounced the age-old lie, and rediscovered truth as God had created it. For truth was not the pathetic residue which remained when garrulous theoreticians and tedious logicians had had their say. It was lyrical in nature, and the humblest of men had a deeper knowledge of it through intuitive and mystic experience than all the scholars who, throughout history, had tried to catch the world and its phenomena in their tattered nets.

He then went on to tell the story of that famous October day in 1749, that splendid afternoon when, as he was reading the

Mercure de France and walking along the road to Vincennes, his eye chanced to light on the question set by the Dijon Academy, which suddenly revealed him to himself and set him free; in 'a sudden inspiration', he had realised that the 'needs' which up till then had caused him such anguish and which he had taken to be those of nature, were artificial and 'created by public opinion'; truth had been revealed to him at last. Thereafter, it was simply this truth that he had tried to explain in his three chief works—the two Discourses and the Treatise on Education now in the press.

'This then,' he exclaimed, 'is how I became a writer almost against my will, and when such a possibility was far from my thoughts.' If he had remained a writer, it was because of controversy, and 'the criticism directed against him by hack-writers'. He was not even sure that he had any talent; it was only his belief in himself which made him eloquent. His motto was not meant to be expressive of arrogance. 'Perhaps,' he added with his usual false modesty, 'it was a subconscious upsurge of self-esteem which made me choose and plan my motto, and which has made me so passionately devoted to the truth, or to everything which I thought to be the truth.'

Such was his picture of himself. He jettisoned whole tracts of his confused and chequered life-story, to retain only the edifying image of the honest, straightforward man, whose sincerity alone had made him famous against his will. He made no reference at all to his early efforts as a dramatist, his work as a musician, his contributions to the *Encyclopédie*, his novel, his repeated attempts to emerge from obscurity, and his squalid existence with the Le Vasseur family.

But he had managed to reconcile his life with his principles, and his very misfortunes had helped him to do so. He had become a music copyist. Notwithstanding all the interference from his so-called friends, he had lived a life of seclusion. In spite of all, he had managed 'to swim against the tide'. He was free. No, not yet quite free; his last works had not been published. But as soon as *Emile* appeared, he would take his final leave of the public and withdraw into even more complete retirement.

Even now, he had not yet done. The most important part of his lyrical outburst was yet to come—the part which was to charm more surely than all the rest, and win him pity and admiration. He had still to describe the joys of retirement, and his happiness. He would not do it well, because he was in pain. 'My soul is estranged from itself,' he moaned, 'and is entirely at the mercy of my body.' He would nevertheless try. How artfully he prepared his introduction!

There followed the most dignified, tender and heart-breaking lament, a sort of hymn to life and joy sung by one who was about to die. At first, the tone was entirely stoical: 'My ills are the work of nature, but my happiness is the result of my own efforts.' Immediately afterwards, however, the lament became suffused with emotion. People had thought him to be 'the unhappiest of men' whereas in fact he had been the happiest. He had derived 'infinitely more pleasure from his illusions than others had from the realities of life'. He went on to describe his world and how he came to create it, his solitary walks, 'those fleeting but delightful days spent entirely alone, in the company of my good and simple housekeeper, my beloved dog, my old cat, with the birds of the countryside and the forest deer, with the whole of Nature and her inconceivable author'. From this point, the narrative flowed smoothly on. He described the magnificence and purity of the universe, and how he filled it with beings after his own heart, worthy of inhabiting it. He described all his dreams, and his encounters with God. . . . And he ended with the following infinitely simple and humble words: 'I would wend my way slowly home, with a rather tired head but a contented heart. . . . '

He knew only too well what gave him his appeal. The timid and the weak have their own special brand of hypocrisy. By making a parade of their humility, they can win back all that it has caused them to lose. By now Malesherbes must have been quite sufficiently touched. Jean-Jacques wrote a fourth and final letter, in which he adopted a curiously firmer tone. The specialist in illusion came back to reality. He had laid bare his life and his soul; what could anyone hold against him? 'It was within my power,' he concluded, 'not to force myself to acquire a different temperament or a different nature, but to make the most of the one I had, in order to be good in my own eyes and harmless towards others. That, Sir, is no mean claim, and very few men can say as much. Consequently, I shall not hide from you the fact that, despite my awareness of my vices, I hold myself in high esteem.' His literary colleagues criticised him for living in solitude, and maintained that a solitary man is a useless member of society. He, for his part, considered the solitary country-folk of Montmorency more useful to society than all those leisured Parisians who 'lived off the fat of the common people in order to hold forth every week in some academy or other.' And reverting to himself, he exclaimed: 'It is indeed an achievement to offer mankind an example of the life all men should lead. It is an achievement, when one no longer has either the health or strength for physical work, to dare to proclaim the truth from one's place of retirement. It is an achievement to warn men against the madness of those attitudes which are making them wretched . . . ', etc., etc. In conclusion, he confessed that he had very nearly committed a sin, but the confession itself provided him with an opportunity of subtly flattering Malesherbes and the Maréchal and Mme de Luxembourg.

The sin was that he had been tempted to return to society. When he had been deserted by all his friends and plunged into the depths of despair, he had been unable to resist offers of friendship made to him by M. and Mme de Luxembourg.

'I have,' he said, 'a very loving heart, but one which can be self-sufficient. I love my fellow-men too dearly to need to choose amongst them. . . . My concern for the whole human race is enough to sustain my heart; I do not need particular friends, but when I have them, it is most important for me that I should not lose them, for when they move away, I am lacerated.' All his friends, as it happened, had let him down, apart from M. and Mme de Luxembourg. . . . He went on to bemoan his fate in the most pathetic manner, so that there could be no possible mistake about his plight. Yet in the very act of flattering Malesherbes, he allowed himself the following compensatory outburst: 'I cannot hide from you, Sir, the fact that I have a strong aversion for all social positions which are set above others. . . . I hate the nobility, I hate their rank, their harshness, their prejudices, their pettiness, and all their vices. . . .' In the château at Montmorency, however, things had been quite different: 'I made the acquaintance of the master and mistress; they came to love me and I, Sir, came to love them, and I shall go on loving them as long as I live. . . .' What he would have wished was that the Luxembourgs, Malesherbes and himself, had they not been so far removed from each other by birth, could have lived together in some country retreat, far from the society of men. . . . But it only remained for him 'to put an end to this long-cherished dream, since other dreams too would now have to be relinquished'.

There was more than just nobility of thought in the above passages, admirable though they are. They contain a certain element of cunning, and by their apparent outspokenness and friendliness tended to make Malesherbes into a sort of accomplice.

A natural aptitude and passion for solitude, or the ostentatious habit of living, as it were, 'against the tide', are hardly enough to set a man apart from the common herd. He must prove, when his chosen solitude becomes dangerous, that he is able to prefer it to any other mode of life and to maintain it. The time had come when Jean-Jacques was to be put to the test. . . .

His books were being printed. The printing of *Le Contrat Social* in Amsterdam presented no major problems. Jean-Jacques received the proofs at regular intervals and corrected them, grumbling, as was his wont, about all the mistakes that had been made. After being mistrustful of Rey for a time, Jean-Jacques now admitted that he was an honest man, and Rey for his part was most grateful: Jean-Jacques' works had brought him in a great deal of money. He asked Jean-Jacques to be godfather to the child he and his wife were expecting, and generously offered, should Jean-Jacques happen to die, to pay Thérèse a life-annuity of three hundred *livres*. During several months, these two issues gave a moving, human note to the correspondence between publisher and author. Jean-Jacques agreed to be god-father, but only on condition that when he wrote to his fellow-sponsor he did not have to put 'Your obedient servant' at the end of his letter, because he never referred to himself as anybody's servant, 'not even when writing to Princes and to Ladies of any rank'. The question of the annuity was more difficult to settle. He thanked Rey wholeheartedly both on his own behalf and on behalf of Thérèse. He was 'touched' and 'charmed', and resolved to bring so generous an action to the notice of the public, since it could not fail to produce 'a change for the better' in the opinion that Parisians had of Rey. But it was not long before he started wrangling even about this matter. His principles were well known, he said, since he had expounded them in *La Nouvelle Héloïse*: no one ought to have the right to inherit from another, because such an arrangement could give rise to 'horrible wishes'. He would therefore have preferred 'Thérèse's allowance to be less but to be paid as from a fixed date, without reference to his death—say, from the 1st of January 1763'! Rey suggested one hundred and fifty *livres*, to be paid from the 1st of January 1762, and then three hundred after Jean-Jacques' death. However Jean-Jacques stood firm, claiming 'that the time of his death should not be used in any way for the fixing of the date'. There were further discussions about whether the deed of gift, in order to be valid, should be registered in Holland or in France. Poor Rey asked for a few more details, such as Thérèse's baptismal name, her age, and 'perhaps', he added, 'further particulars I do not know of'.

This was enough to awaken Jean-Jacques' guilty conscience and to stir up all the murky past. He replied by return of post:

> With regard to particulars with which, you say, you are not acquainted, there are in fact none, as far as I know, relevant to this matter, apart from the fact that you are justifying your kind action by your desire to give me proof of your gratitude for the benefits you have reaped through my having chosen you as my publisher, while I, for my part, as you know, wish to reward my housekeeper for her good and faithful services, and for the care and attention she has shown me during my long periods of sickness. I am afraid, however, that the word 'particulars' may conceal another meaning, and that you, like many other people, may imagine that I am married to her; in which case you must assume that, while unwilling to receive your gifts directly, I would not be averse to receiving them indirectly through her— an assumption which is hardly flattering either to my sincerity or my integrity. Be that as it may, if this is what you imagine, you can keep your gifts, for I have lived, and will die, a bachelor, and my only concern is to ensure that this good and honest girl is not left penniless; and should you persist in your determination to carry out your kind intention, I would now, in spite of my general unwillingness, prefer your first plan, since it is better that you should think you are making an allowance to my widow than to my wife.

He had given vent to his feelings without divulging any secrets. Poor Thérèse was certainly not his wife, and from then on not even his former mistress; no one should be allowed to suppose that such a relationship had ever existed. Everything was finally settled. Poor Rey gave in without a fight. Simple, decent fellow that he was, he floundered hopelessly. Jean-Jacques must have rubbed his nose frequently in embarrassment as he read Rey's reply:

> There is so much corruption among men that many people cannot believe that it is possible to live with a female and not enjoy their favours [sic]. . . . If I happened to suspect that there were certain particulars of your life-story (which I have requested you to grant me, and it would be most flattering to me should you accede to my request) which can harm you, I would abandon the idea rather than be instrumental in casting a slur on your memory. On the contrary, I think your biography can only do you credit and might even have felicitous consequences.

It was finally decided that Thérèse would receive an annuity of three hundred *livres* starting from 1st January 1763. She had suffered no loss as a result of Jean-Jacques' ill-humour.

By now, he had corrected the last batch of proofs and *Le Contrat Social* was due to appear in early April. The printing of *Emile* was quite a different matter. Jean-Jacques, in all honesty, was certain of being within his rights. When he negotiated with Duchesne, he was convinced that the book would be printed in Holland. If preparations were being made to publish it in France, this was entirely Duchesne's doing, and for weeks Jean-Jacques had been unaware of what was going on. Early in February the censors demanded certain changes in the first two volumes which had already been printed. Jean-Jacques complied with ill grace, agreeing to a few minor corrections. But he wrote to Malesherbes, asking flatly that the contract should be cancelled in respect of the volumes which had not yet been printed. Duchesne would continue to be responsible for the two volumes already completed, and Jean-Jacques would place the printing of the last two volumes, including the all-important *Profession of Faith*, in the hands of a Dutch publisher, since he 'did not want to do anything illegal'. Duchesne naturally would not hear of this and carried on with the printing, so that Jean-Jacques found himself committed willy-nilly. As he refused to submit the two final volumes for censorship, the 'tacit permission' of the authorities could no longer be relied upon.

Duchesne decided that the book should be presented as having been printed in Holland by Néaulme. The licence obtained by Néaulme in his own country would cover both editions, the one printed in Holland, and the one printed in Paris. Malesherbes' department would, charitably, turn a blind eye.

Jean-Jacques resigned himself to 'letting things follow their course'. He underestimated the dangers of his position and replied reassuringly to Moultou, who tried to warn him. However, he disliked being involved in all this deceit.

> I confess I find it rather distasteful [he wrote to Duchesne on 26th March], to see the words *The Hague* and *Jean Néaulme* on a book which has been printed in Paris, so that the work of one who is the friend of truth begins with a lie. It even seems to me that if you wanted to use this inscription and make it look convincing, you should not have allowed it to appear on the first two volumes, which are generally known to have been printed in France, but only on the last two, and using Dutch lettering, red titles and any other details that might have given a foreign appearance to the last two volumes. The public might then, perhaps, have been taken in by the inscription; but I consider it to be a foregone conclusion that its use on all four volumes will deceive no one, so that the lie will have served no purpose whatever. You must, however, do what you consider to be advisable; I cannot decide what expedients are suitable in a matter to which I have not been a party.

Two days later, he brought up the question again: 'I am well aware that it is common practice to print a book in one place, while giving the name of another; but it is hardly my practice to be guided by what other people do.' He continued to believe that the last two volumes should have been distinguished from the first two by different lettering for the titles and a different date of publication. But once more he left the decision to Duchesne, though not without warning him that his 'safety was at stake'. As for his own safety, he never gave it a thought, because his conscience was clear.

In Holland, Néaulme was pushing ahead with his edition. However, he himself became alarmed when he received the text of the *Profession of Faith* from Duchesne. He had never imagined that in a treatise on education anyone could 'cast doubt on all beliefs'. Jean-Jacques reprimanded him in no uncertain manner.

The danger might yet have been considerably reduced, if not altogether averted, had Jean-Jacques refrained from signing his book. It is indeed extraordinary that the idea never occurred to him. But Rousseau he was, and Rousseau he had to be in every word and in every deed, especially now when he was publishing the most useful and the most honourable of all his books. Since the police exercised arbitrary and archaic powers, all other writers thought themselves entitled to resort to craft. Montesquieu had not signed *L'Esprit des Lois*, nor would Voltaire sign the *Dictionnaire philosophique portatif*. All through the century the most vigorous and truest ideas had only gained ground in clandestine fashion, anonymously or beneath some disguise. Truth progressed with cat-like stealth. Jean-Jacques however felt compelled to put his signature to everything he wrote. To him it was an obligation, a duty. He despised those writers about whom he was soon to say:

> In order to be useful with impunity, they throw their books to the public and then duck their heads. . . . As long as their names do not appear on the books, these writers remain unknown to the Magistrate, although everybody knows who they are, and may perhaps mention their identity. Several of them are even in the habit of admitting authorship in order to enhance their reputation, while disclaiming it in order to ensure their safety. One man will declare to another that he is, or is not, the author, according to whether they meet in the court-room or at a supper-party. The answer can be yes and no in turn without the slightest difficulty and without raising the slightest scruple. In this way, safety can be reconciled with vanity.

Such shrewd and prudent tactics did not befit him. He was just 'a clumsy writer', in other words, a writer who knows his duty and who is anxious to carry it out; who feels obliged to make no statement to the public that he cannot freely admit, put his name to and be responsible for. A man's right publicly to proclaim his ideas drew its strength from the fact that it was his duty to proclaim them. He was not free as long as he was obliged to hide like a thief or a crook. Freedom was only real if proclaimed regardless of the hazards involved, and exercised in the spirit in which a soldier fights a battle. It was not enough, for the service of mankind, to do what most people did, that is, look for the good they preferred, and speak the truth they knew.

A deeper, more personal, commitment was needed. Truth, if anonymous and unsigned, remained inhuman—a concept without flesh and blood. But it became contagious and changed men's hearts as soon as one man emerged to sign it with his life and to intimate that he was prepared to face disaster for its sake. Then all were aware that it was their own destiny which was at stake.

The latest attack of his malady had made him more churlish and unsociable than ever. He took great pains to safeguard his solitude. The following notice appeared in the April number of the *Mercure de France:* 'To all "writers" and "wits". Jean-Jacques Rousseau, citizen of Geneva, begs all Authors to stop sending him their works, especially through the post, and those gentlemen known as Wits to stop sending him congratulatory letters, even prepaid, since he is not able either to spend so much on postage or to reply to so many letters.' He had no desire to make new acquaintances. Poor 'Julie', Mme de la Tour-Franqueville, asked after his health almost every week, each time bidding him farewell for ever and then sending a further letter. On one occasion, he replied rudely: 'Your heart, Madame is less intelligent than your mind,' then gave no sign of life for months. Suddenly, he had the idea of adopting a mode of dress more suited to his condition; he knew an Armenian tailor who sometimes came to Montmorency. He enquired about prices and had made for himself a 'complete set of Armenian clothes', consisting of a cap of squirrel's fur, and, instead of trousers, a long cloth robe to hide the catheters, and a high belt.

The storm was about to burst.

The packages containing *Le Contrat Social* were despatched to Dunkirk on the 13th April. Rey would have liked Jean-Jacques to approach Malesherbes about the problem of bringing the work into France. He refused, although he was shrewd enough to tell Malesherbes all about Rey's kind action, and the life annuity he had made to Thérèse. On the 12th May, Rey was notified that the packages had been seized, and that it was 'impossible' to allow the book into France. Rey protested in vain that within a fortnight France would be flooded with pirated, clandestine editions. The booksellers who were to have been entrusted with the sale of the book in France notified Rey, who in turn informed Jean-Jacques, that it would be wise 'to remove his name from a work which might well be his ruin'. Jean-Jacques replied that both Rey and himself had no choice but to abide by the decision taken,

> ... but [he continued], it does not thereby follow that you must remove my name from a book which I am proud of having written and which contains nothing but what is highly acceptable to the sentiments of a decent, upright man and a good citizen, nothing that I would refuse to acknowledge and nothing that I am not prepared to uphold before any qualified tribunal. I am aware that, as far as my own person, my behaviour and my writings are concerned I owe obedience and respect to the laws and government of the country in which I am living, and I would be most distressed if, in this respect, any Frenchman were more sensible of his duty than I am. But as far as my principles as a Republican are concerned, they have been published in a Republic, and, in France, no magistrate, no tribunal, no legislative body, no Minister and not even the King himself, has any right to question me on such matters, or to ask me to account for them in any way whatever.

The first copies of *Emile* were put on sale on the 24th May. As early as the 26th, Bachaumont noted in his diary: 'Rousseau's book, which is widely read at the moment, is causing a considerable stir;' and on the 31st: 'Rousseau's book is creating a greater scandal than ever. Church and state are united against the author, and his friends have told him that there is reason to fear for his safety'; 3rd June: 'Rousseau's *Emile* has been seized by the police. This will by no means be the end of the affair.'

The stupidity of the existing system was made glaringly clear. Malesherbes, the Director of Publications, found himself in the position of having to ban a book, the clandestine publication of which he had encouraged. All those influential persons who had prided themselves on being Jean-Jacques' protectors were suddenly at a loss, found themselves overwhelmed by the scandal, and began to take fright. Jean-Jacques was indeed the victim of the Jesuits but not at all in the way he had foreseen. The measures which the government was preparing to take against them were causing a good deal of public uneasiness and, in order to reassure their friends, the government had to prove that its sole aim was to serve the cause of religion. It could give this impression by taking measures against Jean-Jacques.

Secure in the conviction of his innocence, Jean-Jacques does not appear to have been unduly anxious. He was informed that a pirated edition was about to appear in Lyons. He protested to the Lieutenant of Police, M. de Sartine, not in order to defend his own rights, but those of his publisher: 'If the pirated edition is published,' he wrote, 'my publisher will suffer a loss which I shall inevitably share; if those responsible for the fraud remain unknown, I shall be suspected of having been a party to it. This is more than enough, Sir, to justify my present state of acute anxiety, and the trouble I am causing you.' The letter was not without a certain dexterity, if Jean-Jacques intended to give an impression of absolute innocence, show himself in a magnanimous light, and stress at the same time the absurdity of the various plots that were being hatched against him.

He had sent his book to Mme de la Tour-Franqueville. On the 1st June she announced her intention of paying him a visit: 'If it were not against convention to visit you, I would be unable to resist the desire to come and see you and thereby demolish or complete the conception you have of me.' The elderly gallant, putting on all his airs and graces, replied immediately: 'You should consider carefully before making your proposed journey: for I must confess that, despite my condition, I am very much afraid of you.' He was full of dreams of love. On the 4th June he wrote again. He wanted to talk to Mme de Luxembourg about her: 'Am I,' he wrote affectedly, 'to desire or fear the visit you seem to promise me? . . . No, I have never feared any woman as much as I do you. . . . ' He enquired about the date of her arrival.

On 3rd June the book was seized. He made no move.

It was Whitsuntide. Julie wrote to him on the 5th, and again on the 7th, expressing the hope that her name at least would not be involved. 'My husband, my family, all of us, are in a terrible state; my heart is still pounding with the shock.' She did not mention her visit. She was in great distress because of the rumours circulating in Paris, and asked Jean-Jacques to set her mind at rest. 'I always fear imprisonment for those people who dare to tell the truth.'

In Holland Néaulme was becoming more and more apprehensive. He would have liked Jean-Jacques to modify the

Profession of Faith. On that same day, the 5th June, Jean-Jacques wrote to him:

> I am extremely sorry about the difficulties you say you are experiencing with regard to the Profession of Faith, but I tell you, once and for all, that neither censure, nor danger, nor violence, nor any power on earth will make me retract a single syllable of it. . . . In glorifying God, and speaking for the true good of men, I have done my duty; whether or no they turn my teachings to account, whether they commend me or censure me, is their affair; I would not give a farthing to turn their disapproval into praise. Besides, at their very worst, what can they do to me that nature and my own ills will not soon do without their help? They can neither grant me my reward, nor deprive me of it, since it does not depend on any human power.

Jean-Jacques felt the atmosphere around him becoming increasingly tense. The Maréchal asked him some strange questions: had he not spoken ill of M. de Choiseul in *Le Contrat Social* and in *Emile*? Mme de Luxembourg, who was even more embarrassed, said nothing at all. The scandal, and the pressure of public opinion, had reached such a peak that it was no longer possible for anyone to help him. The Luxembourgs and Malesherbes were beginning to be apprehensive on their own account. Malesherbes asked to have his letters returned. Mme de Boufflers even went so far as to ask Jean-Jacques if he would not agree to a stay in the Bastille, 'in order to avoid the jurisdiction of the Parlement which has no authority over prisoners of State'.

On the 7th June the Maréchal sent him a letter from the Curé of Deuil, who said he had information from a trustworthy source to the effect that Jean-Jacques' case was to be brought before the Parlement that very day; a writ was about to be issued for his arrest: 'It is quite openly asserted in the Palais that it is not enough to burn books and that the writers themselves ought to be punished.' He began to be aware of the danger, yet a letter he wrote to Moultou showed admirable sang-froid: '. . . For several days now all my friends have been vying with each other in their efforts to make me frightened: I am being offered asylum everywhere, but since I am not given what I consider adequate reasons for accepting it, I intend to stay where I am, for your friend Jean-Jacques has never learned to take refuge in hiding.' If he had to defend himself—although he could not believe that this would happen—he had decided to challenge his judges.

> But [he declared], the Parlement has very little idea of inter-national law, and in all legislative bodies there are certain interests to which justice is always subordinated, and it would be just as easy for the Paris Parlement to burn an innocent man as it is for the Parlement of Toulouse to break one on the wheel. [Calas had been executed two years previously.] If the motto I have chosen [he concluded] is not just an empty boast, this is the time to show myself worthy of it, and how better can I use the few years of life still remaining to me? Whatever treatment men mete out to me, what can they do to me that nature and my ills would not soon have done without their help? They may take away my life, which has become a burden to me through ill-health, but they cannot take away my freedom: whatever they do, I will still retain it, though I may be bound by their chains and confined within their prison walls. My career is at an end; it only remains for me to put the final touch to it. I have glorified God and spoken for the good of mankind.

It never occurred to him to take flight. Although his protectors were anxious for him to leave, his calmness made them feel uneasy, but he was unaware of their embarrassment.

After the Whitsun holidays, on the 8th June, he re-read Marianne's letters, removed everything 'which might provide an indication or sign of her identity', and informed her of what he had done. In the afternoon he took his usual walk, going as far as Champeaux with Father Alamani and Father Mandard. 'Never in my whole life had I been so gay,' he writes in the *Confessions*. Even when allowances are made for his usual special pleading, it may well be true: danger and fame had combined to produce in him a kind of intoxication.

Late that evening, after supper, as usual he read the Bible. He was reading the story of the Levite of Ephraim when Thérèse burst into the room, followed by La Roche, bearing a note from Mme de Luxembourg: 'I am sending you the Prince de Conti's letter,' she wrote. 'It seems to me that you have not a moment to lose in collecting your papers and putting yourself beyond the reach of all the vexatious measures which may be inflicted upon you by authority which is not always accompanied by justice.

For God's sake, come: you can give me no greater token of friendship. La Roche will tell you why I have sent for you at night.' The Prince's letter contained the information that a 'warrant would be issued against Jean-Jacques that very day'; and that measures would be taken for his immediate arrest. 'There is a danger not only of prison, but of the stake.'

He got ready at once and hurried to the castle. It was immediately decided that he should leave. He makes an embarrassed admission of this, and mentions his anxiety not to compromise Mme de Luxembourg as the sole reason for his flight. And no doubt he would have been unable to avoid compromising her, had he had to defend himself in a court of law. 'It was this', he writes, 'which made me resolve to sacrifice my reputation for the sake of her tranquillity and, in the circumstances, to do for her what nothing would have induced me to do for myself.' There was no need for him to try to justify himself. He had every reason to take flight, and his decision must undoubtedly have brought great relief to his protectors. The entire night was spent in discussion, the main question being: where should he go? Mme de Boufflers was in favour of England. He decided, however, on Yverdon, in Switzerland, with the vague hope that he might eventually get to Geneva, his native city, once he had ascertained what sort of a reception he might expect there. Dawn broke. He spent the morning sorting out his papers which La Roche had brought over from his 'tower'. Meanwhile, the *Grand' Chambre* was in session and passing sentence on *Emile*. At midday the warrant for his arrest was ready.[1] The warrant stated that since the author had had no scruples about giving his name, proceedings would be taken against him with the utmost promptness, and 'that it was important, in view of the fact that he had not concealed his identity, that justice should take the opportunity of making an example'. Jean-Jacques, in signing his book, seemed to have thrown out a

---

[1] At the end of Book XI of the *Confessions*, Jean-Jacques implies that the perpetrators of the 'plot directed against him', were keen to get him out of the country in order to facilitate its operation. He wonders what would have happened if he had stayed in his bed. He draws a distinction between what he calls a 'comminatory warrant' and 'an actual warrant'; But this is meaningless. There was only one warrant, and it is only too clear that if Jean-Jacques had remained within reach of the police, the warrant for his arrest would have been carried out.

challenge. The court decreed 'that the aforementioned book should be rent and burned at the foot of the main staircase in the courtyard of the Palais de Justice by the public executioner' and 'that Jean-Jacques Rousseau should be seized and arrested and brought to the prisons of the Conciergerie of the Palais'.

In the afternoon, Thérèse came to the château, and they bade each other farewell. He promised her that she would soon join him. By four o'clock he was gone. 'Between Montmorency and Deuil,' he writes in the *Confessions*, 'I met a hired coach carrying four men dressed in black, who, smiling, raised their hats.' He had no doubt but that they were the bailiffs who had been sent to arrest him. They may well have been. However, the fact that they saluted him does not imply that they had recognised him. There is no reason to believe that the authorities simply wanted to make him leave the country so as to get rid of him. The bailiffs, if bailiffs they were, may not have been saluting him personally, since he was unknown to them, but rather his impressive turn-out, his post-chaise and postillion. The journey lasted four days. Huddled in his carriage, he composed, so he tells us, *The Levite of Ephraim*, a long poem in the style of the Idylls of Gessner, which he had read the previous winter. Perhaps he played with the idea, but it seems doubtful that he enjoyed enough peace of mind to write the poem. He avoided the main highways, Besançon and Lyons, and went through Salins and Pontarlier, so as 'not to be brought before some officer or other'. At Dijon he had to give his name; it occurred to him to use his mother's instead of his own. 'I could not bring myself to do so,' he wrote to Mme de Luxembourg, 'my hand trembled so much that I was twice obliged to put down the pen: finally the name Rousseau was the only one I succeeded in writing, and my only deception consisted in omitting the J. of one of my Christian names.'

By the 11th June, he was approaching Dôle. In Paris, in the courtyard of the Palais de Justice, the public executioner was tearing up and burning his book 'according to the customary rites'. Books do not burn easily, but the executioner was used to this; he stirred up the fire and soon a thin, comically inadequate, spiral of smoke rose up into the sky.

CHAPTER FOUR

The 'Cause of God' (1762–1764)

He is convinced that his cause is the 'cause of God'. He is in an alarmingly excitable state—A letter from Thérèse—*Emile* and *Le Contrat Social* are burnt in Geneva and a warrant is issued there for Jean-Jacques' arrest—Unrest in Geneva—Jean-Jacques is obliged to leave Yverdon and escapes to Motiers-Travers—Thérèse joins him there—Both the 'atheists' and the 'bigots' are against him—He is protected by Frederick and the Earl-Marischal—Jean-Jacques is allowed to take Holy Communion—Solitude in Motiers—He wears Armenian dress—Death of 'Maman'—He drafts his open letter to Christophe de Beaumont—Jean-Jacques and Figaro—Jean-Jacques' religion: he defines the faith as it is still conceivable. He attacks the Catholics in order to win Protestant support—Jean-Jacques falls ill and makes his will in favour of Thérèse—His health improves: his letters to Marianne—He is bored—The *Lettre à l'Archevêque* appears in March 1763—Geneva forbids it to be reprinted—Jean-Jacques gives up his citizenship—What Jean-Jacques owes to Geneva and what Geneva owes to Jean-Jacques—*'Représentants'* and *'négatifs'*[1]—The *Lettres de la Campagne* written by Tronchin the *Procureur-général*—During the winter of 1763-1764, Jean-Jacques works in great secrecy on the *Lettres de la Montagne*—Jean-Jacques, the soothsayer of Europe—

[1] Translator's note: The term 'représentants' was applied to citizens of Geneva who advocated public liberty; the term 'négatifs' to members of the oligarchy who refused to listen to popular demands.

Jean-Jacques and Henriette—*Pygmalion* or self-love—Publication of the *Lettres de la Montagne*—Voltaire's *Le Sentiment des citoyens*. The night of the 31st December 1764.

IN THE DIFFICULT situation in which he found himself, he decided to go to Yverdon in Bernese territory, to stay with 'his oldest friend', Daniel Roguin, whose acquaintance he had made many years ago when he first arrived in Paris, and who, in fact, had introduced him to Diderot. He arrived during the morning of 14th June. At the frontier he had stopped the coach and, flinging himself on the ground, had kissed the land of freedom!

> Here begins [he wrote eight years later], the work of darkness in which I find myself engulfed, without even once having been able, try as I may, to pierce its terrible obscurity. In the abyss of misfortunes in which I am plunged, I feel the painful effects of the blows directed against me; I can see the weapon with which they are delivered, but not the hand which guides it nor the means that hand employs. Shame and misfortune fall upon me as if of their own accord, and apparently without human intervention. When my grief-stricken heart gives vent to lamentations, I seem like a man complaining without reason, and those who have encompassed my downfall have discovered the inconceivable art of making the public their unsuspecting accomplice, who is not even aware of their plot.

And he implored all generous-minded readers to try to fathom these mysteries and discover the truth by tracing the evil back from one intrigue to the previous one, and from one agent to another. And he proclaimed, with all the conviction of a madman, 'I know full well exactly what the result of their enquiries will be, but I am lost in the dark and tortuous subterranean passages leading to it.'

We are overcome with a feeling of pity on reading the opening words of Book XII of the *Confessions*. Under the immediate impact of the ordeal, everything seemed utterly dark and sinister to him, yet there was no 'darkness' in the whole affair; on the contrary, it was terrifyingly clear. It was another case of the eternal struggle between unfettered genius and tradition. However, the genius himself labours in total darkness when, because of his sincerity, he is unaware of the scandalous originality of his thought, and cannot understand the amazement

and revulsion it arouses in everyone else. Such sincerity amounts
to madness. Jean-Jacques was so sincere that he went mad. He
was so convinced of the simplicity, honesty and obviousness of
what he had written that, being a sick man into the bargain, he
was unable to understand the opposition he met with on all
sides. He was absolutely certain that his cause was 'God's
cause'. To him the attacks upon him seemed quite inconceivable.
So he tried to find, and even invented, reasons for them. The
only explanation could be that he was the victim of some 'plot'.
And who else could have instigated this 'plot' but his 'former
friends', the destroyers of God?

He was not actually mad in June 1762, but in a state of
feverish excitement because of the dangers which threatened.
Sometimes suspicious thoughts shot through his mind like those
illusory streaks of light we occasionally see when we close our
eyes. He had no sooner arrived than he wrote to inform Moultou,
in Geneva. He was rather ashamed at having been forced to
flee, and at having had to 'take a decision of which he fundamentally disapproved'. He had been forced into it in order not to
compromise his friends. He intended to wander through the
mountains looking for 'some wild uninhabited spot where he
would be able to find asylum for the remainder of his wretched
life'. He declared that he had no intention of going to Geneva.
'A poor outlaw should not seek refuge in his own country; he
ought not to impose his shame on his fatherland and force it to
share his humiliations.' This, however, was only his way of
sounding Moultou, who must have fully understood what was
meant. Jean-Jacques was utterly convinced of his own
innocence. 'If only,' he wrote pathetically, 'I could, from now
on, make the people of Geneva forget that I ever existed! Do not
give anyone my address; do not talk about me or mention me by
name. May my name disappear from the earth! Ah! Moultou!
Providence has erred; why did it decree that I should be born
among men, yet made of a different species from the rest of
mankind?'

Letters arriving from Paris must have done something to
comfort his heart. Duclos generously offered him six hundred
livres; Coindet, with whom he had quarrelled, was prepared
to join him wherever he was and 'to go along with him wherever
he wanted to go'; D'Alembert offered to approach the King of

Prussia on his behalf, and recommended him to Earl-Marischal Berwick at Neuchâtel; the Comtesse de Boufflers was trying to find asylum for him in England or Germany.

What would Thérèse decide to do? He had written to her as early as the 17th, beginning his letter: 'My dear child....' Above all, he wanted her to make up her own mind: 'My child,' he wrote affectionately, 'do not despise me because of my wretchedness. Men may make me unhappy but will never succeed in making me vicious or unjust; and you know better than anyone that I have done nothing illegal.' He could put up with everything provided she were once more at his side. He showered her with advice about selling up their humble home. There were three or four *écus* in the lid of the sweet box which would be enough to pay the butcher. And she must be sure not to forget the truss for his hernia and the candle-holders. Thérèse received Jean-Jacques' letter on the 22nd. On the 23rd she got up at 4 o'clock in the morning to undertake the great labour of writing a reply in her very illiterate French. She was so delighted that she went on repeating the same thing over and over again: 'I am waiting impatiently for the moment when I can join you, and I send you all my love.... You know that my heart is yours and that I have always told you it was ... even though I had to cross seas and climb precipices in order to be with you, I would only have to be given the word and I would set off at once. ... it is my heart which speaks and not my lips....' Jean-Jacques deciphered the incredibly misspelt message. It was bound to have a profoundly moving effect on a man of his temperament. They were about to set up house again and would be together until his death.

The indictment brought against Jean-Jacques by Omer-Jules de Fleury, the Public Prosecutor, was being circulated throughout Europe. The tiny fire in the courtyard of the Palais de Justice had kindled other equally ridiculous fires. On the 20th June a note from Moultou informed Jean-Jacques that *Emile* and *Le Contrat Social* had been burnt in Geneva; and that a warrant had been issued for his arrest in that town. It occurred to him that he should go to Geneva and give himself up; then he abandoned the idea, because at least he had not been summoned to appear before a court of justice. He asked the magistrate of Yverdon if he enjoyed the respect and goodwill of the Berne

authorities, since otherwise he would be loath to remain on
Bernese territory. He was now riddled with anxiety. The very
enthusiasm with which his friend Moultou was undertaking his
defence in Geneva aroused his alarm. In terms very different from those he normally used, he urged Moultou to
be prudent:

> Learn to manoeuvre, my young friend, and never try to offer
> direct resistance to men's passions, if you want to make them
> see reason. Envy and hatred of me are now at their peak. They
> will not diminish until long after I have ceased to write, when I
> have begun to be forgotten by the public, and people are no
> longer afraid of hearing the truth from me. Then, if I am still
> alive, you will serve my cause and people will listen to you. For
> the moment, say no more; respect the decision of the magistrates
> and public opinion; do not openly abandon me, for that would
> be an act of cowardice; mention me but rarely, do not appear to
> defend me, write to me only occasionally, and above all do not
> visit me; I absolutely forbid you to do so. In short, if you want to
> serve my cause, do so in my way; I am a better judge than you
> of what is right for me.

The initial effect of danger was to make him prudent and as a
master and a friend he could be difficult and overbearing.

Jean-Jacques suspected Voltaire and the French government,
more particularly Choiseul, of being the cause of all the trouble
with his native city of Geneva. We have no proof of this. As far
as France was concerned, we may suppose that the Genevan
authorities, for their part, were anxious to be friendly. As for
Voltaire, given his mischievous nature, he must have derived
pleasure from the *citizen's* difficulties with his native town, but
he was not responsible for them. The evidence suggests that all
he did was to look on with amusement as the believers fought
among themselves. It is true he had still not forgiven Jean-Jacques
for having denounced the *philosophes*, and for having written the
Lettre sur les spectacles which was responsible for the fact that
Geneva had no theatre. But when he read the *Profession de Foi*
his irritation was only equalled by his admiration. The rest
of the book seemed 'very common-place' to him, but he would
have liked to have those fifty or so pages separately bound in
leather. 'Oh! how we would have cherished him, madman
though he was,' he wrote to Damilaville on the 31st July, 'if only

he had not been a false friend, and what a fool he was to insult the only men who might have forgiven him!'[1]

Such was Jean-Jacques' fierce ingenuousness that he himself was unable to see what far-reaching effect his writings might have. The fact is that *Emile* and *Le Contrat Social*, and the seeds of freedom contained within them, were to start a kind of revolution in Geneva. The two books were to stir up fresh quarrels over the question of liberty.

The Petit Conseil, which was the ruling body, together with their spokesman Jean-Robert Tronchin, the Procureur-général, were to condemn the intolerable spirit of revolution embodied in the *Contrat*, a book whose author was 'oblivious of any reciprocal commitment between the governing body and the governed, since the former seemed to him to be merely instruments that nations can at any time replace or destroy as they will'. The Procureur added in forceful terms: 'This extreme freedom is treated as a divinity by the author: to it he is ready to sacrifice the most sacred principles and since he finds precepts in the Gospels which limit this disastrous independence, he considers a Christian republic to be a contradiction in terms, religion to be merely a reinforcement for tyranny, and Christians men intended to grovel in the most abject slavery'—and as a matter of fact, a good deal of this was implied in his chapter on 'civil religion'. The sentence pronounced by the Petit Conseil proves that Jean-Jacques' political principles, and the *Contrat*, were even more suspect in the eyes of the aristocratic government of Geneva than the religious views he expressed in *Emile*. The two things were linked: 'Religion and government had never been subjected to a more direct attack.' Furthermore, the Procureur-général was able to announce triumphantly that Jean-Jacques was not, as he prided himself on being, a citizen of Geneva. He had been lying in 1754 when he had given people to understand that he had never abandoned his religion. Yet the *Profession de Foi* was in itself an admission. He had in fact abjured his religion, and in so doing had become an alien in Geneva.

We may suppose that this statement was a fair summary of the views of the governing oligarchy who were glad to be rid of

[1] Cf. *Annales Jean-Jacques Rousseau*, I. p. 273. 'Voltaire's unpublished notes on *La Profession de Foi d'un Vicaire Savoyard*,' by B. Bouvier.

such an intractable *citizen*. Voltaire belonged to their class, he was one of them, he was a gentleman of the King of France's Privy Chamber: everything could therefore be forgiven him. Jean-Jacques, whose fame had been a source of pride to them for a while, had become no more than the son of a Saint-Gervais watchmaker, himself a somewhat unworthy citizen. Yet at the same time, in the eyes of the lower classes, the 'avenaires', Jean-Jacques was beginning to emerge as a kind of popular leader. As early as the 22nd, Moultou wrote to Jean-Jacques: 'You may be sure that the secret cause of the severity of the sentence against you was the desire to keep you out of Geneva: you are feared there, you are too outspoken and those in authority are afraid that we might want to become as outspoken as you are.' In his anxiety Jean-Jacques' first impulse was to adopt a conciliatory attitude. He wrote a rather sharp reply to Moultou urging upon him, 'should occasion arise', to assure all the magistrates that he would continue to respect them, even if they were unjust; and all his fellow-citizens that he would continue to have affection for them, however ungrateful they might be. He added that he had no hatred in his soul, and that it was a consolation him 'to know that he retained his kindly disposition even in adversity'.

On 9th July he was forced to leave Yverdon. The magistrate's kindness had proved to be insufficient protection: the Senate of Bern demanded his expulsion. He felt that everywhere he went 'he would be barred from both land and sea'. He crossed the mountain during the night and reached Motiers-Travers the following day. There, in the principality of Neuchâtel, he was on the King of Prussia's territory. A niece of his old friend Roguin, a certain Mme Boy de la Tour, offered him hospitality in a house she had there. Thérèse arrived on the 20th. And once more they were reunited.

Stupidity nevertheless continued to do its work. The Amsterdam magistrates withdrew the licence they had granted the publisher. In Paris the Sorbonne was in session for several days to decide on the wording of its 'Censure' in French and Latin. On the 20th August, Archbishop Christophe de Beaumont issued his pastoral letter denouncing *Emile*; Jean-Jacques was well on the way to becoming the anti-Christ.

In Geneva, public opinion was wavering. The Petit Conseil,

somewhat ashamed of its harshness, hesitated to reveal the terms of its decision to Jean-Jacques' family, and did not even make it known to a delegation of citizens. The Compagnie des Pasteurs (Association of Ministers of Religion) had made no move as yet. Moultou would have liked Jean-Jacques to write a letter which he could have shown the Ministers in order to allay their misgivings about Jean-Jacques' orthodoxy. Voltaire, judging by his own experience, believed that the situation could be patched up. One day Moultou had met him in a Genevan *salon* and he had said: 'Jean-Jacques will come back: the syndics will say to him: "Monsieur Rousseau, it was wrong of you to write what you have written: promise that in future you will respect the religion of this country." Jean-Jacques will promise and may even say that the printer had added some extra pages to his book.' 'No, Sir,' Moultou replied, suddenly abandoning all idea of compromise, 'Jean-Jacques does not sign his works and then repudiate their contents.' According to Moultou's story, Voltaire found no answer. It was impossible to avoid upheavals with a man as stubborn as Jean-Jacques. He was never satisfied to be merely left in peace; if he was in the right, he wanted the fact to be openly admitted. In the lives of others, such as the 'mountebank' Voltaire and the 'juggler' Tronchin, there could be a margin of non-seriousness. They lived in the world and accepted its intrigues and compromises. He, on the contrary, was always completely serious. Voltaire knew that truth is like a carrier-pigeon; it could be counted on to carry out its task spontaneously, unobtrusively and anonymously, once it was released into the world. He did not think of truth as belonging to him, whereas Jean-Jacques' truth bore his signature: it would have been impossible to say which meant more to him, the truth or himself. Pride made him rather clumsy and he could not understand why people failed to recognise his sincerity. That was the root of the trouble. But this having been granted, it was still true that he himself never failed to complicate the issue, and he found it impossible to keep quiet. He was flabbergasted by what had happened and wrote as follows to Mme de Boufflers:

> You cannot imagine what a scare Fleury's indictment of me has caused among our ministers, who are the most active of all. They look upon me with horror; they have to force themselves to allow me into their churches. Spinoza, Diderot, Voltaire and Helvétius

are saints compared to me. The ministers and the *philosophes* have almost become reconciled in their common attack upon me which the believers conduct openly, the *philosophes* by secret, intrigues, loudly bemoaning my fate the while. Voltaire the poet (on other occasions he had called him Voltaire the mountebank) and Tronchin, the juggler, have done their work well in Geneva and in Bern, and you can be certain they will not forget me in Berlin.

This was how he himself saw the pattern of events. It is true that things had reached such a pass that—ironically enough—it was Voltaire, the author of the *Sermon des Cinquante*, who was becoming the defender of the true faith, while it was Jean-Jacques who was being persecuted. As he said, 'The atheists were secretly stirring up the formidable army of religious bigots.'

The 'religious bigots' were quite capable of action on their own behalf. Jean-Jacques could not see that in every partisan quarrel the adversaries whose opinions coincide most closely look upon each other as being the most heretical; his writings were all the more offensive in that he adopted the very tone that the religious bigots themselves might have used, and expressed himself with the same warmth and sincerity. Jean-Jacques' guilt was all the deeper since he was honest and religious. Voltaire's blasphemy was the work of a lost soul, and was accepted as such without further ado. But how could Jean-Jacques' disturbing doubts be tolerated if they were precisely those that the 'bigots' dared not admit even to themselves, and if they were made up of those very things which could make the conscience of every believer uneasy? And how dared he express them publicly and in so moving a fashion? The effect on the faithful was only too obvious. On his very first reading of *Emile*, Tronchin, the doctor, had immediately declared that Jean-Jacques could pride himself on having done a great deal of harm and of having 'stabbed humanity with one hand while embracing it with the other'. Such were the terms of a letter he wrote to Jacob Vernes, the minister at Séligny and a friend of Jean-Jacques. And he added the following charitable conclusion: 'I wish this unfortunate man were dead—yes, I repeat, I would rather he were dead, since his last two works are going to do a great deal of harm.' Also the 'bigots' had their own selfish interests to consider. Once the Petit Conseil, the authorities, had announced their decision, it was to be expected that the Compagnie des Pasteurs would follow suit. Vernes, the recipient of this letter from Tronchin, was hoping for a university chair and immediately adopted a more reserved attitude towards Jean-Jacques. Early in July, he wrote to him saying he was 'the truest of all his friends' yet asking why Jean-Jacques had not consulted him, and how it had happened that he had 'spread such alarm among the faithful', disturbing them in 'that tranquillity bestowed by a lively faith, which is something we greatly need in this valley of tears and wretchedness'.

With every passing day, poor Jean-Jacques was faced with some new judge of his orthodoxy and his virtue. It was inevitable that the theologians should make the most of the opportunity and, preening themselves on their authority, try to teach him a lesson. Jacob Vernes, the minister with whom he had corresponded ever since 1754, had the idea of refuting *Emile*, but in moderate terms. He even declared that *Emile* seemed to him to be evidence of a naturally Christian soul: *Testimonium animae naturaliter christianae*. His intention was 'to convince Rousseau' and not 'to cause him distress'. He said as much to Jean-Jacques in a letter but did not avoid making the most offensive suggestion, since he asked for 'a categorical recantation of as public a nature as the attack had been'. Jean-Jacques was quite dumbfounded! He wrote to Moultou: 'People who set up as judges of Christianity should have a better knowledge of it than these gentlemen have, and I am amazed that no one has as yet pointed out to them that their court is not so supreme that a Christian cannot appeal against its decisions.' He soon came to the conclusion that 'Vernes was two-faced'.

Letters arrived for him from all directions, letters so diverse, so extravagant both in praise and blame, that they were to keep him—obsessed as he was with probing into his own conscience—in a state of perpetual tension. He could legitimately have the impression that the whole of Europe was taking an interest in his fate. The German writer Hirzel, the author of *Socrate Rustique*, sent him his book addressing him as 'the foremost among men'. Rulhière, who wrote to him from St. Petersburg, seemed to be expressing the view of humanity as a whole in begging him to put himself beyond the reach of the law: 'In your place,' he wrote, 'Socrates would have fled and sought some place of refuge.' Everybody explained to him that he owed it to himself to live and to be free so as to serve as an example for others. He had to face, on the other hand, all the vicious gibes which aimed at compromising his reputation, the pamphlets and anonymous letters like those written by 'Philandre' who said: 'Look for some place of retreat among the savages where Nature, it would seem, intended you to be born.' An individual called Comparat—who signed and even published his letter— hoping to achieve some eminence by climbing on to Jean-Jacques' shoulders—wrote to him on behalf of all fathers who had been deeply shocked by *Emile*: 'I am not a writer,' he declared 'but I am a father.' His letter was ridiculous and yet Jean-Jacques was sufficiently perturbed to feel that he had to reply and vindicate himself: 'I do not know you, Sir, and I have never heard your name before. What harm have I done you? What strange depravity of the heart makes you deliberately provoke and needlessly depress an unhappy and wretched man who never gave you a thought? Beware lest your letter is read during your life-time, thanks to the fame my misfortunes have won for me; before you wrote it you were merely unknown, now you will be an object of contempt.' Naturally enough he was convinced only by letters of praise. Towards the end of the year he felt able to write to Moultou: 'Europe has already decided between them (his enemies) and me. What does anything else matter?'

In the Principality of Neuchâtel where chance had brought him, he must at least have experienced some degree of security. The King of Prussia and his official representative in Neuchâtel, the Earl Marischal, treated him with kindness. In a series of very shrewd and eloquent letters he had put himself in their care from the moment of his arrival at Motiers. To the King he wrote:

I have often spoken ill of you and I may yet do so again; nevertheless, driven from France, from Geneva, and from the Canton of Bern, I now seek refuge in your territory. I was perhaps mistaken in not coming to you first: praise of this kind is the praise of which you are worthy, Sire, I have not deserved any favour from you, nor do I ask any; but I felt I must inform your Majesty that I am in your power, which is where I wish to be; Your Majesty can do with me as you wish.

The King readily agreed to play the noble part thus offered him. At the same time Jean-Jacques' meeting with the Earl Marischal was extremely fortunate, for no man was more fitted to understand and comfort him.

He was a Scotsman in the service of the King of Prussia, an old, much travelled eccentric who had more faith in the virtues of mankind than in their laws. He replied to Jean-Jacques' request by inviting Jean-Jacques to his residence and describing himself as being 'an old man rather like a savage, although perhaps somewhat corrupted by contact with civilised barbarians'. He certainly shared a good many of Jean-Jacques' ideas, but in addition he had something the citizen lacked—a sense of humour. He was tolerant of men's follies, remembering perhaps those that he himself had committed in his time.

The King was pleased 'to offer asylum to persecuted virtue', but made the mistake of expressing the hope that Jean-Jacques would cease to write 'about dangerous topics which might over-excite the passions of the people of Neuchâtel . . . who were given to fanaticism.' Jean-Jacques took offence and informed the Earl Marischal that while he had willingly promised himself to give up writing, he was under no obligation to make the pledge to anyone else. This point having been settled, he would comply with the rules of hospitality: 'On the whole,' he added 'there are but few kings whom I respect, and I am not fond of the monarchical form of government; but I have followed the rule of the gypsies who, in their forays, always spare the house in which they lodge.' He was quibbling, as usual. Some time later the King ordered the Earl Marischal to send Jean-Jacques his allowance of wheat, wood and wine, expressing the hope 'that a present in kind would prove more acceptable than money'. Jean-Jacques responded to this generosity by sending the King the most pedantic, arrogant and fatuous letter possible. Prussia, he wrote, had been impoverished by war: 'You wish to give me bread,' wrote Jean-Jacques; 'do none of your subjects lack bread? Remove from my sight that sword which dazzles and offends my gaze. . . . Could I but see the just and feared Frederick fill his States at last with a race of happy people to whom he would be a father, then Jean-Jacques Rousseau, the enemy of kings, would willingly die of joy on the steps of his throne.' The Earl Marischal had asked him if the King's gesture did not warrant some 'polite response' on his part: this was perhaps rather more than he had bargained for.

The Neuchâtel ministers, like their colleagues everywhere, banned *Le Contrat Social* and *Emile*, but no action was taken against Jean-Jacques. M. de Montmollin, who was minister at Motiers, in response to the request made to him by Jean-Jacques, not only 'agreed but was even desirous' that he should be admitted to Communion at the end of August: he took Communion and it was 'the greatest possible solace'. He had written to the minister:

> I am sincerely attached to this true and holy religion, and I shall be until I draw my last breath. I desire always to be united with the Church outwardly, as I am in the depths of my heart, and whatever solace I may find from sharing in the Communion of the faithful, I affirm that I desire to do so as much for their edification and the honour of the Church as for my own advantage; for it is not right that anyone should think that a sincere man who uses his reason cannot be a member of Jesus Christ.

The letter showed little humility. Mme de Boufflers disapproved of this action by Jean-Jacques, suspecting him perhaps of hypocrisy. Jean-Jacques, however, was acting in accordance with the advice of the 'Vicaire Savoyard': he was adopting the customs and religion of the country in which he was born, and just as he had seen to it that Thérèse could fulfil her religious duties in a neighbouring village where there was a Catholic priest, so he himself was careful not to give offence to the flock to which he now happened to belong. Nevertheless the vigour with which he replied to Mme de Boufflers on this score, the pains he took to justify himself, seem to indicate that he was not absolutely sure of not having also been swayed by considerations 'of his own advantage'. He protested that he had not gone back on anything he had said in his book. In any case, M. de Montmollin had not asked him to do so. What he had done afforded him only feelings of joy. 'You have to be oppressed, ailing and at the same time have faith in God to feel how sweet it is to live amongst your brothers.' M. de Montmollin's generosity in recognising him as a member of his Church, in opposition to all his colleagues, made it incumbent upon Jean-Jacques to be guided by him from now on. As regard the charge of hypocrisy, he was able to do himself justice on that score: 'An author who has been banished,' he wrote, 'for whose arrest a warrant has been issued and whose works have been burned because he had the courage to express his opinions, sign his writings and refuse to go back on his word: a citizen who cherishes his fatherland yet prefers to give up his country rather than his freedom of expression, and go into exile rather than renounce his beliefs, is quite a new sort of hypocrite.'

'O peace, which comes from being forgotten by men, O precious tranquillity, where are you? Ah, if only I could find you among these mountains, I would spend the rest of my days here. I am trying to wipe out all memory of the past.' Such was his lament to the Marquise de Verdelin, when he wrote to ask for news of his cat, 'la Doyenne', which he had left in her keeping. Could he henceforth be expected to be no more than one of the good M. de Montmollin's silent and submissive parishioners? He had arranged for some repairs to be done to the house lent to him by Mme Boy de la Tour. He had taken to wearing the long Armenian robe which was so convenient in view of his disability. For want of clients he did no more copying, but he had learned to make laces, and offered to give some to any young girl who, at the time of her marriage, pledged herself to feed her child herself. He was more than half a woman, he said. At last he had found peace, and all he wanted was peace. But winter came, bringing cold and snow, that his 'machine' might not be able to endure. His health worsened and once more he thought of making his will.

At the beginning of October a letter from M. de Conzié informed him of Maman's death which had occurred two months earlier. Henceforth, wrote M. de Conzié, she would be 'happy', 'her noble soul would receive the reward for her virtues and sufferings'. M. de Conzié invited him to spend a few days in his 'hermitage' at Les Charmettes where there was 'a tiny cell, good milk, beautiful fruit, good chestnuts and peace in plenty'. All this awakened memories in Jean-Jacques. His thoughts turned once more to the story of his life that Rey was urging him to write. What better course was open to him than to concentrate his thoughts on this and seek repose within himself? He asked M. de Malesherbes to send him a copy of the letters he had sent him at the beginning of the year and which were a kind of preliminary sketch for his self-portrait. Then, such was his nature, that on a sudden impulse he again threw himself into the fray. He was still in the grip of a kind of resentful anger. It occurred to him to write a pamphlet frankly entitled: 'Jean-Jacques Rousseau, citizen of Geneva, to Christophe de Beaumont, Archbishop of Paris.' He had reached a point at which he felt he could and should address a prince of the Church as his equal. 'How does it come about, Your Grace,' he exclaimed 'that I find myself addressing you? What language do we have in common with which to speak to each other? How are we to understand each other? And what is there between you and me?'

Here again he showed a certain guile. By attacking the Catholics, he was reckoning on gaining the goodwill of the Protestants. A Genevan minister, called Sarrasin, had expressed to M. de Montmollin his astonishment at the readiness with which the latter had allowed Jean-Jacques to take Communion. Subsequently Jean-Jacques had discussions with M. de Montmollin about the teachings of the *Vicaire savoyard*. He asserted that it had never been his intention to attack the Reformed Church, but that his sole aim had been to fight the intolerant and murderous dogmas of the Roman Church, and to protest, if not directly, at least quite clearly, against the abominable work of Helvétius, and confound the new philosophers. All this he proposed to restate in his letter to the Archbishop. By attacking 'Papism' and 'Roman idolatry' he hoped to win back the confidence and respect of the Genevan ministers.

The Archbishop's 'pastoral letter' cut him to the quick. The fact was that some parts of it were quite well written and it put rather splendid rhetoric at the service of tradition and order.

From the very heart of error [the Archbishop had written], there has arisen a man who is filled with the language of philosophy without being a true philosopher: his is a mind endowed with a great variety of knowledge which has not enlightened him and which has spread darkness in the minds of others; his is a character subject to paradoxical opinions and behaviour, combining simplicity of manners with pretentiousness of thought, fervent admiration for ancient maxims with a passionate advocacy of innovation, the obscurity of retirement with the desire for notoriety: he has inveighed against those very forms of knowledge he was cultivating, he has preached the excellence of the Gospels while destroying the dogmas they contain: he has depicted the beauty of those virtues which he was stifling in the souls of his readers. He has set himself up as the teacher of the human race only to deceive it, as a public guide only to lead everyone astray, as the oracle of his age only to consummate its ruin. In a work on social inequality he had reduced man to the level of the beasts: into a more recent work, he introduced the poison of sensual pleasure while seeming to proscribe it: in this particular work he takes advantage of man's early years, in order to establish the supremacy of irreligion.

The opening pages of Jean-Jacques' reply are admirable. Strangely enough, Beaumarchais was to adopt the same rhythm, feeling and even the same ideas in some passages of Figaro's monologue. I recommend students of literary sources to make a comparison between the two texts: Jean-Jacques writes: 'As I begin this letter I cannot help reflecting on the strangeness of my fate: some features are peculiar to me alone.' And Figaro asks: 'Can anything be stranger than my fate?' Both the hero of Beaumarchais' play and Jean-Jacques express the same astonishment at this strangeness, the same surprise at having suffered so much injustice, the same rebelliousness: they use the same violent language, the same biting epigrams, and occasionally the same linguistic ambiguities. Jean-Jacques speaks out as if he were addressing the audience from the front of the stage. Never before had he used such simple and direct language: never before had his style been so relaxed and so telling. He declared that all these things had happened to him through no wish of his own. He recounted his life-story, or rather the myth he had made of it. He had been born 'in happy obscurity' and he had never had any intention of becoming a writer. He had been plunged into authorship by a wretched question set by an academy and found himself transformed into a writer through his very contempt for that profession, and at the same time into a victim of the public. He was extolled, fêted, sought out, insulted, threatened and cursed and all for the most futile reasons. Now, weary of the heady fumes of success which puff a man up without completely satisfying him, he thought of laying aside his pen. All he wanted was to die in peace. This, bailiffs had just informed him, he would not be allowed to do: as a Genevan and a Protestant he had had a book printed in

Holland, and a warrant had been issued for his arrest by the Paris Parlement which no doubt thought itself qualified to judge the human race. This was the sum total of his crimes . . . and of his virtues. But everybody, 'great and small' alike, had become involved in the matter; the dreariest pedant felt entitled to give his expert opinion: there was not a stupid minor cleric nor paltry parish priest who did not want the honour of aiming the last kick at him.

There follows a furious passage in which we can catch a glint of madness.

> All this, Your Grace, forms a combination of circumstances to which I alone am subject; yet this is not all. I am now faced with one of the most difficult situations in my life, one of those in which vengeance and self-respect could most easily be satisfied and which least encourage an upright man to behave with moderation. A dozen lines would suffice to pour everlasting ridicule on my persecutors. If only the public could be informed of two incidents, without my having to reveal them! If only the public knew who had planned my destruction, and what has been done to encompass it, they would see through the agency of what contemptible insects, by what sinister means, the powers that be seek to operate! They would see what noisome decay had been at work within the Parlement to produce this state of ferment! They would see for what ludicrous reasons the States of Europe were leagued together against a watchmaker's son! How greatly I would enjoy their surprise, were it in my power not to be the instrument of it!

But he would not divulge these incidents. His pen, 'fearless in telling the truth yet innocent of all satirical intent', would compromise no one. Consequently we will never know for sure what the two incidents were which his madness was feeding on; to whom, to what, he was referring. He was probably thinking of events at L'Ermitage, of the behaviour of the *philosophes*, and Grimm's jealousy, and perhaps also his disagreement with his Jansenist neighbours in Montmorency who, when in Paris, lived in the same house as D'Alembert, and had, he believed, denounced him. In his present state of anguished brooding any memory could revive and fill his whole mind, and anything could serve as a proof.

Jean-Jacques' skill was shown in the way all through the letter he maintained an admirably dignified tone. Addressing the Archbishop again in the style of Figaro he said:

> You thought you could humiliate me by ill-treatment, but you were mistaken: without weakening my arguments you have prompted generous hearts to take an interest in my misfortunes. ... Your Grace has shown himself neither humane nor generous towards me: not only could you have displayed such qualities without sparing any of the criticisms you have made against my book, but had you done so, those criticisms would have been more effective. I confess too that I had no right to demand such virtues of you, nor had I any reason to expect to find them in an ecclesiastic. Let us at least see whether you have been fair and just, for such a duty is strictly incumbent upon all men, and the saints themselves are not exempt from it.

Contemporary critics have made touching efforts to bring out the deeply religious, and even Christian character of Jean-Jacques' thought. But such leniency on the part of men whose judgement is backed by their own faith as believers is perhaps a striking sign of the exhaustion and weakening of the Christian religion during the nineteenth century. Archbishop de Beaumont was no doubt right to be more exacting. It is true that Jean-Jacques himself exclaimed: 'I am a Christian', and this was enough to earn him the hatred of the *philosophes*, but not the respect of believers. In such matters the individual is not the only judge, and heresy consists precisely in believing that he is. He further declared: 'I feel my soul within me: ... ' such a statement can only be an adequate justification in a debased Church which is more sensitive to the aesthetic quality of attitudes than to the truth of the dogma. What sort of Christian could he be, since he argued against the revelation and the miracles, and believed neither in the Trinity nor in Christ's mission, nor in His Redemption of mankind? It was possible that Jean-Jacques was a deeply religious person, but, if so, this only made him all the more dangerous. By proclaiming *his* religion and nothing but *his* religion, he set a shocking example of freedom. 'I wanted God to say to me what he had not said to others.' Such was the *Vicaire savoyard's* claim, and in making it he expressed Jean-Jacques' own unacceptable pretension. In his pride, not only did he have the effrontery to deny the revelation contained in the Gospels, he was not far from believing that, if there were any revelation, he alone had proved worthy of it. His *Profession of Faith* was tantamount to a new Gospel. He dared to talk as if he were another Christ, and he was very near to believing that he was.

Compared to the *philosophes*, Jean-Jacques may appear today, in the history of ideas and manners, to be an upholder of religious sensibility. Yet he undid that which he upheld. Religiosity is not religion; from the point of view of a dogmatic religion, which is still in its prime, it means very little to say only that one is aware of God. Which God? it asks. But at a time when dogma was in decline, when the majority of thinking people found it impossible to believe in miracles, Jean-Jacques happened to describe a faith that was still possible: he freed God from the Churches, yet kept the great vague name of God as a powerful consolation. But M. de Beaumont, who had no intention of surrendering his Archbishop's crook, was right to condemn him as a heretic. *Emile* heralded the end or the inevitable transformation of a religion for whom man, by his very nature, was suspect, and which set out merely to curb his passions. Jean-Jacques had no fear of God and rejected the concept of a God of fear. He believed in the first place in himself and believed that he was authorised by God to do so. He believed that man was free to the point of not needing to ask anything of God. Divine Grace became superfluous. The fundamental issue which the Archbishop rightly stressed was the belief in original sin. It was the existence of original sin which justified the Church and its clergy in keeping a close watch on all human activity, in loading men from childhood with chains, so as to accustom them to submission. Jean-Jacques had asserted on the contrary: 'Let us take it as an irrefutable principle that the first impulses of nature are always sound: there is no original perversity in the human heart.' He thus undermined the whole structure of Christian belief, and shared in the mad passion of his century and of the *philosophes* whose aim, according to M. de Beaumont, 'was nothing less than to appropriate the heritage of Jesus Christ'. Jean-Jacques believed still more in man than in God. To be exact, he made no distinction between the cause of God and the cause of humanity. His letter is the best possible expression of the fact that God himself is never anything but a concept and a word used by man.

Two or three pages of his letter were intended more especially for the ministers. Affecting rather too cleverly to address the Archbishop, he said: 'Because the Vicaire raises certain objections against his Church which is the Catholic Church, you are trying to make me out to be an enemy of mine.' He protested with all his heart that he was happy to have been born into the most reasonable and most holy of religions, and to be 'inseparably attached to the creed of his forefathers'. Priests were within their rights to attack him, but not Protestant ministers.

Deeply grateful as I am [he wrote], to the worthy minister who resisted the overwhelming pressure of example, judged according to the truth, and did not exclude a defender of God's cause from his Church, I shall retain all my life a tender memory of his truly Christian charity. I shall always be proud of having been considered one of his flock, and I hope I shall in no way shock its other members either by my opinions or my behaviour: but when priests unjustly assume rights they do not possess and set up as the arbiters of my beliefs and say to me arrogantly: Retract what you have said, conceal your opinions, explain this, deny that, their haughty manner does not in the least impress me, and they will never force me to tell lies in order to be orthodox, nor say what I do not believe in order to please them. If my vigorous language offends them and if they wish to expel me from the Church, their threats will inspire little fear in me, for it is not in their power to carry them into effect. They cannot prevent me remaining united with the faithful in heart: they cannot delete my name from the list of the elect if it is already inscribed there. They may deprive me of consolation in this life but not of the hope of the life which is to come, and that is why my most ardent and sincere wish is that Jesus Christ should be the arbiter and judge between them and me.

Here again he was manoeuvring quite shrewdly. He could not prevent the ministers behaving towards him as the priests had done! But he was obliging them to admit that he represented Protestant tradition and was using the very language of its founders. Luther had declared: 'I am neither able nor willing to retract anything . . . for it is neither safe nor honourable to act against your conscience.' Like the great founders, Jean-Jacques' only concern was with the truth which it was his duty to communicate; apart from that he was humble and simpler than they had shown themselves to be, because, like Christ, he had no taste for doctrinal subtleties or theological jargon, and was more interested in charity and virtue than formulations of belief and articles of faith.

In his conclusion, Jean-Jacques, ceasing to deal with the religious issue, reverted to the theme which gave his letter its true grandeur. He, an ordinary man of humble birth, addressed one of the great ones of the earth, and in tones never before heard. Over and above all the incidental disagreements, his deepest concern was clearly evident—it was to force recognition of the equal dignity of all men.

> Men like you, sitting in the seats of the mighty, can discourse at will. Recognising no rights but your own, and no laws but those you yourselves impose, far from making it your duty to be just, you do not even feel yourselves called upon to be humane. In your pride you ruthlessly crush the weak without being answerable to anyone for your own iniquities; insults come as readily to you as acts of violence: and whenever it suits your own interests or those of the Church you sweep us out of your way as if we were no more than dust. . . . If Your Grace . . . were a private person like myself, and I could summon you before an impartial court, where we could both appear, I with my book and you with your pastoral letter, you would certainly be found guilty and condemned to make me reparation as public as your offence has been. But your rank relieves you of the necessity of being just, and I count as nothing.

The stage was obviously set for Figaro's entry, and the very language he would speak was ready waiting for him.

On the 1st January 1763, Jean-Jacques sent his manuscript to Rey to be printed. A few days later he was still uncertain about publishing it, then finally he let matters take their course. Then, now that the excitement of inspiration had subsided, he was bored. It was a strange experience to be at once a very important man in the eyes of the world and yet so solitary. The courtesies shown him by the one or two people who came to visit him were not enough; he had quarrelled with his neighbours in the village. As long as the weather was not too inclement he had sometimes been able to pay a visit to the Earl Marischal at Colombier. Winter, however, forced him to remain indoors and he was reduced to building 'castles in the air'. It was all

settled that as soon as the Earl-Marischal had found a husband
for his adopted daughter Emet Ulla, and some occupation for
his other children, his illegitimate son Ibrahim, the two bastards
Motcho and Guinée and Stephan the Kalmuck, he would go
back and live in Scotland and take Jean-Jacques with him.
David Hume, 'the kind and gentle David', and a friend of the
Earl Marischal would join them and all three would found a
small republic and at last experience *placidam sub libertate
quietem.*

Meanwhile, however, Jean-Jacques had to endure the rigours
of the climate and was ill during the whole winter. 'The
machine' was becoming more seriously impaired and once more
he made a will in favour of Thérèse: 'I hope,' he wrote, 'to die as
poor as I have been in life; a few clothes and a small sum of
money will probably be all I will leave behind me, and it is
hardly worth making a will for so little. But the little there is
does not belong to me: I must dispose of it according to the laws
of gratitude.' He was even bored by the countryside because it
was no longer the same as it had been in his youth; everything
had changed. The truth was, as he pointed out to the Maréchal
de Luxembourg, he himself had changed and grown old. 'When
we become incapable of pleasure, we imagine pleasure has
everywhere ceased to exist.' The local inhabitants appeared to
him to be vain and 'over-ceremonious'. True, he had received
letters from all over Europe, but most of them were burdensome
because they prevented him concentrating on himself. Moreover
the large number that actually arrived made him wonder about
those that were, he was sure, being intercepted. The letters he
treasured most were those from Paris. His attitude to France
was uncertain—France was the cause of all his misfortunes, yet
Le Devin de Village was being performed again at Versailles and
Duchesne the publisher was offering to reprint all his works.
The Luxembourgs wrote less often; but unhappy women like
Mme de Verdelin, Mme de Chenonceaux, remained faithful to
him—together with Mme de la Tour whom he had never met
and whom he had at first treated so harshly.

Poor Marianne, he had even forgotten her Christian name.
He had to write and ask her to remind him of it. He also asked
her to give her age, and a description of herself. 'I think,' he
said, 'that your features disturb me even more than if I had seen

them.' They vied with one another in coyness. He would have been very distressed if their sentimental correspondence had come to an end now. When, in December, Mme de la Tour was again urging him to write without delay, he had replied: 'Everything I receive from you appeals to me and attracts me— apart from one small detail.' The small detail was simply Marianne's insistence on being replied to promptly. Marianne, however, did not understand what he was referring to and for more than a year the 'small detail' was a great subject of discussion between them. Marianne was very keen to know what the 'small detail' was, and Jean-Jacques, who had quite forgotten what he had written, was very hard put to it to enlighten her. All this romantic cajolery was a great solace to him. When it was in danger of being interrupted, he would set it going again by some unkind remark, as was his wont. . . .

The absurdity of the world struck him more and more and he was at a loss to know what he was doing in it. It occurred to him that he might change his name. But, as the Earl Marischal pointed out, such a step would be quite useless: 'Since you will alter neither your habits nor your mind, the citizen of Geneva will soon be recognised.' There was no getting away from his identity. To add to his uncertainties, he received a curious piece of news from Moultou: the latter had been sent for by Voltaire who had talked to him at great length about Jean-Jacques in tones which, Moultou swore, left no doubt about his affection. Jean-Jacques was not altogether convinced, but declared that he was ready to let bygones be bygones, feeling certain, moreover, that 'for the sake of his own reputation, it was in Voltaire's best interests to make up their quarrel'. The Earl Marischal, who was a man of sense, did his best to ensure a modicum of safety for the bewildered fugitive who was in danger of finding himself with no possible refuge anywhere in the world. As the Earl Marischal was planning to leave Neuchâtel and go first of all to Berlin, then to Scotland, and in fact did leave on the 30th April, he took care beforehand to see that the King issued 'letters of naturalisation' to Jean-Jacques in the principality of Neuchâtel.

On all sides people were engaged in refuting the *Profession of Faith*. On the 3rd March, Jean-Jacques received a refutation from Bitaubé, who was a minister in Berlin. According to his calculations this was the twenty-fourth refutation. He simply did not have time to read everything that was being written about him. Nevertheless he was well aware of every attack and on occasions ready to fight back. A certain Méreau, dancing-master to the Duc de Saxe-Gotha and a relative and pupil of the famous dancer, Marcel, whom he had referred to somewhat disparagingly in *Emile*, wrote to avenge his master. Jean-Jacques enjoyed replying to this letter. Méreau had recognised that he was a 'singular man', and this at least gave him pleasure. He was more irritated by the attacks of the Neuchâtel *Mercure* which never let a month go by without condemning his 'sophistry' and his 'inconsistencies'.

In March, his letter to the Archbishop was brought out in Geneva, and for several weeks Jean-Jacques and his friends watched carefully to see what effect it was producing. Moultou and De Luc maintained that 'Jean-Jacques' enemies had been thrown into confusion', that he only had to appear in Geneva to realise that he had won the day. He himself was more cautious and rightly so. The first syndic did not forbid the sale of the letter, but under pressure from the Resident of France forbade that it should be reprinted in Geneva, and his decision was ratified by the Petit Conseil. From that moment Jean-Jacques' mind was made up. On the 12th May he sent his letter of renunciation to the first syndic.

Having at last recovered [he wrote], from the astonishment into which I was plunged by the unexpected behaviour on the part of the Magnifique Conseil, I now take, at however great a cost to myself, the decision which honour and reason prescribe. I therefore declare to you, Sir, and beg you to inform the Magnifique Conseil on my behalf, that I renounce for ever my rights as a burgess and citizen in the town and Republic of Geneva. I have tried to honour the name of Genevan: I have loved my fellow-countrymen dearly; I have done all I could in order to be beloved of them; no one could have been less successful. I wish to gratify them even in their hatred: the final sacrifice which I can still make them is to give up a name which once was dear to me....
But, Sir, my native city may become foreign to me, it can never leave me indifferent; I remain bound to it by tender memories, and forget only its affronts. May it prosper always, and see its fame enhanced. May it abound in citizens who are better and above all happier than I am!

In his view this was a great gesture and it perhaps caused less stir than he had hoped. The idea had long been in his mind, ever since those sombre days in June 1762 when in his distress he had expected Geneva, his native city, to recall and welcome him, and had been obliged to accept the asylum offered him by foreigners. He had felt enraged and humiliated, because no one had done more for his country than he had. He had always linked Geneva to his thought and his fame and he had always quoted Geneva among servile peoples as the guarantor of his integrity of purpose. He was Rousseau of Geneva and insisted on the title. He had signed himself Citizen of Geneva every time he wished to give men some idea of what freedom and virtue were. Through him, Geneva was in process of changing the world. And yet Geneva despised him. Now the world would have to choose between his native city and himself. His letter of renunciation would bring eternal shame on Geneva. It could sometimes happen that a man's conception of his fatherland was more truly representative of it than the fatherland itself, which was a confused and fortuitous conglomeration of petty interests, petty traditions and petty events. He might give up his title; but he would retain it for ever in the memory of men and Geneva, after condeming him, would owe to him its true life and true greatness.

When writing to individual Genevans he adopted a humbler tone: 'You who know my feelings, pity me for having to take so heart-rending a step. But after the affronts I have suffered in my native city, affronts for which atonement has not, and never can, be made, to consider myself to be still a Genevan citizen would be to accept dishonour.' Forty years ago, in 1722, his father Isaac Rousseau had chosen to go into exile on a point of honour. He had cried: 'I am Rousseau! I am Rousseau!' and had left the town and had never made his peace with it again. Perhaps his gesture had been forgotten by now. At the time the powers that be had laughed at what seemed to them to be a misplaced demonstration of pride. Things would not be as simple in the case of the son who was now in his turn crying 'I am Rousseau! I am Rousseau!' but in a voice with quite a different ring.

It was the decision taken by his father which had started him off on his chequered existence. He had almost always lived a long way from his homeland. It is true that for quite a long time he had given it but little thought, and he does not appear to have suffered much from the *heimweh* which he describes in a letter to the Maréchal de Luxembourg as the characteristic 'and sometimes fatal disease' of the Swiss in exile, nor did the strains of the *ranz des vaches* ever bring tears to his eyes when heard in a foreign land. As a matter of fact for a number of years he had been inclined to let it be forgotten that he was Swiss, and if he did admit his nationality, it was to excuse his clumsiness. He had rediscovered his fatherland in the year 1750 at the same time as he had rediscovered himself. His wasted efforts, all his fruitless attempts to become a fashionable writer, the very fact of failure, had reconciled him to Geneva, and from then on he had ostentatiously behaved as a citizen among subjects and as a free man among slaves. This had been the root cause of his success. He had become the citizen of an ideal Geneva which he created in his resentful day-dreams. But what did he know of the real Geneva? For him it was no more than a few child-hood memories. Geneva was something he had dreamed of rather than known. Even in 1754, when he returned there in order to become reinstated in the Protestant religion and recover a title which for the past four years he had publicly assumed although he had no right to do so, his stay had been short, and he had seen very little of the town. The kind manner in which he had been treated had only served to increase his illusions. No doubt he was literally a 'citizen of Geneva', but he was also an *émigré*. He had travelled a good deal and owed more than he realised to the spirit of freedom and tolerance which he had discovered among the 'enslaved' peoples, to the atmosphere of Paris, to the enlightened knowledge of the *philosophes*, his 'former friends', to Diderot, Grimm and even Voltaire. He had meditated at great length on the Genevan word, Republic, but his dreams had been nourished by his reading. It was in France that he had learned to think for the whole world. The *Profession de Foi du Vicaire Savoyard* and the *Contrat Social* would never perhaps have been written if he had not been born in Geneva, but had he never left the town they would have been nothing more than insignificant pamphlets about local politics. It was his experience as an exile which turned them into universally valid meditations.

He was now beginning to find out what the real Geneva was like—it was a theocratic republic infected by the unwholesome air blowing over the mountains from France, and he found himself out of harmony with everything in Geneva, because he had lived too long among the *philosophes* to have any liking for theologians, and had suffered too much from the politeness and ceremoniousness of French manners to tolerate the Genevans' awkward imitation of them. He had nothing but contempt for the kind of hypocrisy which brought both the ministers and . . . Voltaire into his enemies' camp. How could he tolerate the supervision and restraints which the New Zion thought fit to impose upon him at the very time when all its own standards were being debased? He took his stand against the whole of his native city, as he had taken his stand against the Church, in writing his letter to the Archbishop. The gesture was the same and prompted by the same pride, but it was more extraordinary in this case. Can one imagine a man declaring that he is no longer French, English or American and expecting that this declaration alone would be enough to recall France, England and America to their true nature? No society can be lawfully constituted except on the basis of a contract. He considered that in his case the contract had been broken; he had been denied the justice due to him, and the whole world had to be called to witness. All nations would benefit from the lesson that a single conscience can outweigh a State. At once the town was in an uproar. Moultou wrote to Jean-Jacques:

> I have shed tears for your country, and felt admiration for you: I would never have advised you to take the decision you have taken, but you were right to do so. It was the only one worthy of you. I have seen how dejected the good citizens are because they must be reproaching themselves for their own weakness: I have seen the cruel jubilation of the others, which was disturbed by shame and remorse. Oh my friend, you are indeed great; I have enough greatness myself to feel the nobility of your soul.

In a letter which has not come down to us another of his friends, Marc Chappuis, disapproved of his action. Jean-Jacques replied by laying bare his soul: 'After having been publicly disgraced in my native city,' he wrote, 'and after waiting ten months during which no one has protested against the stigma, I was compelled to take the only course capable of protecting my honour which has been so cruelly attacked.' He explained that he owed some account of himself 'to the public to whom he had the misfortune to be known, and to posterity who might one day come to know him'. The burgesses of Geneva had the right to make representations: why then had they not done so when he had been treated so shamefully by the Petit Conseil? Since his decision harmed no one but himself Geneva had nothing to complain about. 'By breaking its pledges,' he concluded, 'it has freed me from mine; and by making them appear ignominious to me, it forces upon me the duty of renouncing them. O Genevans! I had put my honour in your safe-keeping and my mind was at rest: but you have proved so unworthy of this trust that you oblige me to withdraw it.' The letter was read by the whole town: people said that 'it sounded the signal for revolt'. Through no wish of his own his name was becoming the rallying point for a kind of revolution. During this last year he had spent in exile, he had even tried to moderate the turbulent zeal of his friends. But deep within him he felt embittered and thought that everything done on his behalf was inadequate. Certain individuals such as Colonel Pictet, Marcet de Mézières, and De Luc had espoused his cause. The Procureur-général had been re-elected at the end of the year 1762, but with some difficulty since he lost four hundred votes. But that was not enough for Jean-Jacques. He had hoped for more, and had expected that the entire Genevan bourgeoisie would rise up in his defence.

On 18th June 1763 De Luc, accompanied by forty or so citizens, presented an initial *Représentation* (remonstrance) to the First Syndic. They were not only protesting against Jean-Jacques' condemnation, but widening the issue, and in fact relaunching the offensive against the Petit Conseil which had been interrupted by the Act of Mediation of 1738. Jean-Jacques declared himself 'glad indeed to find in his former fellow-citizens vestiges of an affection that he had thought quite dead', but considered his friends' action 'too belated to be of any use'. The government responded by rejecting the remonstrance. Tension mounted and the Petit Conseil put up a weak defence.[1] There was a second then a third remonstrance. The dispute now reached its height and dealt with the scope of the remon-

[1] Cf. Rod, *L'Affaire Jean-Jacques Rousseau.*

strances, how and to what extent they could limit the power of the oligarchs of the Petit Conseil, the rights of the mass of the population, those of its rulers, who seemed to reject every check on, and supervision of, their authority and always adopted a negative attitude to popular demands. Geneva was divided between two parties: the '*Négatifs*' and '*Représentants*'. Towards the end of the summer, Tronchin the Procureur-général published his *Lettres de la Campagne*, which was a clever and eloquent defence of the oligarchic tradition. This was followed by a fourth remonstrance more biting and vigorous than the preceding ones, but the main result was that De Luc succeeded in persuading Jean-Jacques to reply in person to the Procureur at the same time as the *Représentants* were drawing up their collective reply.

He took his time about it and worked in great secrecy for months, right through the winter and spring. For he was quite capable of discretion and secrecy, and he is mistaken when he declares in the *Confessions* that 'by nature he found it absolutely impossible to keep anything hidden that he felt or thought'. He felt he had finally to settle his account with the authorities and with the ministers who continued to bombard him with pamphlets.[1] His pledge never to write again had been taken in vain; calumny forced him once more to take up the pen. He wrote to De Luc: 'Being ill, listless, disheartened, passionately longing for the peace I am not allowed to enjoy, I feel the greatest possible distaste for this task whose difficulties I am well aware of, especially since it must be done superlatively well, or not done at all. I have no love for childish baubles: if I touch them they fall to pieces in my hand.'

Having an inadequate knowledge of the history of Geneva he set about studying it, and De Luc provided him with all the necessary books. He at once saw how dangerous it would be for him to allow himself to be restricted to the history of Geneva. The aim was to interest the whole of Europe in this revolution that was taking place in a small town. He was always most effective when he adopted a certain plaintive and humble tone. It was exactly the right tone to win him the support of humble people everywhere. He began with a sort of preface:

[1] Cf. Jacob Vernes, *Lettres sur le Christianisme de J.-J. Rousseau.*

It is somewhat late in the day, I know, to return to a hackneyed and almost forgotten subject. My state of health which forbids sustained effort, and my dislike of polemics, are responsible for my slowness in writing, and my reluctance to publish. I would have destroyed these letters, or rather I would never have written them, if my own interests alone were at stake: but I am not so far estranged from my native city as to be able to look on calmly while its citizens are oppressed, especially since it was to defend my cause that they have endangered their rights. I would be the most despicable of men if, in such circumstances, I heeded a feeling which passes beyond gentleness and patience to become weakness and cowardice, when it prevents a man fulfilling his duty.

I agree that the subject-matter of these letters can be of no importance to the general public. The political constitution of a small town, the fate of one petty individual, the stating of a number of injustices, the refuting of certain sophistries—these are not in themselves matters of sufficient consequence to attract a great many readers. But if my subject-matter is slight, the objects I have in view are great and worthy of the attention of every decent, upright man. Let us disregard Geneva, and leave Rousseau to his depression; religion, freedom and justice! These matters are not unworthy of your attention, whoever you may be!

It is clear that he had not lost his old fire and had an ability to generalise. Tronchin had entitled his letters, *Lettres de la Campagne*. Jean-Jacques called his: *Lettres de la Montagne*. He withdrew nothing whatsoever of what he had written in *Emile* and the *Contrat Social*. He maintained that the Petit Conseil's condemnation of himself and his books had been illegal and he proved as much by quoting certain facts from the history of Geneva. But his attitude was one of aggression much more than one of self-defence.

What right, he asked, had magistrates to pass judgement on his religion? By law they were required to ask the opinion of the Consistoire, but they had been careful not to do this. His books had been 'torn to shreds' in the search for reprehensible statements. The Gospels themselves could not have stood up to so 'infamous an inquisition'. But he felt that all those early Reformers who had broken away from the Church of Rome purely because of their belief in tolerance and liberty of thought were on his side. 'What,' he asked, 'was the true spirit of the evangelical Reformation?' and gave the answer.

The individual reason decides by deducing the tenets of faith from its accepted common standard which is the Gospel, and it is so essential a quality of reason to be free, that even if it wished to submit to authority it would not be at liberty to do so. If this principle is in any way weakened, the whole doctrine of Evangelicalism at once collapses. If it can be proved to me today that in matters of faith I am obliged to submit to anyone's decisions, I will become a Catholic tomorrow and every sincere and consistent man will do likewise.

Had the pastors, and ministers, understood and still been attached to their religion, they would have greeted the publication of his book with cries of joy. But 'their mania for wrangling and intolerance is such that they no longer know what they believe, what they want, nor what they are saying . . . they are no more than clumsy hirelings of the Priests'.

As regards his political thought, it is true that he was at times too argumentative, proving only too well that had he remained within the narrow confines of Geneva he himself would have been no mean wrangler. But as soon as he broached the problem of the relationship within the Republic between the people and the government he raised the level of the argument, and, addressing the burgesses of Geneva, exclaimed:

Most honoured and sovereign Lords, your magistrates themselves call you magnificent. . . . But the body entrusted with the execution of your laws is at the same time their supreme interpreter and arbiter: it gives them the meaning it chooses; it can render them ineffectual. . . . You may be sovereign Lords within the Assembly, but once outside it you are of no consequence. Four hours a year you are subordinate sovereigns, for the rest of your lives you are subjects. . . . There remains therefore only one active power in the State, the executive. The executive power consists only of force, and where force alone prevails, the State is dissolved. That is how all democratic States eventually perish.

He explained how freedom had been lost, through the action of time, and the inevitable and stubborn determination of a permanent body to increase its power. Slowly, imperceptibly, without anyone being able to foresee what the ultimate outcome would be, the gentlemen of the Petit Conseil introduced their innovations . . . and when finally they were noticed and efforts were made to remedy them, it was the Petit Conseil itself which accused others of being innovators. When he came to examine the underlying principle of the remonstrances which the *Négatifs* refused even to consider, Jean-Jacques showed that they provided the only means 'of ensuring that the Magistrates remained subject to the law'. If, in a Republic, there had to be a 'negative power' which could oppose all innovations liable to destroy freedom, he asked to whom it should belong.

> On the one hand [wrote Jean-Jacques], I see a population restricted in numbers, sober and peace-loving, composed of hard-working men, anxious for prosperity, subject in their own interests to the laws and to their ministers, and entirely absorbed in their commerce or their different trades; since they are all equal as regards their rights, and there are few differences between them as regards wealth, there are neither leaders nor dependents among them: because of their commerce, their social situation and their possessions, they are all very much dependent on the magistrates, and are obliged to treat them with deference and are afraid of displeasing them: if they want to intervene in public affairs, they only do so at the expense of their own interests. . . . On the other hand, in this small town, whose affairs are, when all is said and done, of no great significance, I see an independent and permanent body of Magistrates, almost professionally idle, who devote most of their energies to what is the very vital and very natural concern of all those in power, which is to extend their authority unceasingly. For ambition, like greed, feeds on its advantages, and the further man extends his power, the more he is consumed with the desire to become all-powerful. . . . Such [Jean-Jacques explained] were the relative positions of the Petit Conseil and the Genevan Bourgeoisie.

It was clearly within the scope of the bourgeoisie to put a stop to the encroachments of the Petit Conseil. After expressing this 'opinion', Jean-Jacques reverted in conclusion to a plaintive and pathetic tone. In giving his opinion, as he had been asked to by his fellow-citizens, 'I have,' he said, 'fulfilled my final duty towards my native city. I now take leave of its inhabitants; there is no further harm they can do me, and there is no good I can do them.'

Opposition always produced the same reaction in him: it made him advance one stage further in the elucidation of his thought. He had been accused of having questioned the truth of the miracles, and as a result launched a furious attack against miracles. A hundred years before Renan, he showed that the miracles were the greatest weakness of Christian theology: 'Yes,' he exclaimed, 'I shall always maintain that the support which people seek for their belief is the greatest obstacle to it: remove the miracles from the Gospels and the whole world will bow down before Jesus Christ.' And he added in a note: 'I do not know what these fine, fashionable Christians think in their heart of hearts; but if they believe in Christ because of his miracles, I believe in him in spite of them, and something tells me that my faith is better than theirs.'

On one point only perhaps his 'fine rhetoric' did not succeed in concealing the weakness of his defence, but served rather to reveal a certain contradiction in his thought. Even his friends had been somewhat embarrassed by the chapter on 'civil religion' in the *Contrat*. His justification of it was inadequate. The *Contrat*, he explained, was a purely political work, and that in it he was arguing purely from a political point of view, when he showed how impossible it was for Christianity to establish the unity of a country. The very arguments he uses justify a belief that when he wrote the *Profession de Foi du Vicaire savoyard*, and then again the chapter on civil religion in the *Contrat*, he had yielded to different and contradictory impulses, both of which were equally strong within him, and as usually happened, his very eloquence had led him to carry each one to its logical conclusion. The *Profession de Foi* affirms man's right to freedom of thought. 'Civil religion' grants the 'Sovereign' power to limit that freedom, and can turn the Republic into an unbearable prison. He was, as we would say today, both an anarchist and a totalitarian. The truth was he had both these tendencies from Geneva itself where they had been reconciled by history and tradition. But they remained irreconcilable in his own mind. What right had he to do what he forbade the Petit Conseil to do, that is, impose some particular creed on the citizens of his ideal republic? But each one of his readers has since discovered these same contradictions within himself; and the tension in every democracy springs perhaps from the fact that it is constantly striving to resolve and reconcile them.

The manuscript of the *Lettres* was ready by June (1764). Winter and spring had been fairly peaceful. In his own way he exercised the same kind of authority as Voltaire at Ferney. It seemed as if fame had finally conferred wisdom upon him. The *Confessions*, even his letters, show him perhaps as being sadder and more anxious than he really was. *Emile, La Nouvelle Héloïse*, the *Contrat* had ensured him an income. Mme de Verdelin and Mme de Boufflers wanted to give him money but he refused. The edition of his works being prepared by Duchesne, and the *Dictionnaire de Musique* which he hoped to publish soon, seemed to safeguard the future. All those who visited him at this time mention his amiability. He was rather proud of his eccentricity, and of his Armenian costume which he kept in good trim and even enhanced with silk sashes and fur trimmings. He went on making laces: 'I have thought like a man,' he said, 'I have written like a man, and people have disapproved of me, so now I will become a woman.' He declared that 'he was savouring the pleasure of existence'. Many people came to see him, among them friends such as Sauttersheim, who was not a spy as he had feared at one moment, but merely a sponger and adventurer, with a certain fascination for Jean-Jacques: then D'Ivernois, D'Escherny, Du Peyrou, and De Pury. It was at this time that he developed an interest in botany. It was, in his opinion, 'the true occupation for an active body and a lazy mind' such as his. On fine days, they used to go up into the surrounding mountains, and even attempted longer expeditions. D'Escherny never found him in anything but good health. 'To complain of being ill is a form of coquetry dear to geniuses and pretty women,' he comments. However, according to Jean-Jacques' account, which is contained in a letter to Julia Bondely, he could only ensure himself a tolerable night's sleep by chopping wood all day in spite of his weakness, so that he was in a constant state of perspiration, 'the briefest interruption in that state having very painful results'. The truth was that his state of health varied from day to day. During the fine weather he was out and about, in winter he was shut up in Motiers. He would have liked to find some other place of residence but he did not know where to go.

He was very happy to be the centre of so much attention and the happier it made him the more he affected to disdain it. He complained about receiving so many letters some of which, however, were extremely gratifying. On one occasion Marianne wrote to him that at Montmorency the peasants spoke of him as

being 'a father to them all'. They added, with tears in their
eyes, 'no wonder he has been treated like that, *because he could
foretell the future*'. A legend had already grown up around him,
and in his own village he was well on the way to being hailed as
the soothsayer of Europe. A daughter having been born to the
Prince de Wurtemberg, he called her Sophie, and announced
that he was relying on 'the sublime tutor of *Emile*' to see to her
education. Jean-Jacques, full of self-importance, immediately
despatched to the Prince what amounted to a veritable disserta-
tion on the subject. He concluded it with the following somewhat
insincere remarks:

> These are perhaps no more than the incoherent ravings of a
> feverish mind. The contrast between what is and what should be
> made a romantic of me, and has always made me a stranger to
> common practice. But you command, Sir, and I must obey.
> Since you ask for my ideas, here they are. I would be misleading
> you if I presented my follies to you as if they were the product of
> other people's reason. In submitting them to the scrutiny of so
> sound a judge I do not fear the harm they may cause.

For several months the Prince kept him informed of little
Sophie's progress, and Jean-Jacques wrote obsequious and
formal letters in reply. They contained not a single cry from the
heart. Not the slightest hint of remorse. Jean-Jacques, as the
spiritual foster-father, never descended from the heights of the
sublime. When young men asked for his advice he made his
oracular pronouncements with great authority. A certain
marquis called Séguier de Saint-Brisson was very anxious to be a
writer; Jean-Jacques advised him to 'concentrate on actions
rather than words'. The young Abbé de Carondelet wanted to
be confirmed in his desire to leave the Church. Jean-Jacques
replied: 'Before deciding on a profession, it is impossible to
study its purpose too carefully: once the decision has been taken,
the only course is to fulfil the duties of your profession.' His
readers were misled by the passionate tone of his books. Aristocrats feeling the restrictions of the tradition in which they had
been brought up wrote to him simply in the hope that he would
encourage them in their rebellious attitude, and were astonished
when he turned out to be a cautious plebeian, strongly attached
to the fundamental order of things, who uttered warnings and
chided them for their behaviour. His very admonishments

served to enhance his prestige, and everyone was anxious to have a letter from him. When none was available, people would make copies of the letters he had sent to more fortunate correspondents. He protested violently against such indiscretions, but they were balm to his soul. He never enjoyed fame so much as he did during these first years of his wanderings: it followed him wherever he went. Everywhere he was conscious of arousing curiosity and even a sort of love.

Letters addressed to a famous writer vary in quality, but there are always some that are moving. No doubt a number of the correspondents are crazy. But among the many appeals for help there is inevitably from time to time some letter so sincere, some cry so heart-rending, that however convinced the professional writer may be of his own sincerity, he is forced to realise how much facile padding there is in his writing, and to make some effort towards self-improvement. Some unknown, anonymous man or woman speaks out. In some unexpected and very simple letter, but one which is dictated by the experience of a lifetime, a reader, full of awed respect for genius and fame, bears witness, in the way the writer himself was trying to do, and his testimony transcends his anonymous individuality, and is as telling a revelation of the wretchedness that the writer was anxious to depict and cure, as he himself was ever able to give.

In April 1764 a young woman, of whom we know only that her Christian name was Henriette, wrote this kind of letter to Jean-Jacques. She must have been about thirty-five. She timidly revealed which passage in *Emile* had made her decide to write to him: it was the passage in which he condemned bluestockings. She was afraid that he might think she was one of those ridiculous creatures whom he so rightly condemned. But she was certainly not a bluestocking. 'I have no thorough knowledge of anything,' she said, 'still less do I try to put forward any pretence of knowledge.' She had had, however, to undertake certain studies, because, given her situation, this had seemed to her a 'reasonable, useful, and perhaps even necessary' thing to do. It was on this point that she requested his advice.

She explained that she was no longer either very young or very pretty. She had been born rich but had lost her wealth, 'just at the age when one is beginning to appreciate its advantages'. Then for the next fifteen or sixteen years she had had to face one trouble after another. She had learned that 'misfortune is a fault for which one is never entirely forgiven, that the consideration one is shown is always proportionate to the degree of one's wealth, and that this attitude was a failing which can be found even among sensible people'.

The entire letter was written with the same admirable lucidity. 'In short,' she wrote, 'I learnt enough about the human heart to despair of my own ever being satisfied. It was full to overflowing and needed to unburden itself, and to find some kind of consolation, but I knew no one in whom I could have that absolute trust which brings relief.' Being poor she had had to abandon any hope of the married state. She was gradually developing into an old maid and the prospect filled her with horror. 'There is nothing I would find so humiliating,' she wrote, 'as to be like a young woman who has been left on the shelf, and who is waiting in vain for someone to seek her out.' That was why she had started to study; first her aim had been to escape from herself, to fix her attention on something outside herself, then because she had developed a liking for study, and finally she had continued through pride, in the hope 'of seeming to be through choice what she was forced to be through necessity'.

But she herself was not deceived: she had trained herself to 'think like a man' but she still had 'a woman's heart', which rebelled against the very rules she had imposed upon herself. In diverting her mind, she had deluded her heart. Now she had abandoned any feeling of pride. 'All I wish to achieve is a more serene and more tranquil state of soul,' she wrote. She asked if Jean-Jacques could not give her some advice about what she should do. She described her character, her proud nature, her horror of mediocrity, her appalling loneliness. She wished she could always remain asleep, because as soon as she awoke her anguish started all over again. She could not busy herself with embroidery or spinning, because society having rejected her she had no one to work for. 'In my isolation, I belong to neither sex, I am merely a thinking and suffering creature, living on the fringe of a society in which I have been granted no place, like an unused stone lying by the side of a building of which it has not become a part. It is neither a corner-stone nor a foundation-stone, it serves no purpose, it has merely been pushed to one side so as not to be in the way of passers-by.' She had tried to become a church-goer, but could not manage to be a believer. She had consequently taken up studying again. She would soon grow old and she dreaded the prospect of living among old women. 'She had therefore to try and find some sort of companionship among the other half of the human race.' Studying would perhaps help her to do this.

> I protest once more [she concluded], that I am quite devoid of vanity: I am not trying to set up as a philosopher or a wit, but simply to acquire a little strength to use it against myself. I am no more than a poor weak creature. . . . The pleasure of listening to reason has always been obliterated by the pain of being obliged to comply with it, and thus deaden my sensibilities to everything. As long as my inclinations remained alive, my whole existence was one long agony, in fact a death I relived at each moment.

Jean-Jacques, mistrustful as ever, did not at first sense the suffering that was present in this letter; all he saw in it was a talent for writing. He had recently met at Neuchâtel a young woman who was both a bluestocking and a wit and who 'was always putting herself forward'. He imagined that she was his correspondent and replied at length, assuming that he was writing to a conceited highbrow. 'Above each line you write I can see the following words written in large letters: "Just see if you have the temerity to condemn anyone who can think and write as I do to give up reading and thinking".'

A few months later, Henriette, who had become the victim of further misfortunes, corrected his mistake. She had no desire to shine, or to 'put herself forward': 'My prime motive', she said, 'is to be able to do something with a life which up till now has only been an encumbrance to me. Teach me how to live, Sir, I beg of you—in other words tell me by what means I can come closest to happiness.'

This time Jean-Jacques was touched and apologised for the misunderstanding. . . . 'You cause me too much concern,' he replied, 'for me to leave your letter unanswered. There are few people who appeal to me as much as you do, and nobody who surprises me more. For me you are an enigma, at once distressing and humiliating. I thought I knew the human heart, but I fail altogether to understand yours. You are suffering and I am unable to comfort you.'

The truth was that he found himself up against his own limitations and discovered a kind of solitude he had never experienced and could not understand. It so happened that when he was thinking of telling his life-story and drawing his self-portrait in words, he had jotted down the following note: 'For the wicked man, being compelled to live alone is hell, for the good man it is Paradise; for him there is no more delightful spectacle than that of his own conscience.' But here was a woman, who was both good and virtuous, and yet who did not find pleasure in being alone with herself.

I have related the Henriette episode at some length and quoted from these letters, because, I think, they give a good idea of the nature of Jean-Jacques' happiness. He was not alone: supported by himself, his work, his fame and his belief, he could do without 'other people'. He wrote to Henriette:

> Should that sensitivity, which makes you dissatisfied with everything, not turn back upon itself? Should it not sustain your heart with a sublime and delightful feeling of self-regard? Does it not always provide a resource against injustice and the discouragement which comes from insensitivity? It is so rare, you say, to encounter a soul. This is true: yet how can one have a soul oneself and not find delight in it? If one sounds other souls and finds them cramped and narrow, one becomes disheartened and indifferent: yet being so ill at ease with others is it not a pleasure to come home again? I know how much the need of attachments makes the impossibility of forming any painful for sensitive hearts: I know how sad this situation is, but I know that it is not without its charms: it causes us to shed abundant tears: it induces a feeling of melancholy which makes us conscious of our own beings, and which we should not like to be without; it makes us seek solitude as the only refuge in which we can find ourselves alone with everything we are right to love. I cannot repeat to you too often that in my experience there is no happiness or peace of mind in estrangement from oneself; on the contrary, I become more conscious every day of the fact that we are only happy on this earth in so far as we shun outward things and draw nearer to ourselves. If there exists any sentiment which is sweeter than self-esteem, if there exists any occupation more pleasant than that of enhancing this sentiment, I may be wrong: but such is my view: you may understand from this how impossible it is for me to share your attitude, and even to imagine your condition.

Henriette, for her part, admitted that she did not feel 'detached' from outward things, nor from other people.

> . . . To be nothing [she said], to hold nothing dear, to have nothing dependent on me, in short, to live without knowing why, is a dreadful sensation . . . being neither daughter, mother, nor wife . . . I serve no purpose, nobody has any need of me. I could leave this world whenever I liked and no one would notice, so why should I stay here? I am just an encumbrance to myself. Is it possible to be self-sufficient and all in all for oneself? The human heart likes to overflow, and how can it overflow into itself?

She wrote one or two more letters, but Jean-Jacques felt he had nothing more to say and did not reply. Philosophy had been proved to supply no remedy for a life of despair. He had discovered that it was possible to be even more lonely than he was, and that in such a case the word 'solitude', which he loved, took on a different meaning.

At the end of May, a letter from La Roche informed Jean-Jacques of the Maréchal de Luxembourg's death. He was very genuinely sorry, but correspondingly sorrier for himself. For months he had heard nothing from either the Maréchal or his wife. He wrote a curious letter to Mme de Luxembourg, apologising for bothering her: 'Alas! What have I done?' he wrote. 'Is it not my only crime that I have loved both of you too much, and have thus prepared for myself the sorrow with which I am now consumed? Until the very last moment you enjoyed his most tender affection, of which death alone has deprived you. But I lost both of you while you were both still full of vitality. I am more to be pitied than you are.' That was how his mind worked: it was as if Mme de Luxembourg owed him some justification on her own behalf and on that of her dead husband.

He could not forget himself for a single moment: this is a risk which every great writer runs: for him the essential thing is always to pursue his own train of thought, and everything must be organised, as it were, naturally, in relationship to it: that is as it should be. Everything, however, is thrown into confusion, both in the world in which he lives and in his own mind, if he takes the mistakes of his wounded susceptibility to be a form of thought. In the end everything becomes poisoned. Jean-

Jacques had been obliged to withdraw within himself, but he derived too much pleasure from doing so; he was too fond of his own company. Some Protestants were surprised that he did not defend their cause, as Voltaire was doing. A certain Pourtalès ventured to say this to him, but he met with a sharp rejoinder. Jean-Jacques replied by recalling the letter he had written to the Archbishop of Paris which provided adequate proof of 'his lively concern for their troubles'. 'But,' he added, 'being oppressed, persecuted and hounded like a criminal wherever they are in power I have found them united against me. . . . If I continued to defend their cause, would they not ask me why I was interfering in their affairs? . . . Finally, I am depressed, disheartened and ailing, and so many worries are thrust upon me that I no longer have any time to spare for those of others.'

The work of men like Montesquieu, Voltaire or Diderot is dictated by the object it has in view. It represents an effort made by a human mind to grasp something which is outside itself and which has a form and a life of its own. The mind tries to embrace it, but does not attempt to take its place. Jean-Jacques, however, always remained confined within himself. For him, understanding the world meant projecting himself into the world and contemplating his own image therein. It was no mere accident that, during the first weeks of his stay in Motiers, after finishing *Le Lévite d'Ephraïm*, he should have set about writing another poem entitled *Pygmalion*, in the kind of silence that was ensured him by the seclusion and remoteness of his retreat. Having created all his books out of his 'illusions', it was inevitable that, carrying this tendency to its ultimate conclusion and extending it as it were outside himself, he should imagine that his illusions had become reality. He himself confesses that he doted on those delightful girls, Claire and Julie, 'like a second Pygmalion'. He was fond of everything he had created in his mind. He cried, as his Pygmalion did to Galatea: 'O vanity, weakness of men, I never weary of admiring my own work; I am intoxicated with pride; I worship myself in what I have created. . . . No, never has nature ever created anything so beautiful, I have surpassed the work of the Gods.' In certain moments of concentration and ecstasy his work appeared to him to be truer and more alive than himself. The statue would come to life, touch its own body, recognise the fever of life

127

within it, and speak in the first person. And he, distraught with happiness, replied: 'Yes, precious and delightful object, yes, worthy masterpiece of my hands, my heart and the gods, thou, and thou alone dost exist: I have given thee my whole being: from now on I shall live only through thee.' Thus the sincere Jean-Jacques was perhaps moving towards a new kind of fallacy. He was no longer aware of the limits imposed by the body, and had transferred his being to the soul in his writings.

His attitude towards Geneva was beginning to be that of an *émigré*: 'The fervour I used to feel for my native city,' he wrote to Lenieps, another *émigré* like himself, 'has been replaced by the most profound indifference. It is as if, for me, Geneva no longer existed: and the stupidities issuing from that country no longer even have the power to amuse me. The change has not been brought about either by reason, or indignation, it has occurred spontaneously, and independently of my will.' Deep within him, he was still full of resentment. On 1st August he set off to walk to Aix-les-Bains, ostensibly to have treatment for incipient sciatica, but got no further than Thonon. 'When I saw the spires of Geneva in the distance, I found myself succumbing weakly to the kind of yearning I would have felt in the past for some false-hearted mistress.' The preceding sentence is from a letter to the Earl Marischal in which he also complained that illness and continuous rain had forced him to turn back. He was not telling the whole truth: in actual fact, the chief object of his journey, perhaps the sole object, had been to meet the leader of the *Représentants* at Thonon. The details of the publication of the *Lettres de la Montagne* and of the reply which the *Représentants* themselves were to make to Tronchin's letters were settled between them and they agreed on a code to be used in their subsequent correspondence on this matter. The arrangement was virtually a conspiracy. It was particularly important that the *Lettres* should appear before Christmas 1764, that is before the elections of January 1765. Jean-Jacques brought constant pressure to bear on his publisher. It was arranged that the books would be taken into Geneva 'in a securely fastened packing-case, wrapped in oil-cloth with another layer of stout material on top, labelled *standard cloth*', and addressed to Jacques Vieussieux, one of the conspirators.

That mad desire to be active to which, alas, almost all human beings are subject, occasionally took hold of him too, and involved him, perhaps not unpleasurably, in these conspiratorial details. But the essential part of his life lay elsewhere. A letter which he wrote in August to Mme de Boufflers testifies to the fact that he was reasonably happy throughout that year, in spite of his melancholy tone:

> Nothing could be more uneventful than my life, nothing could be less ambitious than my plans: I live from day to day without a thought of the morrow: rather I am bringing my life to a close but more slowly than I had expected. I will not depart until it pleases nature to call me, but her dilatoriness is proving burdensome, for I have no further business here below. The repugnance that everything now inspires in me makes me sink yet further into indolence and idleness. My abode, although healthy enough for other men, is harmful to someone in my condition. Consequently, to escape from the deleterious effects of the air and the unwelcome intrusions of idle folk I wander through the countryside during the fine weather: but at the approach of the winter which in this region is very long and severe, I have to return home and suffer. For a long time I have been looking for somewhere else to live, but where can I go, and how can I arrange for the removal? I am hampered at one and the same time by poverty and riches; any kind of effort fills me with alarm; the carrying of my rags and books through the mountains would be awkward and expensive. And why should I quit my house when I expect soon to quit my body? Whereas if I stay here I enjoy delightful days of aimless, carefree wandering from wood to wood and from cliff to cliff, absorbed in my dreams, my mind empty of thought. I would give everything in the world to be a skilled botanist; it is the true occupation for an active body and a lazy mind. I might even be so mad as to study botany, if I knew where to begin. Do not be anxious about my financial situation: until now I have not lacked the necessities of life, even in abundance, and there seems no likelihood of any lack in the immediate future. Far from scolding you for your offers of help, Madame, I thank you for them; you will agree, however, that they would be out of place, should I avail myself of them before the need arose.

He had a vision of himself becoming the Solon or the Lycurgus of his day. He had made no secret of his admiration for the Corsicans who were at that time fighting for their independance. The following passage from the *Contrat Social* had not failed to touch the emotions of Corsican patriots: 'There still exists in Europe one country susceptible to legislation—it is the island of Corsica. The valour and steadfastness with which this brave people have shown themselves able to recover and defend their freedom might well prompt some wise man to teach them how to preserve it. I have a feeling that one day this tiny island will surprise Europe.' In September, a letter from Buttafoco, who wrote to him on behalf of Paoli, 'the Corsican leader', asked him if he himself would not undertake to be their legislator. He was enchanted by the idea. However, he at first hesitated to accept, because of age, exhaustion, ill-health and his ignorance of the country. Buttafoco, however, finally persuaded him. The news spread through Europe and Grimm wrote in his correspondence that it was strange to see a man become the legislator of another country at the very time when he was spreading dissension in his own.

At last the *Lettres de la Montagne* were ready. They reached Geneva during the first fortnight of December, and Paris a few days later. The secret had been well kept. Even in writing to his closest friends Jean-Jacques denied that he had composed the 'letters by *the man* of the mountain' that people were talking about. But when the bomb was about to go off he was seized with a kind of panic about what might happen. He had written his letter to the Archbishop in the style of a Protestant pamphlet in order to gain the goodwill of his own country. The device had met with little success. This time, on the contrary, he was careful to be tactful towards the Catholics, no doubt because he still had some hope of returning to France. He was groping his way and looking round for allies. He sent his book to the 'venerable Abauzit', inviting him to act as arbiter. 'The ministers of Geneva, those gods of flesh and blood, could have punished me if I was guilty,' he wrote, 'but if Cato exonerates me, they have only subjected me to oppression.' He sent a copy to the French resident minister along with a rather obsequious letter. The diplomat rejected his compliments somewhat curtly. At once Geneva was in an uproar. The *Négatifs* denounced him as 'a fire-brand'; the 'Petit Conseil' did not know what to do; the *Représentants* were exultant. The impressionable Moultou, with whom he had been recently reconciled, was transported to the point of using prophetic language:

I have read your book [he wrote], it contains the lamentations of a hero.... Now Europe must utter its verdict.... But, Sir, what will be the effect of this work amongst us? God alone knows whether you will one day wipe out the memory of it with your tears, or whether your fatherland will owe you a debt of gratitude. ... In just another hundred years, Sir, your vigorous writings will break Europe's chains, and religion having become more enlightened, will cease to make victims suffer and will no longer consecrate their persecutors; endure the insults of your contemporaries, they represent the seal of truth.... Even Geneva, which now rejects you, will one day be proud to honour you. ... This prophecy is as certain as your fame.

Jean-Jacques remained anxious. It was perhaps because he wished somehow to indicate his loyalty to old memories and his affection for the common people of Geneva that it occurred to him to send 'his darling Jacqueline' eighteen *livres* with which she bought a silver cup and went round from door to door in the Saint-Gervais district 'with her silver cup in one hand, and a bottle of wine in the other, begging people to dance a round and drink to the health of Jean-Jacques'.

On the 31st December, just when he was in this state of excitement and anxiety induced by fame, the post brought him a kind of New Year's gift—a small, anonymous eight-page pamphlet entitled innocently enough *Le Sentiment des Citoyens* ('The Opinion of the Citizens'). The author claimed that he was voicing the 'opinions of the town' in response to the *Lettres de la Montagne*. It began: 'We are sorry for a madman: but when he becomes a raving lunatic we tie him up. Tolerance which is a virtue would in such a case be a vice', and the author proceeded to accuse Jean-Jacques of having insulted Jesus Christ and the ministers of the Gospel.

Jean-Jacques read on and came to the following paragraph:

Can a man born in our town be allowed to offer such affronts to our ministers, most of whom are also our relatives and friends, and who act sometimes as our comforters? Who is the person who is behaving towards them in this way; is he a scholar disputing with scholars? No, he is the author of an opera and two unsuccessful plays. Is he an honourable man deceived by misplaced zeal and levelling rash accusations at virtuous men? We confess with shame and sorrow that he is a man bearing the dreadful taint of his debauchery, who dresses up like a circus clown and drags with him from village to village, and from mountain to mountain an unfortunate creature whose mother died because of him and whose children he abandoned on the door-step of a poor-house, after refusing to allow a kind-hearted person to take care of them, and spurning all natural feelings, as he renounces those of honour and religion.

It was as if the whole light of the heavens was suddenly trained upon him: he looked into the depths of his own being, saw there everything that he had forgotten. It was fifteen years since he had condemned himself to a life of virtue, and God knew how courageously he had endured his punishment. Could fifteen years of virtue and industry have been in vain? Now the whole of Europe would know the shameful secret of his life! Everyone would see him as the greatest hypocrite who had ever lived. Letters he wrote that same day reveal that never before had he been in such a state of 'turmoil'.

He did not attempt to vindicate himself: he fought back: 'Oh, Sir', he wrote to D'Ivernois, 'if all these people had been less brutal and condescending, and had tried to win me over with kindness, I feel that I would never have been able to resist them: but by behaving as they have, they have put me on my mettle. Thanks to their efforts they will make me great and famous, whereas I was never intended to be anything but a nobody.' He sent the pamphlet to Du Peyrou, specifying that he should return it so that it could be included 'among the documents connected with his life-story'. 'Oh, when all has been revealed,' he exclaimed, 'how posterity will love me! how it will bless my memory! You, however, should love me now and believe that I am worthy of your love.' He took care not to discuss the facts of the matter, but his prose panted with anguish. He was writhing like a hero under the lash.

Misled by the tone of the letter, he was convinced it had been written by Vernes the minister. In fact it was by Voltaire, who had not forgiven him for revealing in one of the *Lettres de la Montagne* that he was the author of the *Sermon des Cinquante*, nor for the fact that the *Représentants* had intimated to the Petit Conseil 'that if the writings of a Genevan were to be burnt it was regrettable that those of a Frenchman had not received the same treatment'. Such behaviour, he said, was worthy neither of a philosopher nor a gentleman.

It was true that Jean-Jacques had denounced him as the author, but in any case this was an open secret: everybody knew Voltaire was the author and no one believed him when he denied it.

We can see only too clearly how one stupid provocation after another, combined with the profound temperamental disagreement between the two men, had brought them to this point. It had all begun with a rather entertaining piece of mischief on the part of Voltaire. A year before, a certain Mme de Beaugrand, who was not well informed as to their relationship, had sent him a letter addressed to Rousseau asking him to pass it on. Voltaire's only reply had been to send her the *Sermon des Cinquante*. She, not understanding what it was all about, and having finally discovered Jean-Jacques' address, asked him to give her an explanation. Jean-Jacques had been furious. At the time he was busy on the *Lettres de la Montagne,* and he inserted a venomous paragraph in which he made Voltaire himself reveal his authorship of the *Sermon.* Voltaire was now getting his own back. He had probably been told of Jean-Jacques' secret by Tronchin, the doctor, who had probably been informed of it by Mme d'Epinay. ... A few weeks later the stupidity of the quarrel was to be made abundantly clear: Jean-Jacques' *Lettres de la Montagne* and Voltaire's *Dictionnaire philosophique portatif* were to be reconciled by being burned on the same fire, in the courtyard of the Palais, in Paris.

Jean-Jacques was completely overwhelmed: for six days he did not know what to do. Then he decided on the most unlikely and the most brazen course: he sent the pamphlet to Duchesne his publisher in Paris, and instructed him to reprint it, with the addition of a few notes and a kind of preface in which authorship was attributed to Vernes. The document is still extant[1] and it makes somewhat sad reading; it is made up of a number of lies written out in Jean-Jacques' best handwriting. He no doubt thought that appearances were on his side. The accusation would appear incredible since he had made a public profession of virtue: he had only to issue a denial for the scandal to be silenced once and for all. As far as his ailment was concerned he could with a clear conscience give the following convincing details:

[1] The facsimile can be found at the end of Vol. XII of the *Correspondance générale.*

No disease, major or minor, of the kind referred to here by the author, has ever defiled my body. My affliction has nothing whatever to do with any such disease: it has been with me since birth, as it is known to people still living who looked after me in childhood. Messrs Malouin, Morand, Thierry, Daran, and Brother Côme are acquainted with my disability. If it bears the slightest trace of debauchery, I beg them to contradict me and make me feel ashamed of my motto.

Having made this point and thus rehabilitated his virtue, he went on to deal with the question of Thérèse and the children, displaying a rather despicable form of prevarication and deceit:

The discreet and universally esteemed person who looks after me in my sickness and comforts me in my afflictions, is unhappy only because she shares the fate of a very unhappy man: her mother is at the moment very much alive and in good health in spite of her age. I have never exposed any infant on the doorstep of any poor-house or elsewhere nor have I caused any to be thus exposed. Any person as charitable as is suggested here, would have been charitable enough to keep the matter secret; and everyone knows that Geneva, where I have never lived, and where there is so much animosity towards me, is not a reliable source of information concerning my behaviour. I shall add nothing further about this particular passage, unless it be to say that, murder excepted, I would rather have done what the author accuses me of having done, than write a similar passage.

No, he had never 'exposed' any infant nor 'caused any to be exposed', since he had deposited five at the Foundlings' Hospital, or caused five to be deposited there. . . .

But the brazen denial served his purpose. Given the frivolousness of the period Jean-Jacques' moral prestige remained unimpaired both in Switzerland and in Paris. The most that happened was that during the following months a few lampoons were published, including a letter purporting to be written by Jean-Louis R . . . natural son of Jean-Jacques. He had managed the affair so skilfully that people felt nothing but pity for him in his unfortunate plight. However, Grimm, even though he was acquainted with the facts, published an ambiguous but on the whole fairly kind note in his *Correspondance*: 'M. Rousseau has deemed it fitting to have this little pamphlet reprinted in Paris, adding a few notes in which he simply denies the facts. Those who are not deceived by words will say that a denial is not the same thing as a reply, nor is it easy to see what his aim can have been in publicising a disgraceful lampoon which would never have been heard of in Paris, and for which he had already been avenged in Geneva by public opinion.'

Jean-Jacques was the only person who could not be taken in by his sophistry and his lies. With diabolical accuracy, and a mere flick of the finger, Voltaire had undermined the monument of virtue and sown the seeds of doubt and fear within him. For the first time Jean-Jacques realised that we cannot escape the consequences of our actions. It was obviously not as easy as all that to practise what he preached—*Vitam impendere vero.* Even the most sincere attempt to reform left everything unsettled. He had yet to take the final step in his spiritual development. He had to accept responsibility for his whole life, and, going back beyond recent years in which he had assumed the mantle of greatness, even for his sins and crimes. He had to be such as he would reveal himself to God on the Day of Judgement, naked pure and vindicated.

CHAPTER FIVE

The Genevan Controversy : Jean-Jacques and the Ministers (1765)

Jean-Jacques, in a state of great internal 'turmoil', undertakes the writing of his *Confessions*—The first opening and the first version of the *Confessions*—Jean-Jacques and St. Augustine— Attacks of depression and excitement. He attributes *Le Sentiment des Citoyens* to Minister Vernes—The argument with M. de Montmollin and *La Vénérable Classe*—Jean-Jacques does not know where to go 'to die in peace'—His letters are no more than 'a string of lamentations'—*La Vénérable Classe* commands him to appear before it—he does not do so and is saved by the intervention of Frederick of Prussia—He plucks up courage once more —He promises the State Council of Neuchâtel that he will never again write about religion—But his friends carry on the fight and he helps them—'The usual procedure adopted by the gentlemen of the Church'—He composes *The Vision of Peter of the Mountain*—He looks for another refuge during the summer—The 'stoning' at Motiers—Jean-Jacques on the Ile Saint-Pierre—The Bern government orders him to leave—He suggests that he might become its prisoner—His excitement borders on madness—Jean-Jacques in Bienne, Bâle, Strasbourg and Paris—Flight, but at the same time triumph—He leaves for England on the 4th January 1766.

HE UNDOUBTEDLY spent the first days of the year 1765 in a state both of inner 'turmoil' and concentration on himself, such as he had rarely experienced before. Voltaire's little pamphlet faced him with the question to end all questions: what was he? What was he worth?

One of his most constant thoughts was that there could be no pleasanter feeling than self-esteem. It will be remembered that this had been his reply to the unfortunate Henriette, the unknown young woman who had complained to him about her useless solitude. As for him, he liked himself, he was at ease with himself. He had to like himself; this was an essential condition of his happiness. Among the notes he had been jotting down from time to time during the last two years in preparation for his 'portrait' and the story of his life that he one day intended to compose, was the following curious remark: 'Social man wants other people to be pleased with him. The solitary man is obliged to be pleased with himself; otherwise life is unbearable to him. Thus the latter is compelled to be virtuous, whereas the former may be only a hypocrite.' Doubtless, he applied this sophistical maxim to himself and normally found it adequate. He was a solitary man, who enjoyed his solitude; therefore he was virtuous.

But the little pamphlet lay on the table, in front of him.

It was a reminder of the fact that life was not over in a moment, but goes on from day to day for a long time. Could it be that the bliss he felt away from society and the inner certainty of the moment were not justified?

Memory was not to be denied. A man was a very strange mixture! The little pamphlet lay in front of him and when he had first read it, he had been filled with a sense of his own innocence and had exclaimed: 'Oh, how posterity will love me, when the veil has been lifted!' He had to believe this in order to be happy, but it was perhaps neither certain nor simple. He wondered if it would be wise to lift 'the veil'.

A month before, Duclos had asked him about these 'private memoirs of his life' that he had promised to write. He had given the evasive reply that they would be too difficult to produce without compromising other people and that they demanded more quiet than he was now allowed. Then, in the second week of January, he suddenly set to work; the little pamphlet had made up his mind for him. He wrote again to Duclos on the 13th and by then he had definitely set to work, because the final sentences of his letter are more or less identical with the opening of his book:

> They [his former friends] are doing a great deal to make it easier for me to undertake the task of writing my life-story, which you urge me to continue. There has just been published in Geneva a shocking piece of libel, based on information fabricated by the Lady of Epinay, which information is such as to allow me great freedom of action both with regard to herself and to the people around her. May God preserve me, however, from imitating her even in self-defence! But without revealing any of the secrets she confided to me, I know enough from other sources to make known all that is necessary in respect of her relationship with me. She does not know that I am so well-informed but since she has forced my hand, she will one day realise how discreet I have been. Yet I assure you that I still have great difficulty in over-coming my repugnance, and I shall at least take steps to see that nothing appears in my life-time. But I have a great deal to say and I will say it all; I will not omit any fault of my own, or even any evil thought. I will describe myself as I am; the bad will in almost every instance eclipse the good, yet notwithstanding, I find it hard to believe that any one of my readers will dare say to himself: I am better than that man was. Dear friend, my heart is heavy and my eyes are swollen with weeping; never did a human being suffer so many evils at one and the same time. I keep silent, I am in pain, I am choked with grief. . . .

And so his book came into being. He had already found the title and written it out on a large blank sheet: *The Confessions of Jean-Jacques Rousseau, containing a detailed account of the events of his life and of his private thoughts in all the situations in which he has found himself.*

He composed a long introduction, which he was later to cut out when he realised how much the opening pages would gain through being concise, but for the time being he was still excited by the novelty of the undertaking and could not curb his pen. He was not so much concerned with self-defence or revenge as with self-expression. His book was meant to be something extra-ordinary and admirable. Age, madness and suspiciousness were eventually to turn it into an apologia, but when he began it, he was sure that his innocence would be radiantly obvious. He was confident in the outcome. He proposed to describe a man, himself, and thus to help everyone towards self-knowledge. Up till then, such knowledge had been beyond them; since each person took himself as a yardstick and judged others according to his own nature, a point of comparison was lacking: each person, in order to know himself, 'must be acquainted with himself and one other individual'. That individual would be Jean-Jacques.

'Yes, myself, myself alone, since I have never met any other man who has dared to do what I propose to do.'

The fact was that, in this respect too, the peculiarities of his destiny made him genuinely inventive. True, many men before him had told the stories of their lives and published their 'memoirs'. But they had done so, more often than not, in the light of the great events in which they happened to have been involved. When they came to speak about themselves, they had done so as 'social beings', bent on pleasing, with a show of 'false sincerity', like Montaigne who had described his faults, but had admitted only to agreeable ones. One exception had been that madman, Cardan, but his self-portrait was hidden away in 'ten in-folio volumes of wild rantings'. Jean-Jacques would do what no one else had ever done; he would write the history of a soul. It was not events which mattered but the soul that experienced them: 'Souls,' he wrote, 'are more or less great and noble only in so far as they entertain great and noble feelings.... Facts, in this connection, are no more than incidental causes. However obscure a life I may have led, if I have thought more, and more effectively, than kings have done, then the story of my soul is more interesting than the story of theirs.' Besides, although he might not be famous because of his rank or birth, he was 'celebrated for his misfortunes'.

Above all, he would speak as only a solitary man can speak. He would say things that no one had ever dared to express: 'I shall be truthful,' he proclaimed, 'and without any reservation; I shall tell all, the good, the bad, in short, everything.... The most timid Christian lady never examined her conscience with the thoroughness I shall bring to the task....' He would expose to public gaze all the recesses of his soul and would unravel 'that vast chaos of feelings so diverse, so contradictory, often so base and sometimes so sublime' that had always seethed within him. He blushed at the mere thought of the disgusting admissions he would have to make. But everything was interconnected, and he had to tell all in order to explain that 'weird and peculiar amalgam', that 'singular creature' he was conscious of being. He knew what mystery lay within a man and that 'what is visible is only the smallest part of reality'. As for the other people with whom life had brought him into contact, he would speak about them as freely as about himself, but out of respect for his enemies he would take all necessary steps to ensure that his book did not appear until such time as the facts recounted in it had become 'a matter of indifference to everyone concerned'. Not that he had any fear for himself.

> For my own part [he concluded], I am in no hurry to see it appear during my life-time, and I should scarcely lament the loss of the esteem of anyone who might think fit to despise me after reading it. I admit some very hateful things about myself, for which I would be loath to try to find excuses; the explanation is that this is the secret history of my soul and a most rigorous confession. It is only fair that my reputation should have to expiate the evil that the desire to preserve it has led me into. I expect public admonishment, severe condemnation loudly uttered, and I submit to it in advance. But let each reader do as I have done, let him examine himself in the same way and see whether, in the depths of his conscience, he dare say: *I am better than that man was.*

These sentences contain the same 'turmoil' as was in his heart. He knows his faults and, even so, the loathing they inspire in him is less than his loathing of the apologia he might be led to write; the distinction is an important one: his faults do not make him feel guilty, but he would be guilty if he tried to make excuses for them. The most serious had been the concealment of the birth of his children, through the false shame characteristic of a man who was still too 'social', and then the silence he had maintained for fifteen years, again typical of 'social' man, in order 'to preserve his reputation'. He had kept the base secret to himself. But the little pamphlet had made him decide to 'lift the veil'. And since his name was destined to live on the lips of men, he was proud enough to reject a false reputation and to insist on being unknown and loved as he was.

He would confess to posterity the great fault he had been ashamed to admit and that he had just denied in replying to *Le Sentiment des Citoyens*. The facts seemed to prove his responsibility. Morally, he was not in the wrong. Against the brutal facts of life he would set the pure claims of his heart. He would tell the truth and grant himself forgiveness. No man would have been better than he had been 'in the situations in which he had found himself'. And no doubt the peculiar greatness of his admission would win back for him the prestige and fame he would lose by making it. He would appear in his proper light as the most truthful man who had ever existed.

It cannot be doubted that, when he chose his title, he was thinking of the *Confessions* of St. Augustine, and it is very strange that he should make no mention of them. He refers to Montaigne and Cardan, but he is shrewd enough to leave us the initiative of comparing him to a saint, at the same time as his title forces us to think of the comparison. His book had to be a justification both of himself and of his faith. *Confiteor*. . . . At the beginning of the Christian era, Augustine had called 'the human race' to witness, 'confessed' both his own shortcomings and the glory of God and painted a great picture of a man in the grip of Grace; similarly Jean-Jacques, at the dawn of the new era that he felt approaching, was going to paint the portrait of a man, and this man would be himself. But when Augustine told of his sins, he was speaking 'against himself' and against man in general. Jean-Jacques was less severe; he would speak for himself and for mankind. As he had written to Archbishop Christophe de Beaumont, 'I am far from thinking that the doctrine of original sin, which raises such terrible difficulties, is contained in the Scriptures as clearly and inexorably as Augustine, that master of rhetoric, and our theologians have been pleased to elaborate it.' For his part, he had quite a different conception 'of the justice and goodness of the Supreme Being'. He himself had turned himself back into natural man, and natural man was without sin. The progress he himself had made within himself against the world and society was within the reach of all men. His book and the example of his life would teach them how they could recapture happiness, be content in their own company and commune with God in the surety of a quiet conscience.

Throughout the collapse of religious and social disciplines during the last two centuries, this curious apostle has never failed to go on increasing his flock and, all things considered, has done as much as any saint to restore the sense of the inner life to mankind, to the pure and the impure. It is not enough to say that his example has given rise to a whole literature although private diaries have been published by the score; more than anyone, no doubt, he altered the relationship between the writer and his readers, introducing the kind of complicity or connivance that Baudelaire refers to in the line:

Hypocrite lecteur, mon semblable, mon frère

(Hypocritical reader, my fellow-being, my brother)

Since his time, there have been innumerable books, the writing and reading of which has been a kind of delicious rehashing of the self, providing both writer and reader with the pleasures of the confessional. Literature has competed with the churches and writers with Protestant ministers and Catholic priests. Jean-Jacques was the first of these fishers of souls.

Geneva was in a state of confusion. The 'représentants', in their turn, had published their own *Réponse aux Lettres écrites de la Campagne* ('Reply to the Letters written from the Country'). With every week that passed, some new pamphlet came out. The members of the Petit Conseil were in a quandary. Jean-Jacques had denounced them as tyrants and at first they thought of resigning, then, adopting an attitude of offended honesty, decided to ask the citizens for a vote of confidence, failing which they would withdraw. Both parties were afraid of carrying things to extremes. Jean-Jacques was following developments from afar but, truth to tell, the whole business no longer held much interest for him. He had thrown his bomb and said what he had to say. D'Ivernois and De Luc kept him informed of events but he was now advising even them to show restraint. Besides, he claimed to have a thorough knowledge of 'the Genevan middle-class' and was sure 'that it would go no farther than was necessary'. It was like 'Georges Dandin who thanks his wife for the honour of being a cuckold'. He saw himself in a sentimental light as the prophet Moultou had described: 'One day, Geneva will count it an honour to have produced you, and our descendants will see the Genevans weeping over your mausoleum and, turning their eyes away from the stake with its burning faggots, point to the inscription engraved on the base of the monument: *Luget et monet.*' The thought of this moving scene appealed to him. The future would be his, and this was a further reason why, for the time being, he should yearn for peace and quiet. He had been deeply hurt by Voltaire's little pamphlet; the wound was still raw and refused to heal. During that month of January 1765, he was entering upon the most terrible period of his life. He was going through alternate phases of depression and feverish excitement. Whenever he managed to regain his self-control, he wrote edifying letters to his friends:

> I may tell you [he informed Du Peyrou], that I have felt an astonishing change within myself during the last few days. The most recent events, which ought to have completed my feeling of dismay, have, in some inexplicable manner, tranquillised me and even made me quite cheerful. I have the impression I was attaching too much importance to childish pranks. There is something so silly and stupid in all these burnings of books that one has to be more childish even than these people are in order to get worked up about them. My mental life is over. Why should I take such trouble to choose the piece of earth where I shall leave my body? The most precious part of me is already dead: men cannot alter that, and I no longer look upon this crowd of lying barbarous and contemptible magistrates as being anything more than so many worms gnawing away at a corpse.

But his anxiety had not abated. He had now decided that 'he would defend himself no longer'. He 'would lay down his pen' and 'withdraw within himself'. 'To live in peace for the rest of his days without eating anyone else's bread' was the height of his ambition. But he had to make sure of the means to do so. Duchesne was going to publish the *Musical Dictionary* and this would provide him with some ready money. A group of his friends in Neutchâtel were trying to form a society which would bring out a general edition of his works and, in the meantime, pay him an annuity that Thérèse could inherit. He had asked Du Peyrou to look after his interests and the idea seemed to be making progress, although the Marischal, who was well acquainted with the people of Neuchâtel through having been their governor, had warned him against them and had advised him to negotiate rather with the Dutch or the English. But another question was nagging at him: 'Where should he go?' He thought his references to France in the *Lettres de la Montagne* had been very kind, but they had been of no avail. In that quarter, the same unbending attitude seemed to be maintained. Should he go to England, as the Marischal advised him to do? To Italy where he would find 'the inquisition less strict and the climate softer'? Or to Corsica? At the end of January the *Lettres* were publicly burned in Holland. 'Whichever way I turn,' Jean-Jacques wrote to Mme Verdelin, 'I can see nothing but claws ready to scratch and mouths open to gobble me up.'

At the beginning of February, Pastor Vernes wrote to him, denying authorship of *Le Sentiment des Citoyens*. Jean-Jacques instructed Duchesne to withhold the edition which had been ordered and announced his willingness to spread the news of the denial. But two days later, he became suspicious of Vernes again and changed his mind. About the same period he was given the text of a letter by the Abbé de Mably, which was being circulated in Geneva and in which he was denounced as 'a kind of conspirator', an 'Erostratus' or a 'Gracchus'. He writes in the *Confessions*: 'I sent the Abbé a copy of the letter, and informed him at the same time that he was said to be the author. He made no reply.' This is untrue; we have Mably's reply, in which he freely admits authorship: 'I was sorry for you in your misfortunes,' he wrote, 'as I have felt sorrow for Socrates; but allow me to tell you that Socrates did not try to stir up rebellion in Athens in order to be revenged on his judges', and, pointing out the contradictions between Jean-Jacques' former compliments to the Republic of Geneva and his present criticisms, he added rather mischievously: 'I do not doubt that the people who disapprove of you have your approval.' From then on Jean-Jacques counted Mably as one of his enemies and despised him as someone who, while close to his way of thinking, ran no risks and, in plagiarising his ideas, gave them the prudent and respectable air appropriate to a new conformism.

'The inhabitants of Neuchâtel flare up like match-wood,' the Marischal had written, and, as a matter of fact, the situation did suddenly become worse. The Venerable Class of Ministers of Neuchâtel persuaded the Council to ban the *Lettres de la Montagne* and requested that the plan to produce a general edition of Rousseau's works in Neuchâtel should be abandoned. At Motiers itself, the people who had read *Le Sentiment des Citoyens* began to gossip about Jean-Jacques and Thérèse. The bigoted little town secreted poisonous and malicious rumours. Jean-Jacques was becoming the anti-Christ and Pastor Montmollin who, two years earlier, had been very proud to have such a parishioner and to admit him to Holy Communion, now took fright, under the pressure of public opinion and because of letters from his Genevan colleague, Pastor Sarrasin. 'The ironical scepticism' of the *Lettres de la Montagne* suddenly seemed 'to deal a more serious blow to religion than unbelief itself.' The relationship between the two men had never been very intimate; Jean-Jacques considered his minister to have 'a sombre countenance' and 'a sinister gaze'. Montmollin, a vain man, had a grudge against Jean-Jacques because the latter had never admitted him into the closed circle of his little household. On the 8th March, when Jean-Jacques, 'in the depths of depression', was busy writing to Mme de Verdelin, the minister suddenly called on him. During this meeting, Jean-Jacques recovered 'all the vigour he thought he had lost'. The Venerable Class was due to consider Jean-Jacques' case in four days' time and the minister, feeling acutely embarrassed, was looking for a compromise and had come to suggest that Jean-Jacques might refrain from taking Communion for the time being. Jean-Jacques summed up the proposal in the following humorous formula: 'Sir, I am instructed to break your skull, but if you will have the goodness to break your leg, they may be satisfied with that.' He refused point blank and they went into the whole question of his recent writings. Montmollin claimed that Jean-Jacques had promised him never to write about religion again. Rousseau replied that this was to misinterpret as a promise what had, in fact, been his intention, but that he was not responsible for a course that had been forced upon him, and could not allow himself to be dishonoured. But 'if the Class were willing to let the matter rest', he now offered 'to refrain all his life from writing on any point of religion'. The minister said 'he would do what he could'; Jean-Jacques, for his part, retorted that 'he would do as he wished', and the minister went away.

Jean-Jacques was violently angry, but at the same time defeated. Again he had only one thought which was to go and 'die in peace' somewhere or other. Even a man with a steadier head would have had difficulty in withstanding the strain. He felt himself to be surrounded by calumny and plots. There was a rumour that a book against the Bernese government, entitled *Les Princes*, had just come out and that he was the author; he had to publish a denial. In the state of anxiety in which he found himself, he had to be careful to do nothing that might prevent him obtaining entry to Bernese territory. Then there was the affair of the anonymous man who came to see him, purporting to be a Knight of Malta bearing information from General Paoli; he was just an adventurer but Jean-Jacques was convinced that he was a spy sent by his enemies.

He wrote to Buttafoco to say that he must give up all idea of writing the constitution he had been asked to supply: 'My soul, exhausted with worry, is no longer in a fit state for thought; my heart is still the same, but I have no brain left.' But he was ready to go and live in Corsica, if they would be willing to let him settle in some quiet place where he would try to pass unnoticed. He asked Mme de Verdelin to obtain a passport for him and permission to pass through France, in case he should decide to go and live in England. All his letters were 'litanies of woe'.

He was now at the end of his tether. Two years before, no one would have managed to get any offer or commitment of this kind out of him. Jean-Jacques insinuates that Montmollin's pastoral zeal had only been aroused by his resentment at not being admitted to the society which was to bring out the general edition of Rousseau's works. This may have been so, since greed and hypocrisy go well together. Montmollin felt he had the upper hand, so much so, indeed, that when, on the evening of 10th March, Geyenet, a friend of Jean-Jacques, took him the written agreement that Jean-Jacques would abstain from all writing on religion, he found the wording inadequate and it had to be recast. The text then ran:

> Out of deference to Professor de Montmollin and respect for the Venerable Class, I offer, if this is acceptable, to pledge myself in a signed statement never again to publish any new work on any religious issue and even never to deal incidentally with any such issue in any new work on any other subject; moreover, both in my feelings and conduct, I shall continue to show how much I value the happiness of being united with the Church. I beg the Professor to bring this statement to the notice of the Venerable Class.

The account in the *Confessions* has a prouder ring. The Venerable Class ordered Jean-Jacques to appear before the Motiers

Consistory on the 29th March. He would have to state clearly
(a) whether or not he, Jean-Jacques, believed that Jesus Christ
had died for our sins and had been raised from the dead for our
justification; (b) whether or not he believed in the Revelation
and looked upon Holy Scripture as divinely inspired. There is no
trace of the fine speech he claims to have written and learned
by heart and then decided not to deliver. But we may suppose
that, in the terrible mental turmoil caused by persecution, he
ceaselessly reiterated for his own benefit all the arguments in his
favour. He did not appear. 'When I was summoned,' he wrote
to Du Peyrou a few months later, 'I was too ill to go out and had,
in fact, been confined to my room for six months; it was winter-
time, the weather was cold and it is a strange remedy for a
poor invalid to have to stand several hours on end, while being
questioned without pause on theological matters, in front of
elders the most learned of whom declare that they understand
them not at all.' It would have been a truly remarkable scene had
Jean-Jacques appeared before that parish council to render an
account of his being and his faith. He restricted himself to writing
a very dignified letter. He rejected the very principle of the
procedure that was being used against him. 'Once I have been
received within the Church,' he proclaimed, 'I am responsible
to God alone for my faith.' He included with his letter a copy of
the statement, made in 1872, and on the strength of which
Minister de Montmollin had admitted him to communion.
He had friends in the *Consistoire;* the vote was equally divided and 'the meeting broke up without any decision being
taken'.

Jean-Jacques, surprised and delighted, immediately despatched the news to Mme de Verdelin. He thought he had won;
the *ministraille* (monstrous regiment of ministers) was heading
for disaster, and so was Voltaire who, of course, was in his eyes
the person responsible for all this wretched commotion. He
would stand firm, as he had promised himself he would do, and
would not leave the country until it was clear to everyone that
he was free to remain if he wished. On the 30th, a rescript
published by Frederick placed him under the protection of the
Neuchâtel Council of State and removed him from the jurisdiction of the *Consistoire.*

It was at this point that one of his Genevan friends who had met Diderot in Paris brought him 'peace proposals' from the latter. Diderot admitted that he had wronged Jean-Jacques, but said that this was through 'carelessness, haste and misunderstanding' and not through any 'deliberate intent to harm'. Jean-Jacques, on the other hand, had 'mortally wounded' him by the note in the *Lettre sur les spectacles*. Diderot asked him to disavow this note. 'I do not fully understand', 'Jean-Jacques replied, 'what it is that Monsieur Diderot is suddenly demanding of me, after seven years' silence. I ask nothing of him; I have no disavowal to make. I am far from wishing him ill; still less would I do him wrong or speak ill of him; I am capable of respecting even an extinct friendship to the very end. But it is my most rigid maxim never to rekindle it.' The frivolous, talkative and generous Diderot was labouring under a misapprehension; no reconciliation was possible. Diderot, like Mme d'Epinay, had betrayed one of those secrets with which Jean-Jacques had to live and that he was proposing to reveal in his *Confessions*. Jean-Jacques was sure that there was nothing disgraceful about these secrets, but by publishing them his 'former friends' had sought only to dishonour him. To forgive them, he would have had to admit to himself that he had occasionally been guilty of dishonourable action. On the contrary, the resentment he felt was a justification and seemed to him to be proof of his virtue. Only when he was alone, betrayed and abandoned, did he deserve to be thought highly of by himself and the world at large. Such were the necessities and logical sequences of his destiny. Everyone else had to be in the wrong so that he could be in the right and his life appear to posterity as an eternally lamentable example of the wretchedness of virtue. His very solitude was a guarantee of his greatness.

His victory gave him renewed confidence. It was suggested that he might go to Couvet where the minister and Consistory seemed likely to be more amenable, but he refused. The very people who had helped him were now advising him to send the Neuchâtel Council of State the written pledge he had offered to the Venerable Class and with which the latter had not been satisfied. But now that he thought himself out of the wood, such a course was repugnant to him. He hesitated and gave the evasive reply: 'The promise I make to the whole world (which was asking nothing of him) is never to do anything except what is honest and just; greater promises I make only to myself alone.' He had never had less self-control. Vernes, too, was still waiting for him to make a withdrawal. He could not bring himself to do so. Vernes thereupon published their correspondence and called upon the public to take cognisance of Rousseau's dishonesty. At this, Jean-Jacques answered with a published 'Statement'. There was no longer any question, at this stage, of him making a personal reply to Vernes; there could be 'no understanding or intercourse between Jean-Jacques and the wicked'. There are few more hypocritical passages in Jean-Jacques' writings than this statement. It was entirely based on a subtle distinction: 'It is not,' he wrote, 'a matter of determining precisely whether or not M. Vernes is the author of the pamphlet but whether I should or not believe that he is. . . . I do not wish to prove that Jacob Vernes is a scoundrel, but I must prove that Jean-Jacques Rousseau is not a slanderer.' Never before had he shown himself to be such a master of the legalistic quibble. After listing all the reasons behind his own conviction, he made a show of generosity and invited M. Vernes to take the matter before the Council of Geneva which would make an enquiry and was in a position to establish the truth. He would accept the Council's arbitration. Strangely enough, the statement never appeared; it remained among his papers, no doubt because he was too unsure of himself to publish it.

Throughout the battle he had had the continuous support of the King himself and the Neuchâtel Council of State. He eventually decided that such kindness imposed 'new duties' upon him and, on the 26th April, he sent the procurator-general the pledge which, in his view, would ensure his tranquillity for good. He still harboured serious illusions about himself:

> I dare to affirm [he wrote], that no man ever made less effort to propagate his opinions or was less of an Author, either privately or publicly. In the course of a life chequered with mishaps, I have been forced from time to time to take up my pen to defend myself and others, because I was requested to do so, or compelled thereto by duty or honour, but I have never fulfilled this melancholy duty with anything but sadness and I have always looked upon such a cruel necessity as a further misfortune for myself. Now, thanks be to Heaven, I have been relieved of it and I can hold fast

to my rule of silence; for my own tranquillity, as well as that of the state in which I have the good fortune to live, I freely pledge myself as long as I enjoy the same advantage, never to deal with any matter that might give offence, here or in any of the neighbouring states. Further, I return with pleasure to that obscure state from which I should never have emerged and I hope never again to arouse public attention.

But this concluded nothing. During that same April, his friend Du Peyrou was preparing his *Lettre de Goa* (Letter from Goa), a detailed account of the persecution to which Jean-Jacques had been subjected during the previous two months. It in itself would have been enough to revive the controversy. Jean-Jacques, rather hypocritically, refused to see it before publication. 'It is fitting', he wrote, 'that I should be able to say that I have had no part in it and have not seen it,' but he was very gratified that his cause was being defended in writing. Meanwhile Montmollin, who refused to admit defeat, 'was giving free rein' to his spite and using his sermons 'to rouse the rabble'. To win over the women, he spread the rumour that Jean-Jacques in his last book had written that 'they had no souls'.

Jean-Jacques had made up his mind to leave, but he was no longer in any hurry. As the Marischal wrote to him, he was now 'beyond the clutches of the Sacro-Gorgons' and he was enjoying the illusion of peace. Visitors came to see him from all parts of Europe and he was proud of the fact. In Paris, at a concert of religious music, M. d'Epinay engaged Mlle Fel to sing the motet that Jean-Jacques had composed long before for the festivities at La Chevrette. He had not been forgotten. At this point he took it into his head that his friends should always address him as the Citizen, which was the name he had once been given in Paris. He had paid dearly enough for the title: 'I was, and I am, the Citizen', he said. 'Whoever loves me should give me no other name.' He wished he could 'empty his head of all ideas and stuff it with straw'. For a few weeks he had a vague notion of going to live in another village, further down in the valley. But he did not wish to give the impression of running away. As the weather became finer, he began to go for walks again and to botanise enthusiastically. It was during one of these walks that he spotted a periwinkle, a flower he had first seen almost thirty years before with 'Maman', on that spring day when he had gone to stay at Les Charmettes.

'Rousseau is a Christian, as Jesus Christ was a Jew', Diderot rightly remarked, and he would have liked Jean-Jacques himself 'to explain this problem.' Jean-Jacques had no more been able to escape being conditioned by Christianity than Jesus by his racial origins. This was enough to cause him to be hated even more by those Christians who had remained orthodox than by the *philosophes*. He seemed to be betraying everybody.

Du Peyrou's pamphlet came out in June and Professor Montmollin immediately published a refutation, to which Du Peyrou at once retorted. Jean-Jacques appeared to be keeping quiet, as he had pledged himself to do. However, no one could contest his right to send a letter to his friend. Accordingly, on the 8th August, he wrote Du Peyrou a long account of what his relations had been with M. de Montmollin during the previous three years and Du Peyrou added the letter to his second pamphlet as a piece of supporting evidence. After devoting twenty pages to describing Montmollin as a hypocritical and petty tyrant, Jean-Jacques boldly concluded:

> The usual procedure of the Gentlemen of the Church seems to me to be admirably suited for the achievement of their aims: after theoretically establishing their authority to deal with any scandal, they provoke a scandal about a subject of their choosing and then, exploiting the scandal they themselves have caused, take charge of the affair in order to pronounce judgement on it. By this means they can make themselves masters of all nations, laws and kings, and indeed of the whole world, without its being possible to say a word against them. Do you remember the story of the surgeon who had a shop opening onto two different streets and who would go out by one door to attack passers-by and then steal back again and come out by the other to dress their wounds? Such has been the history of all the priesthoods in the world, with the difference that the surgeon at least cured his patients whereas these gentlemen handle theirs in such a way as to finish them off.

This was not bad going for a man who had 'laid down his pen', and it was certainly enough to invest Du Peyrou's boring prose with spice and readability.

Jean-Jacques went further; carried away by the excitement

of this village warfare, he broke his word and composed a farce which he entitled *The Vision of Peter of the Mountain, called the Seer*, which Du Peyrou published anonymously. He is wrong to accuse the inhabitants of Neuchâtel, as he does in the *Confessions*, of showing a lack of humour in not giving this 'trifle' the welcome it deserved. Jokes were never his strong point, and this one was very feeble. But all this quibbling was bound to lead to disaster; it was an activity in which he would inevitably be the loser in the face of fanatical and popular stupidity.

He thought he had time to spare and misjudged the situation. The image of himself he saw reflected on every side was quite impressive. An artist, whose name remains unknown, came to paint his portrait in August. Another, called Liotard, was to come in September. His innumerable visitors, who were at once a source of gratification and irritation, restored his confidence whenever he had been insulted by the villagers. Things reached such a pitch that he no longer received letters, since the post-office clerk had gone over to Montmollin's side. But he stayed on at Motiers through sheer stubbornness. During June and July he had made a tour of the neighbouring villages and had gone as far as the Ile Saint-Pierre, where he spent ten delightful days. Du Peyrou offered him accommodation in his own home at Neuchâtel from October onwards. Other possibilities were Berlin, Gotha or England, but he could not make up his mind and still had hankerings after Paris. In spite of all his denials, that was undoubtedly where he would have preferred to be. He suggested that his publisher might find him 'a furnished room' near the Luxembourg Gardens, where he could spend the winter incognito, while supervising the publication of his *Musical Dictionary*; of course, in the spring, he would go back to his edifying solitude.

On Sunday the 1st September, he was happy. The Marquise de Verdelin had arrived the day before after spending the summer at Bourbonne to look after her daughter. She had come as far as Motiers to keep her promise to visit Jean-Jacques, formerly her 'dear neighbour'. They spent the day reviving old memories. Then, towards midnight, the whole household was roused by shouts coming from the verandah and stones shattered the windows of the bedroom occupied by the Marquise. Already, on previous nights, marauders had removed the bench outside the front door and set up a barrier of harrows. Now they were attempting to storm the house. In his sermon that morning, Pastor Montmollin had taken as his text a verse from the *Proverbs*: 'The sacrifice of the wicked is an abomination to the Lord; but the prayer of the upright is his delight.' He had, of course, uttered no names, but his whole sermon was clearly directed against Jean-Jacques, the 'elders' who had not sided with him in the Consistory and the *Châtelain*. The faithful could bank on the lavish promises of their loving Redeemer but the wicked must tremble. Mme de Verdelin had to leave on the following day, and Jean-Jacques remained alone. On the Tuesday he was insulted and threatened in the street. During the night of the 7th September, his house was again attacked: as the *Châtelain's* report states, 'the adjoining verandah was filled with stones to a terrifying degree.' Jean-Jacques decided to move, leaving Thérèse at Motiers while he looked for a place of refuge. The *Châtelain* saw to it that the house was guarded, since the rowdiness continued. One morning a week later an effigy was found stuck on the village fountain and, in its pocket, a piece of paper inscribed with a threat against poor Thérèse and 'that old grey-beard', the *Châtelain*.

Jean-Jacques went back to the Ile Saint-Pierre, thus putting an expanse of water between the world and himself. The island was small, and there was just one house on it, which was occupied by an official of the Bernese government, a 'collector' and his family. Jean-Jacques was not sure what sort of a reception he would get from the Bernese government, but the official, a kind man, had written to say that he would make him welcome provided he 'created no trouble'. Thérèse joined him after spending a few days with Du Peyrou at Neuchâtel. Jean-Jacques botanised, sailed on the lake and day-dreamed. It is not really so surprising that this very troubled period should have left him only with happy memories. It was natural that his mind should go back to it when, in 1777, as an old man, defeated and resigned, he was writing the fifth of the *Rêveries du promeneur solitaire*. The old man reverted to that gentle mood he had experienced on the shores of the quiet lake during those autumn weeks when, after so much fighting and debating, he found himself utterly exhausted, 'alone and naked', having broken off all relations with mankind, devoid of both past and future, defeated and happy.

At last, everything around him was profoundly peaceful. He could at last 'experience the sensation of existing, without taking the trouble to think'. He could enjoy his own being. He was at one with the material universe and it with him. 'Like God, he was sufficient unto himself.'

However, his day-dreams were occasionally interrupted by anxiety. Three years previously, Their Excellencies of Bern had forbidden him to sojourn within their frontiers. What attitude would they now take up? 'Governments,' he wrote to his publisher in Paris, 'repeal the good they have done, but never the evil: throughout the world, this is one of the first maxims of state.' For his part, he was ready 'to end his miseries and his days' on the island. He had been in this state of tranquillity for exactly four weeks when he received a letter from M. de Graffenried, the bailiff of Nidan, who was responsible for the island. Very sadly, the bailiff conveyed to him Their Excellencies' order that he must leave 'the lands under their domination'. It was now October and the weather was cold. Jean-Jacques was ill, as was always the case with the return of winter. On the 17th, he wrote to the bailiff to ask for a postponement of the order. On the 20th, after further thought, he wrote again, this time making the most extraordinary proposal to Their Excellencies.

> May it please them [he wrote], to let me spend the rest of my days in prison, in one of their castles or in some other place in their States which they may see fit to choose. I shall live there at my own expense and shall guarantee never to cost them a penny. I submit to being without pen or paper and to have no communication with the outside world except in matters of absolute necessity and through the people in whose charge I shall be. If I am only left free to read a few books and to walk occasionally in a garden, I shall be content.

There is no doubt about his sincerity, but none either, alas, about the fact that such wild sincerity bordered on madness. His four weeks on the island had been four weeks of happiness. Once again he had had proof that the desire 'to circumscribe himself' was one of his deepest impulses. Prison held no fears for him. He was never happier than in those moments when he was delivered 'from the anxiety of hope'.[1] This attitude was also

---

[1] The expression occurs in *Les Solitaires*. Cf. Marcel Raymond's critical edition of the *Rêveries du promeneur solitaire*, Introduction, p. xxvii.

caused by what he called his 'laziness'. As early as 1762 he had written to M. de Malesherbes: 'Many a time have I thought that I would have lived quite happily in the Bastille, since nothing more would have been required of me but to stay there.' Since then the idea had developed in his mind with the result that he was now asking to be locked up.

> Do not think, Sir, [he explained to the bailiff], that so apparently extreme a course is the outcome of despair. My mind is very calm for the time being; I have taken the trouble to think the matter over carefully and have arrived at this decision after a serious study of my present state. Consider, I beg of you, that if my resolve is extraordinary, my situation is still more so. My misfortunes are without parallel. The stormy existence I have led for several years now without a break would be terrible enough for a man in good health; judge what it must be for a poor invalid exhausted by his infirmities and worries and whose only desire is to die in peace. All passions have now been extinguished in my heart; there remains only an ardent longing for rest and retirement. I should find both in the lodging I am asking for; beyond the reach of the importunate and safe from new catastrophes, I should await the final catastrophe, and being no longer informed of what is happening in the world, I should be saddened by nothing. True, I love freedom; but my freedom is not within the power of men, and neither walls nor keep can take it from me. Such captivity, Sir, seems to me to hold so few terrors and I am so convinced that it would allow me to enjoy all the happiness of which I am capable in this life that for this very reason I dare not hope to achieve it, although it would relieve my enemies of all anxiety on my score. But I wish to have nothing to reproach myself with either as regards myself or others; I wish to be able to testify on my own behalf that I have had recourse to all practical and honest means of ensuring a peaceful existence for myself and avoiding the fresh storms that I am being forced into.

The unconscious duplicity of such a statement disarms criticism. After all, if he were so keen to be locked up, nothing was easier; he had only to wait for the police to come and arrest him. But this was not what he intended. He required imprisonment to be the result of a kind of contract entered into jointly by himself and the authorities. Were he to take flight, this would mean that the authorities had rejected the proposal. He would have nothing to reproach himself with, not to mention the pleasure he would experience in making public such a magnificent lament which was at the same time a proof of his magnanimity. He did not fail to take the latter step. He had sent a copy of the letter to Mme de Verdelin in Paris by the 3rd November. His pride set a limit to his sincerity.

The bailiff, who was under pressure, refused to allow postponement and apologised for not being able even to transmit the proposals to Their Excellencies. Jean-Jacques had to leave the Ile Saint-Pierre on the 24th October. He did not know where to go. He stopped first at Bienne and, touched by the consideration shown him, at once decided that he would spend the whole winter there. But he had been misinformed; it turned out that the inhabitants of Bienne were not all well disposed towards him, and he had to move on again two days later. He went to Bâle, and from there to Strasbourg, where he arrived on the 2nd November. He was utterly exhausted, ill and alone, except for his dog, Sultan, which was to accompany him on all his journeys. Thérèse had stayed behind at Neuchâtel. He was still wondering where to go, and Mme de Verdelin was strongly urging him to settle for England. She had got in touch with Hume and the latter had immediately offered to act as Jean-Jacques' guide. There was also Berlin, where he could stay with the Marischal. But at that time of the year the thought of any journey frightened him. He could not stand travelling by stage-coach and he could not go post-chaise. He would have willingly remained at Strasbourg, had he been allowed to do so. But as Du Peyrou said so rightly in a letter: 'The newspapers describe you to the People as a man pursued by the wrath of God and whose presence causes barrenness in the land where he is living . . . and the People are stupid and fanatical everywhere.'

However, the unexpected constantly happens. In Strasbourg he was fêted and felt himself to be surrounded by 'universal goodwill'. 'He was no longer in Switzerland.' He was received by the governor, the Maréchal de Contades, who assured him that 'he was just as safe at Strasbourg as in Berlin'. His lodging at the Auberge de la Fleur, kept by M. Kamm, was filled with visitors from morning till night. Everybody wanted to see him in his Armenian dress, with his grey-squirrel, fur-trimmed bonnet which he was reputed to raise to no one. *Le Devin de Village* was put on in his honour; he attended the performance in a closed box and insisted on paying for all the seats in it. He went from dinner to dinner and concert to concert.

Meanwhile, in Paris, Mme de Verdelin had obtained a passport enabling him to travel through France by way of the capital. He received it by the 14th November. Although Hume was expecting him, he still hesitated, and sought advice from the Marischal. He was in no hurry to move; the weather was cold and his fame was as sweet as incense to the nostrils. Rey had the strange idea of sending him a messenger with instructions to bring him back to Amsterdam, as if being at Strasbourg was like being 'hidden in a mole-run'. He informed Rey, in no uncertain terms, that he was not 'the sort of man to hide'. He was caught up in the mood of the moment; the festive atmosphere around him had changed his outlook. The Marischal, his best friend, advised in favour of England. Thereupon he wrote to Hume 'to throw himself into his arms', happy, as he said, 'to be indebted to the most illustrious of my contemporaries, whose goodness surpasses his fame'.

On the 9th December he set off for Paris in a post-chaise that he had managed to borrow.

His journey was both a flight and a triumphal progress. He could gauge the extent of his power over Europe. 'Do not feel too sorry for him,' Saint-Lambert said. 'He is travelling with his mistress, Reputation.' He had urged Mme de Verdelin and his publisher not on any account to divulge the news of his journey, but no doubt he was not too eager to be obeyed on this score. The journey was not too uncomfortable and he was delayed only one night at Epinay by an attack of his illness. On the evening of the 16th he was in Paris 'in fairly tolerable condition'. To begin with, he stayed with his publisher, M. Duchesne. He had no intention, of course, of showing himself in the streets; he would only go to see Mme de Verdelin. Nevertheless, he appeared in the Luxembourg Gardens and how could he resist the blandishments of a prince? The Prince de Conti insisted that Jean-Jacques should stay with him at the Hôtel de Saint-Simon near Le Temple. The Dauphin, who was on his death-bed, had had Jean-Jacques' letter to the bailiff of Nidan read aloud to him and, after marvelling at it, had said 'things that would make the persecutors blush, had they been people capable of blushing at anything'. He had also expressed surprise at the fact that

Jean-Jacques had not been allowed to settle in Strasbourg and had expressed his disapproval of such severity. This was the gossip that was going round and that was reported to Jean-Jacques. He received visitors in a luxuriously appointed room in Le Temple, from nine a.m. until midday and from three to six. One of Mme de Boufflers' men-servants did the honours.

He sat for the sculptor Lemoine who wanted to do a bust of him. He saw old friends again. Women thronged to see him, and among them, one day, was poor Marianne, Mme de la Tour-Franqueville. She had never yet set eyes on her illustrious friend. When she learned he was in Paris, she wrote him two imploring letters but he replied harshly that 'he could not give new friends preference over the old'. On the 28th, she humbly handed in a note; she was 'at his door' and asked him to receive her, if he were alone. He replied: 'I am not alone, Madam, but this will not prevent me welcoming you with the greatest pleasure, if you care to come in.' He promised to go and see her at her house, but did not keep his word. He did, at least, send her a letter: 'I am extremely desirous that you should love me, and level no more reproaches against me, and still more so that I should not deserve them. But it is too late for me to improve in any way; I shall remain as I am, and it no more depends on me to become more likeable than to cease loving you.' His courtesies were a little rough and the pleasures of pride were not softening his character.

He soon had his fill of visitors and ceremoniousness. It also seems probably that the police reminded him that he was liable to arrest and suggested he should be more discreet. It was agreed that he would leave on the 4th January. The party was over: such was his destiny. He was exposed to the glare of fame and, in so bright a glow, it was difficult for him not to be a little drunk with his own importance. But he was the kind of man who always has to pay for everything, who never enjoys happiness except at a cost. The reminder from the Lieutenant of Police made him realise that he was not his own master and that a man such as he had no right to feel at home anywhere.

One person was sorry not to see him: this was Diderot, who wrote sadly to Mlle Volland: 'Rousseau is in Paris. I do not expect he will call on me, but I will not conceal from you that I should be delighted to see him; I should be pleased to know how he can justify his behaviour towards me. It is wise of me not to make access to my heart too easy; whoever has once found his way in, cannot come out again without tearing it apart; the wound never heals properly.' We do not know whether Jean-Jacques thought in like manner about 'his former friend'. Each of them was involved in his own battle.

CHAPTER SIX

'This Infernal Business' (1766–1767)

The night spent at Senlis—'King David' and the 'dear little fellow'—Jean-Jacques in London—The evening of the 18th March in London—'The workings of fate, I know not how . . . carried me into the mountains of Derbyshire'—In solitude, he believes himself to be 'regenerated by a new baptism'—But the idea of the 'plot' germinates in his mind—He cannot escape from himself—He starts work again on his *Confessions* and the news spreads—The legend of the plot—He is afraid and his derangement becomes more pronounced—The first six books of the *Confessions*—He is convinced that Choiseul himself is in charge of the plot—A passage of the *Social Contract* was the source of all his misfortunes—By January, Jean-Jacques is thinking of looking for a new refuge—The King definitely awards him a pension of a hundred pounds—His correspondence with Mirabeau—On 1st May he takes flight and, after a period of wandering, reaches Calais on the 22nd.

I NOW ARRIVE at that period of his life which is undoubtedly the most difficult to describe. All the documents have taken on the character of evidence in a lawsuit. The innumerable commentaries that have been written on it are like so many speeches for the prosecution or the defence. I cannot hope to get nearer the truth than my predecessors, yet I am confident of being devoid of bias or preconceived ideas. Unlike M. Guillemin, the author of *Cette Affaire infernale*, I do not believe that Jean-Jacques

160

was a man of God while the *philosophes* were demons. Nor do I
believe, on the other hand, that the *philosophes* were saints—
writers rarely are—and Jean-Jacques the ungrateful hypocrite
they said he was. He and I have lived together now for seven
years, and have covered fifty-five years of his lifetime. I am
determined now to go on to the end and to leave him only on his
death-bed. I cannot help being fond of him. I refuse to behave
like the prosecution or counsel for the defence. I dislike magistrates and lawyers whose profession leads them into thinking
that every case has been 'judged' from the outset. Through
living so long, and in such close proximity, with this poor great
man, I shall at least have learned, perhaps, that life is never
'judged', and cannot be.

His initial plan was to make the journey in the company of a
Genevan friend, M. de Luze, who was going to London on
business. But Hume, too, was going back to England, so all
three of them set off on the morning of the 4th January. They
passed through Senlis, Roye, Arras and Calais and the journey
was uneventful.

During the first night, however, a strange thing occurred and
the memory of it was to go on gnawing at him ever afterwards.[1]
What he remembered was that, on the first night, the three
travellers slept in the same room in Roye. He could still see the
room, with the fireplace between his bed and that of M. de
Luze, Mr. Hume's bed at the far end, placed at an angle to his
own, and Mr. Hume 'putting on his shirt with narrow, pleated
sleeves'. They went to bed, but Jean-Jacques remained awake.
He did not know whether Mr. Hume was awake or asleep;
however, several times during the course of the night, Jean-
Jacques heard him exclaim, 'in French' and 'with extreme
vehemence', *Je tiens Jean-Jacques Rousseau* ('I have got hold of
Jean-Jacques Rousseau').

It is on facts of this nature, established with just such accuracy,
that critics have to base their judgement of 'this infernal
business'; more than one of them has gravely decided that
Hume was lying and Rousseau telling the truth, or vice versa.
The problem is insoluble. It so happens that the first night was
spent at Senlis, not at Roye, as Jean-Jacques maintains. M. de

[1] Jean-Jacques gives an account of the journey in a letter written on the
10th July 1766.

Luze, for his part, began by denying that the three travellers had ever slept in the same room, and then agreed that such had been the case at Senlis. As for Hume, he declared that he could not be held responsible for what he said in his dreams, that he was, if anything, still less sure about dreaming in French, and asked Jean-Jacques if he was absolutely certain of being properly awake when he heard 'these terrible words'.

But let us pass on. The travellers were held up for two days at Calais by bad weather. At last they set sail; the crossing, which took place during the night, was rough and lasted twelve hours. Hume was sea-sick; Jean-Jacques spent the night on deck and managed to hold out, an achievement of which he was not a little proud. When they landed at Dover, Jean-Jacques, 'transported with emotion on at last setting foot in the land of freedom', threw his arms around Hume's neck and 'embraced him warmly and silently, while, however, covering his face with kisses and tears that were eloquent enough'.

They had had time to observe each other during the week that the journey had lasted, and each was gimlet-eyed. If you come to think of it, they were in a rather difficult situation, having been, as it were, accidentally thrown into each other's arms and condemned to act out their friendship in public. True friendship can only develop from more discreet beginnings. Each of them made resounding declarations which were undoubtedly sincere but could not, in the circumstances, be worth a great deal. There was no real relationship between them; each was a celebrated writer with a keen sense of his own importance. The 'kind David' was very conscious of having performed a good deed, while Jean-Jacques, by now intoxicated with pride, undoubtedly considered his 'dear patron' most fortunate in having to take care of a client such as himself, who radiated fame and virtue. As for their intellectual kinship, they both had the same dislike of hypocrisy, had both spoken disrespectfully of miracles and suffered at the hands of priests, but Jean-Jacques needed to be a believer as much as Hume loathed the very idea, and we may suppose that, temperamentally, they were often nonplussed by each other. Their compulsory friendship did not mean that there was mutual understanding between them. Hume was a big, smooth, phlegmatic, polite and sceptical person, who congratulated himself on always seeing the favourable rather than the unfavourable side of things, 'a cast of mind,' he wrote, 'which is more advantageous than being born with an income of a thousand pounds a year'. Jean-Jacques' impulsive outbursts could only shock him. The 'dear little man', as he called him in his letters, soon struck him as being slightly ridiculous, entirely lacking in self-control and not quite a man. Even so, during that January, they thought they were friends; they wanted to be, and indeed had to be.

Everything went off fairly well during the first few weeks. To begin with, Jean-Jacques stayed in London at the house of John Stewart, a friend of Hume's. It seemed as if his fame now preceded his every movement. Everyone wanted to see the celebrated M. Rousseau. Even the King's brother-in-law paid him a visit. On the 23rd there was a gala performance at the Drury Lane Theatre, and the King and Queen were present to see, not the play but Jean-Jacques, who had promised to put in an appearance. As it happened, Jean-Jacques very nearly failed to keep his word, because he did not want to leave his dog, Sultan, which had got lost once already. An excellent subject for a news-item! He was the popular personality of the day and the papers discussed him with affectionate curiosity. Two painters, Ramsay and Gosset, insisted on making portraits of him. He was quite won over by this initial kindness, but he soon tired of the noise and bustle. Hume settled him in the house of a grocer at Chiswick, on the outskirts of the capital, and he was joined there on the 13th February by the faithful Thérèse. She had made the journey in the company of Boswell, who had visited her at Motiers, and Hume joked about the relationship between them. Jean-Jacques did not feel that his refuge was remote enough as yet. In London, there were compatriots of his, and even a cousin, Jean Rousseau, as well as a number of English friends, such as the Reverend Daniel Malthus and Boswell, who had visited him at Motiers. Hume spent two months looking for some fresh lodging. There was no lack of offers; however, one difficulty was that Jean-Jacques insisted on Thérèse eating with him at his host's table, wherever he might go. A wealthy landowner, Mr. Davenport, who was introduced to him at the house of the painter, Ramsay, on the 1st March, offered him a residence at Wooton, in Derbyshire, a hundred and fifty miles from London. There, Jean-Jacques would be entirely his own master and would pay rent, since he insisted on doing so: the figure, according to Hume, was £30 a year, which was not very much, but Jean-Jacques contests its accuracy, without however quoting what he considers to be the right sum. On the 19th March, Jean-Jacques, Thérèse and Sultan left London and set out for Wooton.

On the previous evening in Stewart's house, a strange quarrel had broken out between Hume and Jean-Jacques.

Jean-Jacques was already full of suspicions and fears. To tell the truth, he had hardly had a moment's peace since leaving Motiers and everything sharpened his anxiety; the slightest incident was enough to make him feel that his 'misfortunes' were beginning again, and he could not get them out of his mind. It was not Hume who 'had him in his power' but fate, the fate that each of us creates for himself at least as much as it is thrust upon us, although, at the same time, we hold it responsible for what happens to us.

Being the kind of man he was, he was anxious about a matter in which he felt more involved than he would have wished. During the evening they had spent together at Calais, Hume had told him of a plan he had to obtain a pension for him from the King of England. It was not a new idea; it had occurred to him as early as 1762, when the possibility of Jean-Jacques' coming to England had been first mentioned. Jean-Jacques had agreed there and then, making only one reservation, which was that he should first obtain the Marischal's agreement. The latter was already paying him a small pension of 600 *livres* and was aware of the fact that Jean-Jacques had refused similar offers from the King of Prussia and previously from the King of France. Why should he now accept what he had formerly rejected? He was not exactly short of money, nor was he greedy for more; the only difficulty was that he had to count his pennies. As he was to say later, 'Being too attached to that which I possess, I do not know how to wish for the things I have not got.' This was true. He had some savings—three thousand *livres* that his friends in Lyons, the Boy de la Tours, were looking after for him, and the arrangement he had concluded with Du Peyrou for the publication of his works was to provide him with an annual income of at least sixteen hundred *livres*, not counting what might come to him from Rey or Duchesne. For several months past, without

164

unduly straining his resources, he had been able to meet all the expenses of his chequered existence and had refused to be helped by his friends, Mme de Boufflers and Mme de Verdelin. However, he was boasting a little when he said he would accept only for the sake of having 'so great a monarch and so upright a man' as his protector. He had enough to live on, but only just. Postage costs and removal expenses were ruinous. The Marischal advised him, even commanded him, to accept, and he did so. He was growing old and entering that stage when diminished vitality creates a fear of total destitution. He was no longer bold enough to allow himself the luxury of a haughty refusal. In any case, how could he refuse and where could he go if he did so?

At the same time, he wondered about the genuineness of Hume who was pursuing the matter with such zeal, for reasons about which he, Jean-Jacques, was not altogether clear.

About the 18th January, Hume had told him 'that copies of a letter supposedly written to Jean-Jacques by the King of Prussia were circulating in Paris', but gave no details. Jean-Jacques had written off at once to Mme de Boufflers to tell her of his earnest desire to be kept in ignorance of all such 'fabrications', adding that he was no longer interested 'in what happened on *terra firma*'. But his imagination set to work and he began wondering about the contents of the letter.

Bachaumont had copied it out in his *Mémoires secrets* as early as the 28th December, although the *salon*, or other source, he got it from, is unknown. It ran as follows:

My dear Jean-Jacques, you have renounced your native city of Geneva; you have been driven out of Switzerland, a country you have often praised in your writings; the French have put out a warrant for your arrest; come, then, to stay with me. I admire your talents, I am amused by your day-dreams, in which, incidentally, you have been too much absorbed, and for too long. You must eventually make up your mind to be wise and happy. You have aroused enough comment through strange behaviour, unbecoming to a truly great man; prove to your enemies that you are not always devoid of common-sense; this will vex them and do you no harm. You can find a quiet haven within my States. I wish you well and shall treat you kindly, if you are so minded. But if you persist in refusing my help, count on it, I shall tell no one. If you go on racking your brains to discover new misfortunes, choose them according to your preferences; I am a

King and can provide you with such misfortunes as you wish; and, unlike your enemies whose attitude is very different, I shall cease persecuting you when you stop taking a pride in being persecuted. Your good friend, Frederick.

It was one of those jokes that have always been found entertaining in literary circles, and seemed especially so at that time. It is not certain that Hume read the letter while he was still in Paris. But when it was shown to him in London by General Conway, who had been sent it by Walpole, he had no difficulty in recognising how it had been 'fabricated'. He must have been rather embarrassed because, as it happened, he himself had had a hand in it. He was both innocent and guilty. A month before, at Lord Ossory's in Paris, he had been with a group of Englishmen who had been teasing him about his courage in taking responsibility for Rousseau, with whom, as was well known, everything always went wrong. He had had the wit to answer them in the same spirit, and had explained how Jean-Jacques had hesitated between Berlin and England. Frederick had been mentioned in the course of the conversation and either Hume or Walpole had imagined the King of Prussia making the amusing remark: 'I shall cease persecuting you when you stop taking a pride in being persecuted.' He was now in a quandary, not being sure how much of this he could tell Jean-Jacques. His fault, if it was a fault, lay in his knowing everyone in Paris and in having met Jean-Jacques' enemies as well as his friends. Walpole had repeated the joking remarks in the *salons* of Mme Geoffrin and Mme du Deffand and had then composed the imaginary letter, without saying anything about it to Hume who 'was very fond of his dear little man'. Frankness required that he should tell the whole story to Jean-Jacques, but he was held back by embarrassment. He was the kind of man who only says what he wants to say, whereas Jean-Jacques was given to saying what he had not intended. On the 14th March, Jean-Jacques, who had received information from Du Peyrou, asked if it was not Walpole who had circulated the letter. Hume 'said neither yes nor no'. All this seemed very suspicious to Jean-Jacques.

In addition, he felt that he was being pulled at from all sides and that all his plans were being thwarted. It was strange that Hume should be so insistent about keeping him near London at the beginning of his stay, when Jean-Jacques himself was the best judge of what would be suitable for him. Also, in London, Mr. Hume lived in the same house as the son of that 'juggler', Tronchin. Mr. Hume was inquisitive to the point of indiscretion. He had asked Thérèse a great many questions after her arrival, as if he were thirsting to know every detail about her. The post was very slow between Switzerland and London. Letters addressed to Jean-Jacques arrived at very irregular intervals and often looked as if they had been opened; all of them, as it happened, 'had passed through Mr. Hume's hands'. Replies to those Jean-Jacques sent off arrived late, or not at all. He was still waiting for the papers he had left behind him in Paris, and Mr. Hume, through naïveté or duplicity, advised him to have them brought over by Walpole (Walpole again!), who was returning to London. And the translation of Du Peyrou's volume had still not appeared, in spite of the promises made by the publishers with whom Mr. Hume was acquainted.

By the evening of the 18th March, the situation was approaching a climax. Jean-Jacques, together with Thérèse, had been invited to dinner at Lord Conway's house, but he had excused himself on the grounds of his own ill-health and Thérèse's unfamiliarity with the great world. The evening, accordingly, was spent at the house of Stewart, Hume's friend. We have two accounts of the appalling quarrel that occurred, one by Hume, the other by Jean-Jacques, and both men claim that the other is lying. But when we come to examine them, the two accounts are not so very contradictory, and it seems a fairly easy matter to reconcile them.

After supper, the company sat around the fire. Jean-Jacques was due to leave the next morning. Davenport had made all the arrangements and, to save Jean-Jacques expense, had hit on the idea of pretending that the post-chaise would cost nothing, since it was, in any case, returning to Wooton. But Jean-Jacques, who was touchy about accepting charity, suspected that some such scheme was afoot and suddenly reproached Hume with being a party to it. Hume says in a letter written later to Rousseau:

> I tried to calm you down and to change the subject of conver-
> sation, but with no ulterior motive. You sat there out of humour
> and either remained silent or gave me very surly replies. In the
> end, you stood up and made a turn or two about the room; then

167

suddenly, to my great surprise, you sat on my knee, threw your arms around my neck and embraced me with feigned warmth, at the same time as you wet my face with your tears. You exclaimed: My dear friend, will you ever be able to forgive my madness? After all the trouble you have taken on my behalf, after the countless proofs of friendship you have given me here, I repay you with ill-humour and surliness? . . . I confess I was very moved and a very tender scene then occurred between us . . .

According to Jean-Jacques' account, there were two scenes. The first happened before supper.

In Mr. Hume's absence [he says], I was sitting at his table writing a reply to a letter[1] I had just received. He came in and was so curious to know what I was writing that he could hardly refrain from looking to see. I closed my letter without showing it to him, and as I was putting it into my pocket, he asked me eagerly to hand it over to him so that the could send it off the next day when the post was due to go. The letter remained on his table. Lord Newnham arrived and Mr. Hume went out for a moment; I picked up my letter again, saying that I would have time to send it off the next day. Lord Newnham offered to send it along with the French Ambassador's correspondence; I accepted his proposal. Mr. Hume came in again as Lord Newnham was preparing the envelope and about to stamp it with his seal. Mr. Hume offered his seal so pressingly that it had to be used instead. Mr. Hume rang for his man-servant to whom Lord Newnham handed the letter, asking him to give it his own servant who was down below with his carriage, so that it could be taken at once to the Ambassador's residence. Mr. Hume's servant was scarcely out of the door when I said to myself: I wager that his master will follow him; the master did not fail to do so. Not knowing how to go out leaving Lord Newnham alone, I hesitated for some time before following Mr. Hume; I noticed nothing but he clearly saw that I was anxious. Consequently, although I received no reply to my letter, I do not doubt that it reached its destination; but I rather suspect, I admit, that it was read before it left.

As for the later part of the evening, he describes it in the following moving terms[2]:

[1] It was a letter to Mme de Chenonceaux, and we have proof, at any rate, of the fact that she eventually received it. Jean-Jacques knew this too, and the phrase 'I do not doubt . . . ', at the end of his account, is not as specific as it might be.

[2] Cf. *Corr. gén.*, XV, pp. 308-9.

After supper, we were sitting without speaking at the fire-side when I noticed that he was staring at me, as he often did, and in a way difficult to express. On this occasion, his unfeeling, burning, mocking and insistent gaze was more than alarming. To be rid of it, I tried to stare back, but as my gaze caught his, I experienced an inexplicable tremor and was forced to lower my eyes. The good David has the countenance and tone of voice of a kind man but how on earth does such a kind man come to stare at his friends with eyes like that?

The impression left by his gaze stayed with me and made me uneasy; my anxiety rose to a climax and I would have choked, had I not given vent to my feelings. Soon I was seized by violent remorse; I became indignant with myself; at last, in a transport of emotion that I still remember with delight, I threw myself on his neck and held him tight; choking with sobs and streaming with tears, I exclaimed in stammering tones: *No, no, David Hume cannot be a traitor; if he were not the best of men, he would have to be the most iniquitous.* David Hume responded politely to my embraces and, patting me gently on the back, calmly repeated several times: *What is it? my dear sir! eh, my dear sir! well now, my dear sir!* He said nothing further; I felt a pang in my heart; we went to bed and I set off the next day for the provinces.

We can only conclude that each of them remembered the evening in his own way, and according to the situation in which he found himself. Hume was unable to understand what was going on in Rousseau's mind, and Rousseau what was going on in Hume's. Jean-Jacques was led astray by his suspicions and remembers only them, whereas Hume had not the slightest inkling of them. Hume understood the scene in the light of the only misdeed of which he was conscious, that is, his conniving in Davenport's trumped-up story of the post-chaise. But they both agree in their recollection of 'a very tender scene'. Jean-Jacques' reproaches, which were unintelligible to Hume, have been rearranged by the former's too eloquent memory into the histrionic exclamation: *No, no, David Hume cannot be a traitor . . .* etc., and whatever the terms in which Rousseau actually expressed himself, it is certainly not surprising that Hume, bewildered by such an outburst of emotionalism, should have responded by patting poor, weeping Rousseau on the back, saying: *What is it? my dear sir! Eh, my dear sir! Well now, my dear sir!* This does not prove that he was a traitor. Indignation and anger, on his part, would have been uncharitable and ridiculous.[1]

On the 14th March, Jean-Jacques had written to Du Peyrou: 'The too great proximity of London, my growing passion for a life of retirement and I know not what fatality, that guides me independently of reason, are driving me into the mountains of Derbyshire. . . . ' *I know not what fatality*. . . . He was quite right to put it this way. From that point onwards, it seemed as if fate took over so that he was obliged to accomplish his destiny. He was sometimes vaguely conscious of the fact but it did not occur to him to resist. The truest, deepest and most unavoidable of his 'misfortunes' was his own conception of them. Of course, he would have found nothing more offensive than to be told that he courted unhappiness, went out of his way to find it, yet when it came, he felt he had to submit to it as if it were his destiny. He thought he was being sincere in declaring that his peace and quiet depended on the public forgetting him, on being given no cause to remember that he existed. He plunged ever deeper into solitude and rapturously gave himself up to his most dangerous tendencies. When Thérèse and he arrived at Wooton on the 22nd March, he thought that all his ills were about to cease.

The weather was wintry. For a week the countryside was buried under a layer of snow and it was difficult to go out. Jean-Jacques thanked Davenport but, after establishing the truth about the post-chaise, paid the cost of it himself and pointed out sharply to the Englishman that frankness was a still more valuable characteristic than generosity. He also thanked Hume in a letter that was half friendly, half hostile in tone, and then settled down to what he thought would be a happy mode of life. The house was 'fine, convenient and pleasant'. The owner had seen to everything and provided all that was needed. The only problem was how to communicate with the servants; Thérèse and he had to resort to sign-language. He was shut up in a silent house with Thérèse and his dog. The surrounding countryside was just as silent. The village parson was good enough to call on him, but conversation between them was well nigh impossible. This time he had really achieved solitude. At

[1] Jean-Jacques' letter of the 22nd March to Hume proves that the business of the post-chaise was definitely discussed by them before Rousseau left London.

first he behaved as if he welcomed it. His ignorance of English 'would keep idle visitors away through fear of boredom'. He was quite determined to go on speaking French, and French only. As he said jokingly in a letter to Hume: 'I am more or less adopting the stratagem used by monkeys who, according to the negroes, refuse to talk although they know how to, for fear of being put to work.'

During the first few days, clad in his fur-lined bonnet and his greatcoat, he explored the park and the garden and went down to the little river flowing in the bottom of the valley. But he saw no one anywhere; not a soul. It was the season of spleen; the English air was heavy and the wintry numbness of the countryside was slow in thawing out. There were hardly any violets and no nightingales were to be heard. 'All the signs of spring disappear before me,' he wrote about this time to a woman-friend in Neuchâtel. Circumstances forced him to withdraw into himself, but he emphasised the withdrawal. He decided that no more letters should be sent to him through the post, because postage dues were so heavy and he had no guarantee that his correspondence was not being seen by prying eyes. Davenport, who was expected in Wooton at the end of May, would bring all his letters from France. At the same time, he notified everyone that he would send news of himself only very rarely. He would make an exception only in the case of the Marischal and Du Peyrou, who were, he thought, the only two reliable friends he had left. Otherwise, he would compose his mind to silence and tranquillity.

On the 29th March, during a kind of lull in his sufferings, he wrote to Hume, Du Peyrou and Coindet. His energy had revived. His letter to Hume was friendly, as if he had recovered his confidence. The one to Coindet was quite admirable:

I feel as if I had been reborn through a new baptism, since I was well and truly soused in crossing the Channel. I have put off the old Adam and, apart from a few friends. . . . I have forgotten everything relating to that foreign land called the Continent. Authors, warrants for arrests, books, the acrid fumes of fame which cause the eyes to weep—all these things are the follies of another world in which I am not concerned and that I am anxious to forget. I cannot yet enjoy the delights of the country here, since everything is still covered with snow; but meanwhile, I am resting after my lengthy travels, I am recovering my breath, I am enjoying my own company and I can testify on my own behalf that during the fifteen years I have had the misfortune to practise the sorry craft of writing, I have acquired none of the vices of the profession; envy, jealousy, the spirit of intrigue or charlatanism have never for one moment entered into my heart. I do not even feel embittered by persecution or misfortune and as I leave the arena my heart is as whole as when I first came in. This, dear Coindet, is the source of the happiness I shall taste in retirement, if I am left to enjoy it in peace . . . What can one be pleased with in life, if one is not pleased with the only man one can never be separated from? . . .

He wrote this during the day but, towards evening, two letters arrived, having been sent on by Hume, and suddenly revived all his supicions. One of them, which dealt with his business matters, was from D'Ivernois and he had the impression that it had been opened and re-sealed. The other was from Du Peyrou and, very probably, supplied him for the first time with the text of the letter invented by Walpole. Now he felt with a kind of despair that 'his misfortunes were only beginning' and that he had been 'delivered helpless into the hands of false friends'. He did not know what the 'intentions' of Hume were but 'he could not help thinking them sinister, since Hume was friendly with Tronchin's son in London and with his most dangerous enemies in Paris'. He imagined that all his friends, in league against him, had formed 'a plot', the purpose of which he could not fathom. He immediately recognised D'Alembert's style in the supposed letter from Frederick. His guess was wide of the mark, because Walpole and D'Alembert hated each other.

The truth of the matter was that a man like Rousseau could not easily escape from society or obliterate the old Adam within himself. The sincerest desire to bury himself in an unknown village with his servant–mistress and his dog was not enough, given the fact that his thought continued to be everywhere present; indeed, his greatness was linked with this very impossibility. A great man's life, especially, has its inevitable concatenation of cause and effect. He had condemned the ways of the world and played the part of the barbarian—*Barbarus hic ego sum*—stirred up revolutions, filled women and young people with enthusiasm, instilled in every individual the yearning to be himself more truly than anyone else had previously succeeded in being, and had thus planted a new torment in every soul; he had denounced all the pharisees and bigots, both in the camp of the *philosophes* and in that of the believers; he had set the passion of a sincere heart against all intolerant orthodoxies; he had demonstrated that a single conscience could counterbalance all the powers that be; it was too much to expect that all this could be brought to an end as if he were shutting up shop. Contrary to what he thought, he had not been a writer for fifteen years, but during his whole lifetime. He had been, and still was, a writer in the loftiest sense of the term, as he might have been a knight at arms. It was not a profession one could enter or abandon at will. He had always been a writer; he had never had any other ambition at Les Charmettes, in Lyons or in Venice; he was a writer and would be one until death, because of an inner necessity from which there was no escape, because he would always have something to say, since he was incapable of indifference about the happiness or misery of men and would never be able to keep quiet about justice and injustice. He himself had been neither tender nor forgiving in the struggle. He had made friends and enemies. He had often appeared to despise his companions, as if he alone were sincere, as if he alone were acquainted with the anguish of truth, as if they were not all fighting the same battle together. His own obsession had made him disregard those of others. And because it had now led him to retirement in a remote village, he expected that everything was over! It was not so; each man would go on defending his obsession; time, the only judge, would decide which was the most valid of these obsessions and corresponded best to the thoughts and hopes of mankind. He was not free to throw in his hand. He had something more urgent to do than 'enjoy his own company'. After all, he was not as dead as all that, and how did he intend to spend, even now at Wooton, the hours of respite that his sufferings allowed him? His one thought was to go on writing, to go on working at the most powerful and dangerous of his books, his *Confessions*, which would cause him to be loved, would be his apologia and his revenge, would, as it happened, urge his obsession on posterity and—he confidently expected—on the morrow of his death and throughout the centuries would keep his name alive while heaping shame and obloquy on his adversaries, who would also be dead, and silent into the bargain. A great debate would begin, and he counted on his genius, on a certain tone of voice that only he could adopt, to ensure him the ultimate victory.

For two centuries now, partisan spirit has kept alive the legend of a 'plot', which had no reality except in the imagination of an unhappy man. When we look at the facts, it is difficult to see what could have been its purpose. Persuade him to come to England to destroy his reputation as an upright man? Get him to accept a pension so as to be able to demonstrate his ungratefulness? For my part, I can see nothing in all this except another episode in the eternal literary comedy, which is adequately explained by the self-esteem and touchiness of the various participants but which, in this instance, takes on a surprising grandeur because of the importance of the ideas at issue and the character of the protagonist. There was no plot, but the comedy veered towards tragedy. Every great writer of the eighteenth century had a pack of pamphleteers baying after him but all of them, except Jean-Jacques, accepted the fact light-heartedly. Previously, when his strength had been unimpaired and his pride at its height, he had been less senstive to insults. Now he was at the end of his tether. Also the quarrels which raged around him were taking a new twist; it was no longer a question of establishing the greater or lesser degree of his talent or wit; the subject of debate was his virtue or lack of virtue. This was his fault, because he had been suspicious of the integrity of others in proportion as they had been more talented. It was a consequence of his system; the Republic of Letters was getting its own back and now the point at issue between himself and others was a question of honour.

He dealt first with what he considered to be the most urgent matter. The very next day he wrote to the King of Prussia, regretting that 'he was forced to live far away from the State' in which he had counted as one of His Majesty's subjects, and expressing the following prayer: 'Permit your kindness, Sire, to follow me with my gratitude and may I always have the honour of being your *protégé*, as I shall always be the most faithful of your subjects.' Then he sent new instructions to his friends, D'Ivernois and Du Peyrou: 'Before breaking the seals, let us examine them carefully, as well as the state the letters are in,

their dates and the various hands they have passed through. . . .'
He stipulated that all future letters should be sent to him through
Davenport.

He felt he was fumbling in a dark cloud, then suddenly an
idea illuminated his brain, as if a flame had been kindled there:
he had been brought to England so as to be ruined and dishonoured. All the facts fitted together. Hume was persisting
in his obscure machinations. The supposed letter from the King
of Prussia was too clever and too well written to be the work of
an Englishman; the author was, undoubtedly, D'Alembert,
another of Hume's friends. And had Hume's servants not treated
Thérèse and himself with disdain when they passed through
London?

The *St. James' Chronicle* brought out Walpole's letter in its April
number. Jean-Jacques wrote a protest and demanded that it
should be published: 'Let me inform you that this letter was
fabricated in Paris and that, to my heartfelt sorrow, the impostor
who wrote it has accomplices in England.'

On the 9th April he wrote to Mme de Verdelin and this time
he launched forth into a thorough denunciation of Hume, and
concluded: 'All my faculties are so upset that I am unable to
write to you about anything else. Do not be put off by my
wretched sufferings, Madame, and deign to go on loving me,
although I am the most unfortunate of men.'

The London papers went on with their gossip and scandal-
mongering. Almost every week for months some new attack
appeared. It was as if Rousseau's mere presence was enough to
stir up passion. A recent critic, M. H. Rodier,[1] has quite rightly
argued that his situation was insecure, since he depended entirely
on the good faith of his protectors. Hume himself, on bringing
him to London, had expressed his fear of 'the bigotry and
barbarousness' of the English. But the peril was magnified in
Jean-Jacques' imagination. Henceforth he was sensitive only to
the ill that people spoke of him, never to the good.

Moreover, it was unbearable to him that his 'misfortunes'
should not be taken seriously. He was an unhappy creature,
obsessed to distraction with his importance and his fame, but
he was all the more insistent on the honourability of his
wretchedness. Because two or three London publications had

[1] Cf. Henri Rodier, *J.-J. Rousseau en Angleterre au XVIIIe siècle*, Boivin & Cie.

brought out inaccurate articles about him, in which it was said that he was a musician's son and that Hume had obtained the passport which allowed him to travel through France, the whole of England appeared suspect. He excepted the few English people who had made him welcome, but only to write to them in the style which he adopted, for instance, with Lord Strafford on the 19th April:

What, my Lord, can secret slander, which should arouse only a just horror of the rogues who spread it abroad, suffice to destroy the effect of fifty years of honourable and virtuous living? Nay, the countries where I am known will not judge me according to the opinions of your ill-informed public; the whole of Europe will continue to render me that justice which I am not vouchsafed in England, and the striking welcome I was recently given as I passed through Paris, in spite of the warrant against me, is proof that wherever my conduct is known, it wins for me that honour which is my due. Yet if the French public had been as prompt to misjudge as yours is, it would have had the same cause. Last year, an appallingly slanderous account of my behaviour in Paris was put about in Geneva. My only reply was to publish the account in Paris, where it was received according to its deserts and where the most illustrious and virtuous persons of both sexes seemed to wish to make up for the insults of my base enemies by bestowing upon me the highest marks of their esteem.

He was afraid and madness was welling up within him. It was caused by, and fed on, his abominable secret. He alone knew his faults and what kind of man he had been. Voltaire's horrible little pamphlet, *Le Sentiment des Citoyens*, the truth of which he knew, was naturally ever present to his mind. Madness born of anxiety became a mad desire for self-justification: his faults had been entirely caused by his 'misfortunes'. No one should be left in any doubt about his misfortunes, just in case his secret were one day to be divulged; this was his only means of protecting his honour. All his faults, supposing he had committed any, were being paid for by the persecution to which he thought he was subject. The whole world had to see him as the victim he was convinced of being so that he could appear, at the same time, as the incarnation of virtue. Every man seeks salvation as best he can. Madness was Rousseau's form of salvation. It helped him to carry on in the midst of the contradictions his destiny had forced upon him; it helped him to resolve them, to contemplate, and even admire, himself.

His letter to Lord Strafford concluded eloquently: 'My lord, the unfortunate meet with misfortune everywhere. In France, warrants are issued against them; in Switzerland, they are stoned and in England they are dishonoured; they pay dear for hospitality.'

The true reason for this outburst was, no doubt, that he had just heard that a letter from Voltaire to him was being circulated in London. He had not yet seen it, but it was on that same day, the 19th April, that he asked Davenport to send him it. Although he feigned indifference, he was obviously dying to know what it said, and Davenport brought it to him a few days later. It was entitled *Lettre au docteur Pansophe* and Voltaire always denied authorship of it, in spite of the fact that the tone, the style and the wit were all manifestly his. It is often difficult to see his reasons for disowning or acknowledging his writings. Denials and avowals were used to conceal the tactics he employed in the ignoble game forced upon him by the conditions of book-publishing in France. Once more he poked fun at Jean-Jacques' contradictions, implied that he was rather too fond of wine and reminded him of the requirements of good faith, common-sense and modesty. 'True merit,' Voltaire wrote, 'does not consist in singularity but in being reasonable.' He went on to flatter the English in his own way. Jean-Jacques was now in England, 'the country of beautiful women and good philosophers' curious by nature, and no doubt he would attract the same attention "as the king's elephant and the queen's zebra" ', but then the English would have a good laugh. He advised Jean-Jacques to go and preach his religion in Hyde Park, since 'the English did not punish follies of that kind . . .'. In the midst of these remarks there was a rapid, venomous allusion to Jean-Jacques' critical references to England in his books.

Thus, it looked as if new conspirators were joining in the plot: Voltaire, now, after Hume and D'Alembert. Compared to this *Lettre*, 'Vernes' pamphlet (*Le Sentiment des Citoyens*)', so he thought, 'was as sweet as honey'. For months he lived in a state of almost continuous alarm. We may suppose that Thérèse did little to help him to keep calm, since she was by nature talkative and had no one to speak to in the village. She lamented her fate and complained of having been slighted. In London, she had been made to sleep in a room fit only for dogs. And at Wooton, the servants of the wealthy landlord constantly pretended not to understand, whatever they were asked to do. Dangers lurked. As he listened to her, Jean-Jacques felt his plebeian pride returning. He had confidence in her; she saw things, he said, that he could not see himself. Mme de Verdelin wrote in vain to reassure him.

> You will be judged according to your way of life [she said], not according to what the newspapers say. . . . Dear neighbour, treat the details related in the public prints with the contempt they deserve. It is these people's occupation to write for a living; they have already spoken well of you and cannot expect to be read further on that subject; they are now speaking ill of you, everyone is attracted by the novelty and the papers are selling. This consideration should help you to be patient and to live in peace and quiet in face of stupidities which will disappear of their own accord and are in any case refuted by other writers who defend you, all for the sake of money.

As far as Hume was concerned, she refused to believe any of Jean-Jacques' improbable accusations: 'No one would consider it an honour to help a man who was despised.' She guessed that Mlle Levasseur was having a bad influence and, in kindly tones, urged her 'not to lose sight of the fact that our facile imaginations and female tongues do well to be beware of what they see and comment on'. . . . However, all this good sense had little effect on the two solitary exiles.

Meanwhile, the Marischal having approved the idea of a pension, Hume had resumed his negotiations and, on the 2nd May, was able to announce joyfully to Rousseau, who had given up writing, that George III had granted him a pension of £100 a year.[1] He added, as tactfully as possible, that it was perhaps

---

[1] It has been held against Hume that he told people about the pension, after agreeing to keep the matter secret. But when he first mentioned it (to a friend of Jean-Jacques', Mme de Boufflers, on the 19th January, 1766), he presented it only as a possibility that had occurred to him. There had as yet been no stipulation about secrecy. After the first letter, Hume merely kept the Countess informed of the progress of his negotiations, and asked her to treat the matter as confidential. Cerjeat, a friend of Du Peyrou's who was in England, heard about the pension as early as March, but this does not prove that the indiscretion came from Hume. Official secrets are sometimes

necessary that Jean-Jacques should notify the Minister, General Conway, of 'his acquiescence in His Majesty's kindness'. Jean-Jacques wrote to Conway on the 12th May. It was an embarrassed, obscure letter. He was, he explained, a prey to such great misfortunes and in such a state of confusion that he lacked the necessary freedom of mind to conduct himself properly and must therefore suspend decisions on all important matters.

> The pride of which I am accused, far from causing me to refuse to accept the King's generosity, would lead me rather to boast about it [he wrote], and the only painful aspect of the matter is that it cannot redound to my honour in the eyes of the public as it does in mine. But when I receive the King's bounty, I want to be able to give myself up entirely to the feelings it inspires in me, so that my heart is full only of His Majesty's kindness and yours. I have no fear lest this way of thinking should diminish the kindness. Deign therefore, Sir, to reserve it for me until happier times. You will then see that I have postponed taking advantage of it only in the endeavour to make myself more worthy of it.

This is a remarkably contorted piece of writing; translated into intelligible language, it meant: I am quite willing to be indebted to His Majesty and yourself, but I do not wish to be indebted to Hume. This was precisely the point that Hume and Conway were incapable of understanding. They could only suppose that Jean-Jacques had changed his mind and now objected to the matter being kept a secret. Hume, nonplussed, wrote to Jean-Jacques to remind him of what had been agreed upon from the beginning and to ask what new 'calamity' had occurred to him. Jean-Jacques made no reply. On the 19th, Hume wrote again, explaining that he had reopened negotiations. General Conway was prepared to ask the King to make the granting of the pension public, but in that case wanted to be sure that the pension would not be refused. This time, Jean Jacques could not avoid replying, and he did so hurriedly, in a kind of fury: 'I know you, Sir, and of this you are well aware. . . .' He had been betrayed. Hume had brought him to England ostensibly to find him asylum, but in fact to dishonour him. As for the pension: 'I owe it to myself,' he concluded, 'to have no

---

common property. . . . In any case, no one in the eighteenth century would suppose that a pension granted by a King could dishonour the beneficiary— no one, that is, except Jean-Jacques.

more dealings with you and to decline any arrangement, even favourable to myself, for which you have acted as intermediary.'

During the past three months, his mind had come to be totally obsessed by the idea that he had been betrayed by Hume. Nothing had been able to distract him from this obsession. A neighbour, Mr. Granville, an English aristocrat who could speak French, had been visiting him. The Davenports had come to spend three weeks at Wooton at the end of May. But these visits, like the occasional walks he had taken on fine days to botanise in the surrounding countryside, had done little to interrupt the sombre fermentation of suspicion which filled him now with fury, now with despair. On the 10th May, in a mood of still deeper sadness, he wrote to several of his Neuchâtel friends. He mentioned the pension to no one, not even to Du Peyrou, because that would have been to touch upon the most painful, the most secret, point. He was filled with nostalgia for the past, the thought of which alone made the present tolerable. It occurred to him to add a further letter to the series he had once written to M. de Malesherbes to describe himself and make himself better known. Once again he needed to give vent to his feelings. During his stay in Paris, Malesherbes had called on him and had expressed sincere regret for having been involuntarily responsible, to some extent, for his 'misfortunes'. Jean-Jacques had been especially touched by this gesture: 'Yes, Sir', he wrote, 'to admit a wrong and declare it openly supposes quite an unusual effort of justice, but to confess one's guilt to the unfortunate man one has ruined, albeit innocently, and to love him all the more is an act of strength of which you alone are capable.' Who was more worthy than Malesherbes of hearing about his new 'misfortunes'? His letter is at once mad and admirable. He expressed resignation and forgetfulness of the man he had once been: 'I lived in Switzerland,' he began, 'a quiet, peaceful man, avoiding society, taking no part in anything, never indulging in controversy and never even mentioning my opinions. . . . ' He had been betrayed. He told the whole story at length and in detail: the London newspapers, Hume's flattery, his jealousy, the terrible look in his eyes, the scene at the fireside on the 22nd March, the night spent in the inn at Roye. . . . But it was not on that score that he asked for pity; he was suffering on behalf of virtue itself.

I am so resigned about my reputation [he concluded], that it no longer occurs to me to defend it; I willingly surrender it, at least during my life-time, to my indefatigable enemies. But that a man with whom I never had any quarrel—a worthy man, estimable because of his talents and esteemed because of his character— should open his arms to me in my distress and then stifle me when I throw myself into them, this, Sir, is a thought which appals me. Voltaire, D'Alembert and Tronchin have never had the slightest effect on my soul; but were I to live a thousand years, I feel I should never cease to think of David Hume.

The business of the pension was the only definite fact about which discussion might have been possible, but he did not breathe a word about it.

Such a letter is quite baffling. We can suggest, but as a pure hypothesis, that one of the cracks through which madness entered was, perhaps, that first lapse from self-respect, several months earlier, when he had accepted the idea of a pension. He both wanted it and did not want it. The collapse of his pride was equivalent to the destruction of his mind. His innermost being protested, felt that acceptance was dishonourable and, consequently, mobilised his soul against it; others, the whole external world, had to be made responsible for the base undertaking. Others were seeking to dishonour him; it was for that purpose that they had conceived the idea of the pension. Once this was realised, everything else became clear. . . .

It would take him only a few more weeks to forget his initial acceptance and thus retrieve his pride completely.

The 'good David' was dumbfounded. The letter to General Conway made no sense, as far as he was concerned. Moreover, Jean-Jacques, whose interests he was serving, had put him into a ridiculous, embarrassing position. On several occasions, Jean-Jacques had definitely signified acceptance of the pension. 'What in the world could be more unimaginable?' he asked Mme de Boufflers. In the ordinary affairs of life and as regards behaviour in society, a little common-sense was obviously better than great genius, and a little good humour more valuable than extreme sensitivity. He did not know what to think; he sensed that Jean-Jacques was 'disgusted with him', but could not imagine why, since he was not aware of having done anything wrong. It was true that he had been curious; he had wanted to know exactly what Rousseau's financial resources were and had been rather amused to discover that Jean-Jacques was neither as ill nor as poor as he made himself out to be. But there had been no great crime in that. He had always been afraid of the effect that his solitary life at Wooton might have on him, being profoundly convinced that man was not made to live alone, and this 'Socrates' lacking in wisdom, this ultra-sensitive being less than anyone else. Something was bound to happen to him at Wooton, where he was without 'occupation, books, society and sleep'. Everything had turned out to be much worse even than Hume had expected.

Jean-Jacques' reply put him into a state of cold fury which lasted for several months. Jean-Jacques was, without comparison, the blackest, the most abominable villain in the world. He at once challenged Jean-Jacques to quote a single fact against him and to reveal the identity of his accuser. He became all the more furious when, having asked Davenport about Jean-Jacques' new 'misfortunes', he had received the reply that Jean-Jacques had never been more cheerful, happy and sociable. This, after all, was quite possible, so changeable was Jean-Jacques' state of mind from week to week, or even from day to day, and he could well have displayed to Davenport only the mood he wanted him to see. But, in that case, what sort of a hypocrite was he?

Jean-Jacques replied on the 10th July, in a letter eighteen pages long and wild with the frenzy of distraught genius. We must try to follow him, and with fraternal solicitude, even in his aberrations; there are not so many men who come to their doom through having too lofty an idea of what is owing to their honour. But a detailed commentary on his recriminations and complaints would be impossibly long.

'I am ill, Sir, and hardly in a fit state to write.' In fact, his health was no worse than usual, unless the term illness is taken to include his mental state. But that was always his opening gambit. . . . Then, at once, he launched into the attack. The basis of his accusation was his 'conviction', which seemed to him to be enough. 'I only know what I feel; but since I am made to feel it keenly, I know it well. The first care of those who plot nefarious deeds is to put themselves beyond the reach of legal proof; it would be no easy matter to start proceedings against them. Inner conviction admits another kind of proof governing the feelings of an upright man. You will know, therefore, on what my feelings rest.'

There is no need to summarise his diatribe. Points from it have, in any case, already been used in telling the story. It is worth noticing, however, that to give his account an appearance of greater objectivity he hit upon the trick of 'always referring to Hume in the third person' (which also, incidentally, enabled him to use lengthy extracts from his letter to Malesherbes). The substance of his charges was nothing but gossip, impressions, insinuations and insane suppositions. He questioned the value of Hume's services to him. Any good he had derived from them would have come to him in much the same way, indeed better, had Hume not been there at all, and he would have been spared the evil. He made Hume entirely responsible for the supposed letter from the King of Prussia, written by D'Alembert (!), as well as for the comments in the London newspapers, which he analysed one after the other. They had been published either by Hume himself or by his friends. As for the pension, he took good care to emphasise that Hume had asked for it 'of his own accord', spontaneously. He did not deny having accepted it. He even admitted that the moment of refusal had been 'one of the most critical in his life', so great had been his fear of offending the King and his minister and so great had been his need of the money, but 'he had done his duty'. He had renounced the pension and his letter to the minister had been a slap in the face for Hume. If Hume had not felt it as such, then 'he could feel nothing'. To crown all, he had insisted that Jean-Jacques should accept. Triumphantly, Jean-Jacques explained his behaviour:

> Mr. Hume, following his plan, must have said to himself: now is the time for action since, if I urge Rousseau to accept the pension, he must either accept it or refuse it. If he accepts it, by means of the proofs in my possession (proofs of what? that Jean-Jacques was prepared to accept the pension if it remained secret?) I can dishonour him completely; if he refuses it after accepting it, all pretexts will have been removed and he will be forced to explain his attitude; it is at this point that I shall catch him out: if he accuses me, he is lost. If, I say, Mr. Hume argued along these lines, his reasoning was perfectly in keeping with his plan and

therefore, in the circumstance, perfectly natural; and this is, in fact, the only way to explain his behaviour in this matter, because it is inexplicable on any other grounds: if that fact has not been proved, nothing ever will be.

Nothing, alas, could be sadder than to watch the dialectical power that had produced so many masterpieces laboriously elaborating such wildly wrong-headed arguments. But at least we can see what had been in Jean-Jacques' mind all the time. The idea of accepting a pension had never ceased to prick his conscience. This was his usual reaction where money was concerned. He would have been very willing to have more of it, because he needed it, or rather was afraid that he might run short, but at the same time he did not want to soil his hands. This attitude was part of his greatness, and his conscience had never, at any point, been absolutely clear. At first, he had been pleased that the King's government, fearing the reaction of the narrow-minded, should wish the granting of the pension to remain a secret. He found noble reasons to justify his satisfaction: secrecy made the King's gesture seem more intimate. But he also realised how much it was in his own interest, too, and he took good care to say nothing to his friends, not even to Du Peyrou who, on two occasions, asked him about the rumours. Du Peyrou's questions seemed to him to prove there had been a leak, that Hume had been indiscreet.[1] He concluded that Hume's generosity was hypocritical, a manoeuvre aimed against him. The end of his letter is deeply moving. He saw himself as a prisoner in Hume's hands, with public opinion and prejudice ranged against him. But he could not be beholden to someone who had betrayed him.

Whatever obloquy may be in store for me, whatever misfortune may threaten, I am ready.... If it were possible to die of grief, I should be dead. Everything in these occurrences is equally incomprehensible. Behaviour such as yours violates nature. It is self-contradictory and yet I have proofs of it. Either way lies an abyss into which I fall to my doom. If you are guilty, I am the most miserable of men; the most base, if you are innocent. You make me long to be that contemptible creature. Yes, were I prostrate, trodden under your feet, crying for pity and going to

[1] It should be noted that Jean-Jacques never explicitly taxed him with this. To do so would have been to incriminate himself, to admit to having hoped that the pension would remain a secret.

any lengths to obtain it, loudly proclaiming my unworthiness and celebrating your virtues, my heart would be in a state of expansiveness and bliss compared to the state of strangulation and death in which you have placed it. I have only one further remark to make. If you are guilty, write to me no more; it would be useless to do so, and you would certainly not deceive me. If you are innocent, be so good as to justify your behaviour. I know my duty; I am attached to it, and always shall be, however harsh it is. There is no state of abjection so complete that the heart not naturally inclined to abjection cannot recover from it. Once again I say, if you are innocent, be so good as to justify your behaviour; if you are not, farewell for ever.

Had Hume held his hand until he received this letter, there might have been no public argument. He would have realised that the unfortunate Jean-Jacques was quite distraught. He himself admitted that he 'quite calmed down' when he read it. But on the 27th June, in the first flush of his anger after reading Jean-Jacques' initial reply, he wrote to D'Holbach in Paris, as he wrote to everyone else, saying that Jean-Jacques was the blackest and most dastardly scoundrel the world had ever seen: that was his real fault. It is true that Jean-Jacques, for his part, had begun to tell the tale, but his letters were not passed round in the *salons*. Mme de Verdelin had, in fact, burned the letter she received from him. D'Holbach promptly spread the information and by the first week of July, all the news sheets in Europe were on the look-out for details. The play had now to be acted out to the end. Hume hesitated for a few weeks, not being sure whether to keep quiet or not. If he did so, he might appear to be admitting his guilt. He did not wish to prejudice his reputation and good name and he had reason to be afraid of Rousseau's talent, since he knew that Jean-Jacques was writing his memoirs, and wondered what sort of figure he would cut in them. He had to take the initiative and forestall Rousseau's eloquent calumny by publishing the documents in the case. His first plan was to write an account of the whole affair and to give all the evidence in the form of a letter to General Conway, of which half a dozen copies could be made for distribution among friends who knew of the circumstances. If and when Jean-Jacques' memoirs appeared, the truth would thus be safeguarded, whether or not Hume or he was still alive. Of Hume's

Paris friends, Mme de Boufflers, Malesherbes and Turgot advised him to say nothing. The others, led by D'Alembert, advised moderation, but thought it would be useful to publish the documents without any comment. It was Jean-Jacques who, unwittingly, made up his mind for him. Guy, the bookseller, had told Rousseau that Hume was thinking of the possibility of publication. Since he was so insanely convinced of being in the right, he replied: 'If he dares to go through with publication, and does not indulge in enormous falsifications of the truth, I boldly predict that he will be unmasked, without any intervention on my part, and in spite of the extreme cleverness of both himself and his friends.' This extravagant remark, when retailed to Hume, seemed like a challenge. He assembled the documents and composed his *Exposé Succinct (Succinct Account)*, which his Parisian friends published in October. When it came to wrangling about details, Hume was as unreliable as Rousseau. According to him, Rousseau had only asked for a pension to have the glory of refusing it and to be rid of his obligations towards him, Hume. The whole of Europe could look on with amusement.

The point at issue was a man's innocence. Jean-Jacques never replied. The signatures on the various documents quoted in the *Exposé*—e.g. D'Alembert and Walpole—were, in his eyes a guarantee that he had not been mistaken and he had been betrayed. When Voltaire added his voice by publishing a letter to Hume, everything seemed to be turning out as he had expected. What really pierced him to the heart was the fact that even his friends appeared not to understand him—neither Mme de Verdelin, nor Mme de Boufflers, nor Du Peyrou, nor (most serious of all) the Marischal. Correspondence with them became difficult and full of quibblings. They replied cautiously but not one of them was on his side in the matter. Only kind-hearted Marianne had publicly supported him. On the 22nd November, the Earl Marischal, having had enough of these 'tiresome arguments', announced that he would 'cut short his correspondence with him as with everyone else, in order to end his days in peace' and never wrote again.

The solitude became more oppressive as Jean-Jacques and Thérèse wandered from one big room to another. He had almost given up reading. His books and etchings had at last reached

London; the customs duties had been high, but the King reimbursed the expense. He decided to sell them. He was told that they would bring in a lot of money if he agreed to its being announced that they belonged to him. He refused to authorise such publicity. His only pleasure was to go botanising. As he explained to his neighbour, Granville, he had switched his affections; there had been a time when he was passionately devoted to freedom and equality, but now he was only interested in peace. His friends and enemies could do anything they liked, in his favour or against him; he himself refused to become involved in a quarrel.

Davenport testifies that he had found him in quite good health at Wooton in June, in spite of all the excitements he had been through. The explanation was that the periods of madness alternated with others when he was lost in his dreams. Defeated and abandoned though he was, he communed with himself in the great work he was engaged upon, his *Confessions*. He had not managed to do much while at Motiers or on the Ile Saint-Pierre. When he took up his pen again, he had reached the passage about his time as an apprentice in Geneva. He had been an engraver, and the influence of the craft could be seen in the elaborate care with which he prepared his manuscripts in copperplate handwriting. He was writing 'from memory', in the fulness of his heart and with a 'pleasure' which he had perhaps never experienced before. He complained to Males-herbes that 'the total loss of sleep exposed him to the most melancholy ideas', but he took advantage of his sleepless nights to conjure up memories of the past, and these memories filled him with so much emotion that he forgot about pleading his cause. It is precisely this which makes the first books of the *Confessions* so direct and moving a testimony.

No one ever understands anyone else; such was his genuine discovery: 'Each one of us knows little beyond himself, and measures everything by his own yardstick.' But he proposed to do something no one else had ever dared to undertake; he was going to 'tell all', to paint so genuine and truthful a portrait of a man that any reader would henceforth have 'a point of comparison', someone with whom he could compare himself so as to get to know himself better. Instead of celebrating his virtues, he expounded his nature. When he declared that no one would dare to claim to be better than he was, this was not a display of supercilious pride, but a sober appraisal. He knew his inadequacies and his vices, but every man has his own. He proposed to describe himself, according to the expression used by Persius: *Intus et in arte.* He was aware of the uniqueness of the individual, his own uniqueness. He himself was conscious of the grandeur of his undertaking. He was about to write a book that would be unique both in substance and form and, in its apparent naïveté, one of the strangest books to appear for centuries and capable, by itself alone, of opening up new avenues for the study and expression of the state of man.

His desire to describe himself was indistinguishable from his desire for self-justification.[1] His admissions, he thought, would be at once an act of expiation and a means of exoneration. In this connection, a critic[2] has rightly quoted a maxim by La Rochefoucauld: 'Sincerity is a desire to compensate for one's defects and even to reduce their importance by winning credit for admitting them.' He himself observed that 'there are cases in which it is better to repent of one's faults than not to have committed any'. It should be noted, however, that his admissions were to have a delayed effect, being meant only for posterity. It is very remarkable that he should never have admitted his most serious faults in a work published in his lifetime. But he knew that when the last act came to an end, his admissions would put the finishing touch to his greatness and lend an air of sublimity to his whole life.[3] He leads that band of

[1] Jansen and Schinz have distinguished two phases in the writing of the *Confessions:* an initial one during which Jean-Jacques' intention was purely psychological, and a second phase during which he was writing an apologia. The *Correspondence,* and even the first draft of the *Confessions* (the Neuchâtel manuscript), seems to make the drawing of such a distinction impossible. The *Confessions* were originally inspired by Voltaire's pamphlet, *Le Sentiment des Citoyens.*

[2] I refer the reader to the excellent passage in Louis Ducros's book: *Jean-Jacques Rousseau,* 1765–1778, p. 267 *et seq.* I disagree with him on only one point. None of Jean-Jacques' contemporaries could, or did, read the passage in *Emile* about paternal affection as a confession. Jean-Jacques is just indulging in a further piece of special pleading when he refers to this 'almost public avowal' of his faults.

[3] L. Ducros quotes a remark by Bernardin de Saint-Pierre: 'The more humiliating the faults of which Rousseau accuses himself, the more sublime the avowal.' (Preamble to *L'Arcadie,* 1781.) Jean-Jacques had achieved his end.

sinners in European literature of the last two centuries who have counted as much on the confession of their faults as of their virtues to demonstrate their intimacy with the transcendental.

One of the purposes behind this work was to test the genuineness of the *Confessions*. At this point, perhaps, I should draw up a careful and derogatory list of Jean-Jacques' insincerities or mistakes, but I feel strangely incapable of doing so and, truth to tell, such a procedure would strike me as being external to the facts, and in itself a distortion.

The first six books of the *Confessions* are everything they could be at the time when he wrote them. The *Confessions*, like each of his other works, is tantamount to an act in the drama of his life, and at the same time the necessary conclusion of the other works, with precisely the same authenticity. Since each of his books had been dictated by 'inner feeling', he eventually found himself obliged to explain the nature of this feeling and to tell 'the story of his soul'. The *Confessions* is the novel or romance of his life, an expression of his idealistic view of himself. Like *La Nouvelle Héloïse* and *Emile*, it is an idealisation intended to influence the future. It would be wrong to say that he presents himself as he wishes to appear; his procedure is not so deliberate. The truth is rather that he had a clearer memory of what he had thought he wanted to be than of what he actually had been.

At the time of writing, he was in a state of profound anguish, yet he had never expressed himself in so vivacious a style. The explanation is that during the long quiet nights he spent over his manuscript, he was living in a poem of his own making, and its quick, light rhythm was constantly stimulated afresh by the memory of happiness. The remoteness of the period he was describing allowed him to achieve a kind of serenity. No, he had not deserved his wretchedness; he did not wallow in it, as people had accused him of doing in order to overwhelm him still further; he was, by temperament, inclined to happiness and peace. He saw himself once more at Mme Basile's feet or timidly kissing Mlle de Graffenried's hand. The blue of the periwinkle he had picked one spring day with Maman dazzled his inward eye. What had he ever wished for other than happiness? He looked back with pity and amusement on the lost child he once was, exposed to every sort of risk and pursuing his course between good and evil. He thought again of Maman: 'She would often say that it would not be justice on God's part to treat us justly, because, not having granted us the wherewithal to be just, He would be asking us to return more than he had given.' He displayed similar tolerance towards himself. Alone, at Les Charmettes, he had eventually discovered his rule of life and the pleasures of virtue. The basis of his nature was indolence, a delicious laziness, which was variegated as a fabric is diversified with patterns, by his 'chimæras', the dreams of a feverish imagination. 'He was slothful in action through an excessive ardour in desire.' But neither his indolence nor his fondness for day-dreaming had turned him into much of a criminal. He was not even responsible for what he had become, for his work nor his fame. He had not wished to become a writer. Had he been more fortunate, he might have remained with Maman and continued to lead an innocent life. He remembered how afraid he had been of Hell; he would ask himself: 'If I die here and now, shall I be damned?' One day he had aimed a stone at a tree, saying to himself: 'If I hit it, that will be a sign of salvation; if I miss, a sign of damnation,' but the stone had struck the tree. . . . When the time came, God would save the elderly child he now was, and, in the great silence of the future, his book, which told 'the story of his life' as he had related it— to Mme de Warens or Mme Dupin, for instance—whenever he had sought to please, would continue to testify on his behalf.

He had never been so strongly fired with the passion for fame and the desire to be loved and to endure in the minds of men. It is one thing to write, as he had done, for one's contemporaries; in that case, the relationship between writer and reader is immediate and harsh; it may involve provocation or anger or any of those feelings that are aroused by the people we come into contact with in the process of living. It is quite a different matter to write for future generations, for readers as yet unborn, to speak with the voice of a spirit outside time, and to become the insistent ghost that eternity will turn you into.

It may be doubted whether his 'admissions' cost him a great deal, or that it was as difficult as he claims to explore the 'obscure and muddy labyrinth of his confessions.' 'It is not,' he wrote, 'the most criminal things that are the hardest to admit but those which are ridiculous and shameful.' He was referring to his delight in being spanked, his exhibitionism and what are called 'bad habits'. In so doing, I suspect him to be not altogether disingenuous. To say too much is not the same thing as telling the whole truth, and he was not unaware that unsavoury details of this kind could have an appeal. But deeper reasons helped him in the making of his more serious confessions; he had a conception of man—and his book would establish that conception—as a manifold being, capable of moving 'from the sublimity of the hero to the baseness of a scoundrel'; he appreciated the delights of public confession, the opportunity it provided for tragic eloquence, a thrilling vibration of the whole being, and the relief it afforded, as if baptismal waters falling from heaven were restoring the sinner to his pristine purity.

It is here, perhaps, that we can see most clearly how the writing of these particular sections was governed by the torment that was nagging away at him at the same time. He had a bad conscience; he was terrified of the revelations that might, at any moment, be published, and trembled every time he opened a newspaper; he felt himself to be suspect since, in the depths of his soul, he was incapable of replying to the questions that everything seemed to be putting to him: 'Who are you?' and 'What do you want?'

He had got to the point where he was describing his life as a young manservant in the house of Mme de Vercellis. At first he did not tell the whole truth but hesitated and skirted around it. Eventually, he made a clean breast of it and told how he had stolen a ribbon and, when the theft was discovered, brazenly put the blame on poor Marion.

The Comte de la Roque [he wrote], in dismissing us, limited himself to the remark that the conscience of the guilty person would see to it that the innocent victim was revenged. His prophecy was not mistaken: not a day passes without its being fulfilled. *But my punishment is not completely internal and David Hume is inflicting on me now only what I once inflicted on poor Marion.* This cruel memory sometimes troubles me and upsets me so much that, during my sleepless nights, I imagine the wretched girl coming to reproach me with my crime, as if it had just been committed. *A hundred times it has seemed as if I could hear her voice whispering in my heart; you pretend to be an upright man, but you are no more than a scoundrel. I cannot tell how much this idea has poisoned the praise bestowed upon me or how often it has made the esteem shown me a source of torment; so much so, indeed, that I have sometimes felt I* *was persevering in my crime in allowing people to have a good opinion* *of me.* Yet I have never been able to bring myself to unburden my heart of this admission to a friend; the closest intimacy has never led me to do so, not even to Mme de Warens. The most I have been able to achieve has been the confession that my conscience is burdened with an abominable action, but I have never been able to say what it was, *because, if I knew someone who* *had committed a comparable action, similar in all its circumstances, I* *feel that it would be impossible for me not to look upon him with horror.* This weight has therefore lain, unrelieved, on my conscience, and I may say that the desire to be freed from it to some extent largely contributed to my decision to write my confessions.

That was the first version, but he went on to modify it considerably.

I have italicised the sentences that do not figure in the final version. His crossings out, his corrections, his constant weighing of the words he used and the subtle shades of meaning implied by those he selected are revelatory of the anguish in which the lines were written and of their genuineness. But the genuineness is peculiar to that particular period; it cannot be given any more general application. The *Confessions* is a document belonging to a specific date. At first, carried away by remorse and the impulse to confide, he had been too sincere. Later, he very carefully cut out everything that might justify the suspicions of his opponents, especially the conclusive self-condemnation. His admission turned into a very skilful argument, admirably suited to proving that he had been led to commit a crime only through his respect for virtue and the shame that crime inspired in him.

Such is the sincerity of the *Confessions*; it is the sincerity of a man who is struggling both with himself and with what he imagines to be the opinion of others. The story of Marion and the ribbon had not, in itself, been enough to make him write the book; the cause was all the terrible embarrassment he felt in his relationship with himself. The past cannot be corrected. He knew that his conscience was not clear, but he was filled with an anxious desire for purity, and so he put all his cards on the table in the hope that the confession of his faults would at least show him to posterity as he wished to appear, permanently worthy of respect and pity. Marion's misfortunes were, in the last analysis, an opportunity to remind the reader of his own. In this respect, his first draft later seemed to him to be weak and inadequate. He heightened the tone, gave it the required eloquence, and concluded: 'If this is a crime which can be expiated, as I dare to hope it is, it must be so by the misfortunes overshadowing the end of my life, *by forty years of honourable, upright conduct in difficult circumstances, and poor Marion has found so many avengers here below that, however great my offence may have been, I have little fear of taking the blame for it with me. That is what I had to say on this score. May I be allowed never to refer to the subject again.*'

His misfortunes had washed away his sins, he granted himself absolution and was lacking in contrition. Whereas Pascal, making proper use of illness and suffering, had constantly felt his heart to be humbly filled with submission to a mysterious God whose infinite demands he was always afraid of being unable to meet, Jean-Jacques' God existed only within himself; he was only too familiar with his God, who corresponded to his demands and was almost his own creation. When he appealed to God he was really appealing to himself, and his inner life became an arrogant delirium fit to burst his brain. His book invented a strange form of apologetics. He knew how infinitely precious souls were. He spoke to them as only the saints had dared to speak, but what they had said to bring souls under the rule of truth, he used to justify their peculiarities and rebellious-ness. Following his example, each individual could think of himself as embodying the truth.

He was really alone and unique. He had restored the prestige of what Christian spiritual directors of later centuries had called 'the inner self', but he left that self without guidance, as he was, on the great, limitless, spireless moors where he went botanising. He had burned his boats and broken off all connections both with the world and the God revealed by the prophets and the miracles.

This was, perhaps, the real origin of the disagreement between him and his 'former friends', for if truth lay within the self and was absolute, it was essential to find, and accept, some trans-cendental guarantee for it, and dogma became a necessity. But when dogma was rejected, inner truth became relative and each individual must check his own sentiments by comparison with those of others, and must give up pretending to be God. Voltaire, arguing against Pascal's *Pensées*, had written: 'I repeat that to think about oneself, independently of natural phenomena, is to think about nothing, nothing at all: this ought to be realised.' In his opinion and that of his brother *Encyclopédistes*, each of us is defined by his relationship with the world of beings and things. A solitary soul which insists on its solitariness soon turns into a narcissistic soul, more intoxicated with itself than hampered, in spite of its complaints; in the last analysis, it is rather lazy. Truth, according to Voltaire, could only be the object of stubborn and patient research on the part of men. It is an aspect of their human wretchedness that they can never achieve it, but its pursuit also redounds to their glory; and to live very consciously in the midst of the relative and the provisional and to work with passion, and to go on smiling, in spite of all, perhaps requires a quiet heroism that has its own kind of greatness. The final volumes of the *Encyclopédie* had come out in February 1766. The truth served therein by the Encyclopædist 'brothers' was, so to speak, external and social. Rousseau and his 'former friends' could no longer agree. But had Jean-Jacques been more modest, he might have admitted that his inner conviction (but it sufficed him, both as regarded his own private affairs and those of the world), being his creation, was open to criticism from others; and the 'brothers', had they been more generous, might have recognised that the work each one of them had done was valuable only so far as they had put into it that honesty, sincerity and even passion, which fired Jean-Jacques.

His mind was not wholly in the grip of madness. The madness flared up whenever some remark or insignificant happening gave him cause to think that his honour, virtue or misfortunes were being called into question and then, once the crisis was over, it died down again, but remained smouldering in readiness in a corner of his mind. After writing his letter to Hume and sending it off, he enjoyed a period of respite. He worked at his *Confessions*, tried out tunes on his spinet and went botanising on the neighbouring moors. At the end of August he paid a visit to Davenport and his children in Cheshire. At Wooton itself, life was, generally speaking, bearable during the whole of the summer and autumn. He had someone to talk to: Bernard Granville, his neighbour who lived at Calwick, only a few miles away. They paid calls on each other; at Calwick, Jean-Jacques had met a great lady, the Duchess of Portland, who went botanising with him, and a young girl, Miss Deeves, Granville's niece; he saw himself in the rôle of her 'elderly shepherd' and she embroidered a magnificent collar for Sultan. This display of affection was as balm to his heart, but anxiety continued to gnaw at him. He was afraid that someone might cause an estrangement between Davenport and himself and thought of the terrible isolation in which he would then find himself.

His anguish increased with the approach of winter. The arguments of his friends, who tried in vain to get him to admit his misdeeds and his mistakes, only increased his fury, and he wrangled with all and sundry. When the *Succinct Account* appeared, he decided not to reply to it, preferring, as he wrote to Davenport, to be 'the unfortunate Jean-Jacques Rousseau, exposed to the full force of public obloquy rather than the triumphant David Hume, surrounded by all his fame'. But his indifference was a pretence. He collected all the information he could, and tried to discover the identities of the people who wrote anonymously in the *London Gazette*. Everything looked black. In November, Thérèse received news of her mother's death at a time when she herself was ill. Then there was a further piece of bad news: his old friend Lenieps had been imprisoned in the Bastille, in Paris, no doubt at the instigation of the *Petit Conseil* of Geneva.

At this point, he added a further, decisive touch to the illusory structure he was making out of his destiny. The fate of Lenieps enlightened him about his own. To Roustan, who had sent him the news, he wrote back in enigmatic terms:

> In the sad but great and noble labours that the misfortunes of our native city hold in store for you, there is one thing that you can reveal or keep secret as you think fit, but of which you must know. All my misfortunes and, as a result, all those of my unfortunate fellow-citizens, spring from so hidden a cause that it is known to no one either in Switzerland or in Geneva; I have not, and will not, tell it to my most intimate friends, not even to the Earl Marischal and neither the public nor anyone else, as far as I am concerned, will learn of it until after my death. I can only add that this cause springs solely from a misunderstanding which is particularly cruel in that, in place of the calamities it has caused, it ought to have produced all kinds of prosperity both for them and for myself.

This is all very mysterious and needs to be interpreted. He had suddenly become convinced that Choiseul was the prime author of all his miseries. He remembered the question put to him by the Maréchal de Luxembourg a few days before he left Montmorency: 'Did you say anything against M. de Choiseul in *Le Contrat Social?*' He had, on the contrary, made him the object of 'the finest eulogy', but couched in such embarrassed and clumsy terms that the Duke had missed the point and, since then, had ceaselessly sought revenge. Such was the 'misunderstanding'. Choiseul had driven him from Paris and hounded him from refuge to refuge until his misfortunes had become those of a whole nation. The policy pursued by the 'mediators' in Geneva against the 'representatives' was aimed solely against him, Jean-Jacques. Had Choiseul recognised the eulogy for what it was, great benefits would have ensued both for Jean-Jacques and his native country. But Choiseul had misread the text or had been misled. And so, day by day, the 'plot' thickened. Small details, sometimes true, sometimes false, were put together and, in the end, produced dark confusion.

Here is the controversial passage from *Le Contrat Social* (Book III, Chapter 6):

A fundamental and inevitable defect which will always make the monarchical form of government inferior to the republican is that, in the latter, the voice of the people rarely raises to the highest positions any but able and enlightened men, who fill these positions with honour; whereas, in monarchies, those who succeed are, more often than not, petty addle-pates, petty scoundrels, petty mischief-makers, whose petty talents, after helping them to reach the highest offices at court, only serve to display their ineptitude to the public, as soon as they have risen to that eminence. The people is much less often mistaken in its choice than is the sovereign; and it is almost as rare an occurrence to find a man of true worth in the position of minister as a fool at the head of a republican government. It follows that when, through a happy chance, a man born to govern is put in charge of the affairs of a monarchy which has been almost ruined by a swarm of shallow-brained stewards, one is quite surprised to see what resources he can call upon, and his administration marks an epoch.

Here, then, was the source and fountain-head of all his

misfortunes: Choiseul had failed to read between the lines and to realise that it was he himself who was being referred to.

Davenport had promised to return to Wooton but was constantly postponing the journey for reasons that Jean-Jacques found obscure. Suddenly, on the 22nd December, he sent Davenport what amounted to an ultimatum; he demanded to be told at once what his position in the house was exactly, 'whether he was in the way there or not'. He was insistent about settling his accounts directly with his landlord. We can guess that relations were becoming strained between Jean-Jacques and Thérèse on the one side, and Davenport's servants on the other. But Davenport arrived at the beginning of January and once again everything was settled. However, Jean-Jacques was now thinking about looking for some other refuge. It was now the depth of winter, there were frequent snowfalls and it was becoming difficult to go even as far as Calwick. He continued his enquiries about the pamphleteers in London and everywhere found proofs of a plot against him. He continued to be bothered by the thought of having refused the royal pension, and was afraid of having offended both the ministers and the King. At one moment he was on the point of publishing a statement to the effect that he had never, either directly or indirectly, 'boasted' of refusing a pension either from a ruler or a private citizen, and challenged anyone to refute this claim. Then he gave up the idea. He next set about composing a cypher to be used in his correspondence with Du Peyrou. A friend of the latter, a M. de Cerjeat who lived in Lincolnshire, offered him accommodation. His reply was full of apprehension and he was afraid to write clearly either about his plans or about certain documents (chiefly his *Confessions*) that he would have liked to deposit with M. de Cerjeat. Another offer came, this time from France, from the Marquis de Mirabeau, 'the friend of mankind', in a long-winded, though generous, letter, which made rather too much play with the concept of 'the heart' and was full of boasting and indiscreet advice. The Marquis had houses everywhere—a fine, large castle at Mirabeau, an ancient country-house near Marseilles, farms in Angoumois, fourteen estates in Poitou, a barony in Limousin, a residence at Villers-Cotterêts and another in the neighbourhood of Montargis. Jean-Jacques had only to state a preference. We do not know what he really thought

o   197

about this welter of dwellings, but he was not to be outdone in eloquence. He sent back a long, carefully composed and edifying reply: 'How fine a thing it would be if the friend of mankind could offer a place of retreat to the friend of equality.' But this could not be, on account of the Parlement's decree against Jean-Jacques and the disfavour under which he laboured, all through a 'misunderstanding'. The letter, pathetic in tone, was not devoid of calculation, since it was addressed to someone who was thought to be influential with Choiseul. Jean-Jacques, with many a rhetorical flourish, presented himself as being in a resigned state of mind; his 'idle and contemplative' life became 'daily more delicious'. 'To wander in solitude, ceaselessly and endlessly, among the trees and rocks which surround my dwelling-place, to dream or rather yield to wild imaginings at will and, as you say, to gaze vacantly into space; when my brain becomes overheated, I calm it down by analysing some moss or fern' . . . such was his 'supreme delight'. This being so, what reason could the Paris Parlement or the Duc de Choiseul still have for distrusting him? This was what Mirabeau was expected to discover and, in due course, report upon.

Towards the end of January, Davenport again brought up the question of the pension. It would be enough, he explained for Jean-Jacques to write to the minister, General Conway, and state frankly that he had been unwilling to be beholden to Hume; the King would thereupon grant the pension. Jean-Jacques refused, on the ground that any such letter would amount to a request and he did not wish to ask for anything. Thereupon Davenport went a stage further and offered to make the necessary approach himself, provided that Jean-Jacques would guarantee to accept the pension. In the end, Jean-Jacques agreed, but with his usual ill-grace: 'If the pension is offered to me on the spontaneous initiative of His Majesty,' he replied, 'I will accept it with suitable gratitude and respect; but if I am to owe it to appeals on my behalf made by anyone at all, I do not want it. Such is my decision, Sir, and you may be sure that it is unshakeable.' It may be that this lofty tone concealed a certain hypocrisy. Davenport swore that he had made no request, and Jean-Jacques was content to take this assertion at its face-value. He was not even affected by the news that Hume, meanwhile, had become General Conway's secretary and was fully informed of the matter and was perhaps even giving a helping hand.[1] On the 19th March, Davenport announced to Rousseau that he would receive an annual pension of a hundred pounds. He added, rather comically: 'All this can only come from His Majesty himself and his immediate servants because I took care to make your wishes known and, in particular, to show your letter to Mr. Conway.' . . . We may wonder if Jean-Jacques was really taken in by his own attitude and that of others. He was happy for a few days, but he had a bad conscience. It is clear that, deep down, his feelings were very unpleasantly mixed. No doubt the pension gave him some satisfaction but as soon as anyone was in a position to think he was pleased to have it, his only thought was how to justify his acceptance. When the naïve Du Peyrou naïvely congratulated him, he was sharply reprimanded: 'Your mistake is excusable, but serious. If you knew in what manner, through whom and for what reason I received this pension, you would congratulate me less. You may ask me some day why I did not refuse it; I think I shall have my answer quite ready.' The extraordinary thing is that this statement is sincere. He had convinced himself that a refusal would be considered as offensive and would have put him at the mercy of the King and his ministers; in the last resort, fear became a justification of his desire.

Mirabeau wrote to him again. He thought of sending back a fine reply in the shape of one of those self-definitions which always won people over to his side, but was unable to finish it and gave up the idea; however, we have the rough drafts. It was a competitive display of talent, the aim being to show a writer of verve that Rousseau could outdo him. He explained, in a brilliant paragraph, why he found society so intolerably irksome:

---

[1] It is clear from one of Hume's letters that he was informed. He wrote to Hugh Blair on the 24th February 1767: 'When I arrived, General Conway told me that Rousseau had approached him, through Davenport, to receive the pension that had been granted to him. The General replied that I would be in London and that he could not embark upon the matter without my agreement and full approval. You may suppose that I encouraged him in so charitable an action. I hope that he does not run into difficulties with the King, who is very prejudiced against Rousseau.'
Davenport, naturally, spared Jean-Jacques' feelings by telling him nothing of all this.

Do you insist on arguing about a matter of feeling? I find myself obliged to talk when I have nothing to say; to stay in one place when I would like to walk; to remain seated when I would like to stand up, or shut up in a room when I am longing for the open air; to go here when I would like to go there; to eat at times fixed by other people, to walk at their pace, to reply to their compliments or sarcastic remarks, to reply to green and red notes of which I cannot understand a single word; to reason with reasoners and follow the conceits of the wits; to make insipid conversation with women; in short, to spend the whole day doing those things at which I am the least competent and which displease me most, while being deprived of doing not only those things I should like to do but also those that nature and the most pressing needs impose upon me, in the first place the need to urinate, which in my case is more pressing and harassing than any other. I still shudder at the thought of finding myself in the company of women, obliged to wait until some speechifier has got to the end of his sentence, not daring to leave the room in case someone should ask if I am going home, then discovering a well-lighted staircase where I am delayed by other fine ladies, a courtyard full of carriages in constant movement and all ready to run me over, chamber-maids watching me and lackeys lining the walls and laughing at me, and not a wall, an archway or a miserable little corner to suit my purpose; in other words, unable to urinate except in full view of everybody and onto some noble, white-stockinged leg.

The important point in this fluent tirade is that he still had difficulty in urinating, and this remained one of the fundamental factors in his story. By now it was April and he was being poisoned by the urea which had accumulated in his veins during the winter. A crisis occurred and he now found Wooton unbearable. For weeks, he had been thinking of moving elsewhere—to London, for instance, since Thérèse, who was also ill, would be able to find doctors there. He had a wild hope of being able to return to France. He would have liked to talk to Mirabeau; what he had to say 'would only take a minute'. He would ask him to clear up the misunderstanding which had turned Choiseul into an enemy. On the 2nd of April he wrote to Du Peyrou and every line of the letter bears the mark of madness. Du Peyrou had written to him through his cousin, Jean Rousseau of London, but this cousin was devoted to David Hume. The letter was badly sealed and had undoubtedly been opened. Wooton was a prison; he was 'caught in a trap' there, and his papers, his memoirs, were in danger. His only remaining hope was M. de Cerjeat to whom he would have liked to entrust them. But how could he get in touch with him? All the letters he wrote only served 'to betray' him and to get him 'deeper into the mire'. He would send off a duplicate of this particular letter in two days time and would include a second cypher in it. But 'a net is spread between London and Wooton and it is impossible that anything should escape'. On the 8th, abandoning his lengthy epistle, he sent Mirabeau a short note, in which he announced that he was going 'to attempt to travel to London' and 'to clear up a peculiar problem in this country of freedom' by which he meant that he was going to verify whether or not he was free. He was in this agitated state for the whole month, while waiting for Davenport who had promised to come. On the 30th a scene occurred with the servants when Mrs. Cooper threw ash into the soup being served to Thérèse and Jean-Jacques. They left the very next morning, leaving behind their luggage and their dog—and, on the table, a letter addressed to Davenport and full of sour dignity: 'A master, Sir, cannot but know what is happening in his own household. . . . If you are unaware of what has been happening in yours since Christmas in connection with myself, then you are in the wrong. . . . I am easy to oppress but difficult to humiliate. . . . Farewell, Sir; I shall often think with regret of the dwelling I am about to leave, but I shall regret still more having had so amiable a host without having been able to make him my friend.'

Once again he was on his travels, as he had been forty years previously on the road to Confignon:

> O saisons, ô chateaux!
> Quelle âme est sans défauts!

But he was now no more than a poor, hunted man, who bore within him the loftiest conception a man can have of himself and was yet reduced to nothingness and ready to accept any renunciation. He gave up his Armenian dress, which aroused mirth among passers-by, and put on an old blue coat. He would have liked to pass unnoticed. Thérèse followed him in her grey dress and little cap. We know nothing of the journey apart from what he himself relates. He had seemed to be setting off for

London, but he did not go straight there because, on the 5th May, he was at Spalding in Lincolnshire. Perhaps he was trying to reach M. de Cerjeat. He was still at Spalding on the morning of the 14th. On the 5th, he had written to the Chancellor: 'Allow a poor foreigner, who ought to be under the protection of the law, to put himself under your protection also.' He could not 'go further alone and in safety'. He was even afraid for his life, and asked to be given, at his own expense, a guide who would take him directly to Dover, where he would embark 'without lodging any complaint against anyone'. On the 11th, since there must be a fool in every tragedy, the local surgeon sent him a fine compliment couched in Latin: 'Quid Reges, quid Proceres, quid Papae ad te? Quaeso igitur, vir doctissime, ut recorderis chirurgum quemdam spaldinensem,' and begged for a reply. Jean-Jacques had a poor command of Latin, and such pompous praise seemed to him ironical. 'I keep silent before mankind,' he replied, 'and I place my cause in the hands of God, who can read my heart.' On the same day he wrote to Davenport, saying that he regretted his decision and was ready to return to Wooton, which he preferred 'to all other forms of captivity'. On the 14th, he informed Davenport that he was leaving for London, but by the 16th he was at Dover, over a hundred and fifty miles from Spalding. When he saw the sea, and realised that no one had interfered with his freedom to come as far as that, he again thought of returning to Wooton. But he abandoned the idea when he read a newspaper article about his sudden departure. He decided to leave England at all costs. The sea was rough, as if the heavens had joined in the plot against him. At this point he wrote General Conway a long, imploring letter which should, by rights, be quoted in full: 'I do not know with what intent I was brought to England. . . . There is opposition to my leaving. . . . Sir, I wish to leave England or this life.' People wished him dead, but his death would inevitably be commented on, and England's honour would not be enhanced thereby. He proposed a compromise: if he 'were allowed to go in peace' he gave 'his faith and his word' that he would keep silent for ever about Mr. Hume, England, captivity and the misfortunes he had suffered. He would abandon his *Confessions* and would admit that the source of his complaints had been entirely in 'an embittered, suspicious humour'. 'I make a solemn vow,' he wrote, 'never to write anything at all, under any pretext whatsoever, to be printed or published, under my name or anonymously, either during my life-time or after my death.' His letter itself would serve as a gauge of his honesty. He would hand over all his papers and manuscripts. Lastly, he would continue to accept the pension that had been granted to him, since he could not be thought so base as ever to speak ill of a government and a nation from which he was receiving aid. He would bury all painful memories, and consider himself happy enough if he were free. 'I see,' he concluded, 'that my final hour is drawing near; I am determined, if necessary, to go to meet it and perish, or to be free; there can be no half-measures.'

He was now a ruined, distraught and terrified man, deserving only of pity. He had one certainty left: even if he did not write his memoirs, his reputation would be rehabilitated by posterity. But for the time being he longed only to rest and 'to end his days peacefully in the bosom of a friend'. The whole world had taken upon itself to judge him. Caught within the circle formed by the ghosts of his accusing friends, he was tortured by the anguish of being what he had always wanted to be. The modern novel has made us acquainted with such characters. His life had begun in humiliation and outrage as if it had been part of a novel by Dostoyevsky; it was continuing as if it were a novel by Kafka.

The next day, it is said,[1] all during dinner he kept going to the window to see if the wind was dropping. Suddenly he ran off down to the sea and climbed aboard a boat that was high and dry in the harbour. Thérèse had the greatest difficulty in persuading him to return to the inn. On the evening of the 21st May, the boat was at last able to put to sea and, on the following day, Jean-Jacques landed at Calais.

[1] Cf. *Annales Jean-Jacques Rousseau*, VI, p. 298 et seq.

CHAPTER SEVEN

Monsieur Renou (1767–1768)

He does not know where to go—He takes the name of Monsieur Jacques, then Monsieur Renou—He spends a few days at Fleury-sous-Meudon, in a house belonging to Mirabeau—The 19th June finds him at the Prince de Conti's château at Trye—Disagreements with the servants—He finishes the sixth book of the *Confessions* and intends to go no further. He is afraid—He feels he is not free and wants to get away. His madness becomes more pronounced—He decides to stay at Trye—His suspicions—His closest friends are becoming suspect to him—The Prince de Conti comes to Trye—In November Du Peyrou comes to visit Jean-Jacques—'That disastrous night, the most terrible night of in my life. . . .'—A visit from Coindet with whom he quarrels—Solitude—Death of Deschamps, lodge keeper at the château—Jean-Jacques believes he is suspected of having poisoned Deschamps—Jean-Jacques again tries to leave Trye—He gives up all his possessions, and decides to be poor—On the 10th June Jean-Jacques suddenly leaves Trye.

HE CAME ASHORE at Calais on the morning of the 22nd. From this point onwards our own memories of recent years help us perhaps to have a more vivid picture of his distress than was possible for nineteenth-century critics. His situation is explicable independently of any 'plot'. The law was shameful enough in itself in that it curtailed his life and liberty: there is no justification for blaming the *philosophes* for the effects of an oppressive system which they helped to destroy. Jean-Jacques was watched and hunted as Jews were in the early forties. The warrant issued for his arrest was still valid, and he was in fact liable to be arrested at any moment. The fact that he was the protégé of a Prince and of a number of aristocratic ladies did not shield him from the relentless cruelty of those dedicated fools responsible for maintaining law and order. Petty police officials, as our own experience has taught us, are often more to be feared than their superiors. Wherever he went his movements were checked and to some extent controlled by the authorities, and we have seen what appalling anguish constant intimidation and supervision can create in the human mind. Jean-Jacques did not escape such anguish. He did not know where to go; during the morning he thought of going to Brussels to rest for a day or two and wrote to Mirabeau, but by the afternoon he re-wrote the letter, saying that he had decided on Venice, but this meant crossing the whole of France and he had no passport. He also wrote to the Prince de Conti, saying that he would stay at Amiens until he heard what he advised.

All those who were fond of him trembled when they heard that he was back in France. He was soon recognised in Amiens, and when it became known that some of the townsfolk were anxious to give him an official welcome, his position was still further jeopardised. The Prince de Conti warned him that he was 'in great danger'. The law was automatic in operation and any attorney could denounce him with the 'inevitable and fatal consequences'. The Prince urged him to leave Amiens at once, quietly and under cover of night. The bearer of the letter would take him 'to a château', which we may suppose was Trye. When the messenger arrived Jean-Jacques had already left; and had got as far as Saint-Denis where he stayed at the Auberge des Trois Maillets, after which Mirabeau had arranged for him to be taken along with Thérèse to his house at Fleury-sous-Meudon. Jean-Jacques travelled under the name of M. Jacques, stayed a few days at Fleury, but was seen in the park at Meudon, which revived the Prince de Conti's fears. Mme de Verdelin urged Jean-Jacques not to provoke the authorities and 'defy the laws'. 'Stay at home and water your garden.' Kind-hearted Coindet, who had been his friend during the sixties and who still worked for the Necker banking house, put himself at Jean-Jacques' service and for several weeks acted as his sole agent. From 19th June onwards he was looked after by the Prince de Conti. As Mirabeau rather jealously commented: 'the oak-tree took him under its protective shade'. The Prince had negotiated with the court for him to be allowed to find some safe place of retirement. At one moment it was proposed to put him in the Château de Vincennes, under some kind of house arrest, but the Prince insisted that he should not be deprived of his freedom, and he eventually found himself at the Château de Trye, near Gisors. Since the name 'Jacques' had seemed an insufficient disguise to the Prince, Jean-Jacques was to be known as M. Jean-Joseph Renou, (since these were the Christian names given him when he was baptised into the Catholic Church), and Thérèse became Mlle Renou, his sister: such were the pathetic lies forced on him by necessity. Letters intended for him were to be addressed to M. Manoury, the Prince de Conti's Master of the Hunt.

A week had hardly elapsed when it was already obvious that Trye would not be his last refuge. M. Manoury and his family struck him as very kind, 'even excessively so'. 'But,' he wrote to Coindet, 'there are other people here who are not at all anxious to have a guest, and who will secretly do their best to turn me out. People of high rank are always doomed to harbour within their own houses the most dangerous enemies of the people they care for. I am very much afraid that our troubles are not over. We must have patience and be prepared for all eventualities.'

The difficulties he always encountered in his dealings with servants were inevitable. They were not simply due to the fact that he was an encumbrance to them and deprived them of the freedom they might otherwise have enjoyed in their master's absence—the main reason was that since servants have no respect for paupers, they must have found it difficult to tolerate a 'pseudo-master' from whom they received no payment. Conversely he, having once been a servant himself, was inevitably all the more touchy through being uncertain of his right to issue orders, and Thérèse, finding herself accidentally transported to a life of luxury, became no doubt very demanding at times. A group of individuals of this kind, one more impecunious than the other, would have had to be exceptionally intelligent for them all to live in peace together, and for Jean-Jacques to be treated by the others with the deference appropriate to his genius.

On 29th June his dog Sultan arrived back from England, and for a brief space this put him in a good mood. When Coindet, in writing to him, added a 't' to Renou, Jean-Jacques protested against the mis-spelling of his ancestral name which threatened to 'give a plebeian taint to the ancient and illustrious House of Renou'. But on the whole he remained gloomy and peevish, as poor Coindet, who was acting as his agent, was made well aware. When he kept up the joke about not spelling Renou with a 't' he was reprimanded for his lack of respect and reminded of his own plebeian origins. . . . He had sent two silver knives and forks: but he would have been better advised to send four, even if they were not made of silver, so that when Jean-Jacques had a guest he was not obliged to eat with his fingers, and so on. . . . What distressed him most was the rumour that he was mad, about which Du Peyrou had, tactlessly, informed him. 'Consequently,' he said, 'since it has been settled that I am mad, it stands to reason that my misfortunes are mere hallucinations.'

Mme de Verdelin would have liked him to go and live in the south-west of France, in the province of Limousin for instance, where he would not be under the jurisdiction of the Parlement. She would buy him a little house, for which he would naturally pay her rent. He replied that he was weary of everything, and only wanted to drift along from day to day. But he was exposed to the servants' scorn and the jeers of the common people. Because he had neither braid, ribbons, plume nor sword, he was looked upon as a spy. Because he used to go botanising, he was taken for an apothecary and a quack. The Master of the Hunt was definitely not as kind as he had thought, and was envious of the accommodation Jean-Jacques enjoyed. The new lodge-keeper, who was called Deschamps, would deliberately shut him inside or outside the grounds. The gardener refused to give him any vegetables and had stirred up the village people against him. The parish priest had joined in and there had been disturbances. When the Prince's representative had arrested a villager, Jean-Jacques had interceded on his behalf. But the official had replied that he ought to be allowed to do things in his own way if Jean-Jacques wanted to be protected. . . .

Jean-Jacques did not know who was behind all these disturbances, but somebody most certainly was.

Mirabeau, partly out of kindness, and partly out of self-interest, had tried to interest Jean-Jacques in his new economic theories, and was urging him to read his works. But Jean-Jacques had no desire to write or read about any subject, no matter what it was. He wanted to be 'dead to every form of literature', and neither would nor could 'emerge from his present state of mental non-existence'. On Mirabeau's insistence, Jean-Jacques finally gave his views on 'legal despotism', but he had no real interest in the matter. The expression 'had no meaning for him' since it seemed self-contradictory. He had had enough of arguments and henceforth wanted to 'acquiesce and be silent'. Botany was his chief hobby. Sometimes he signed his letters 'herbalist to the Duchess of Portland', to whom he continued to write letters in a ceremonious style. And so the weeks went by. He finished the sixth book of the *Confessions*. He had reached the point when he was describing his return to Chambéry after the escapade which took him as far as Montpellier. He recalled that wonderful time when he had passed himself off as an English Jacobite. But between Mr. Dudding and M. Renou, what a long succession of misfortunes there had been! Only his love of virtue had brought him back and made him decide to 'dedicate himself unreservedly to the service of the best of mothers'. He had hurried back along the road to Les Charmettes, but had found his place taken by Wintzenried. And he was no doubt re-arranging the facts a little to make them agree with his profound conviction that 'the quickening force of adversity' had had the effect of developing his virtues. He had got to the end of the story of his youth, the time when he had been happy. 'I must stop at this point,' he wrote. 'Time may lift many veils. If my memory survives posterity may perhaps one day learn what it was I had to say. It will then be known why I remain silent now.' He was afraid. Mme de Verdelin had told him that people dreaded the publication of his 'memoirs', and that they had not forgiven him for writing *Le Contrat Social*. He dared not embark on an account of the period during which he had first met all those whom he now considered as his enemies, and he hoped, by thus refraining, to placate them and soften their hearts. From then on he gave up writing, and madness, like vegetation growing on fallow land, could more easily invade his empty mind.

On the 12th August, following further unpleasantness on the part of the servants, he wrote to the Prince, as well as to Mme de Luxembourg and to Mme de Verdelin, asking to be allowed to submit to his fate and lead his own life as he thought fit. The Prince (who himself was taking the greatest possible precautions to keep Jean-Jacques' whereabouts secret because, as experience has taught us too, no one is to be trusted), replied to him through Coindet, that he had no wish to 'restrict his freedom', but that he would be safe 'nowhere else in France', and that he should 'have patience'. He himself would come to Trye and put things to rights. All Jean-Jacques' correspondents wrote to him very guardedly as if they were afraid of adding fuel to the flames. They dared not contradict him—and made only some slight attempt to make him see the facts of the situation in their true light. Only Mirabeau, generous and expansive as ever, ventured to warn him against the danger of 'drifting to and fro in uncertainty and in the ocean of his own peculiarity', and urged him to have a 'cheerful heart'. Mme de Verdelin promised to find someone who could intervene with Choiseul. Jean-Jacques was in a fever of impatience, and convinced that his new name, Renou, was an 'open secret'. Anything which occurred in the castle or in the surrounding countryside aroused his suspicions. He saw it as part of that 'continuous, clandestine coming and going, the effect of which was only too obvious in the attitude of the local inhabitants'. Village rumour had it that he was an Englishman who had come to buy up corn and starve the population.

> The entire neighbourhood is swayed by the lodge-keeper. I can bear everything except disgrace [he wrote to Coindet]. If only someone would enlighten me as to my situation, and tell me what I must, or must not do! Am I allowed to choose an abode for myself in some remote corner of the kingdom? Or would it be better if I left France altogether? I was allowed to enter without hindrance: I can at least hope to be allowed to leave in the same way. But how and where? I ask only to do as I am told. Let me be informed of what is expected of me, since as long as my wretched existence continues, I must perforce be somewhere. But it is no longer possible for me to remain here. . . . Pity me, my

young friend, pity my poor grizzled head which, having no place in which to rest, goes floating through the void, and which feels, to its sorrow, that the rumours which have been spread abroad concerning it are still only half true.

The poor man felt he had no other course open to him but total oblivion and madness. When the servants, who had been summoned to Paris by the prince, came back to Trye, Jean-Jacques felt that they mistrusted him even more than ever. He was now convinced they thought he was a spy: he gave up his resounding title of herbalist to the Duchess of Portland and sadly signed his letters to Coindet: spy to the Prince de Conti.

We can only guess at the steps his friends—and they had no easy task—were undertaking on his behalf in Paris. Coindet would have liked Jean-Jacques to write a letter which he could use as evidence stating his determination never to write or publish anything again. But he had already written precisely this kind of letter time and time again. The Prince was more afraid of the Parlement than he was of the Court. Jean-Jacques received no reply to his letters, and the very secrecy surrounding the negotiations on his behalf, filled him with panic. At the end of August he became unwell and suddenly changed his mind. After doing everything in his power to leave, he decided to remain at Trye, come what may, and to 'allow himself to be put out of his misery' there.

He was hoping for a visit from Du Peyrou, whom he had seen again at Fleury where the two friends had greeted each other with emotion. Du Peyrou had come post haste from Switzerland in order to meet him and had since been on a business trip to Holland. But when he returned to Paris he had promised to call at Trye before going back to Neuchâtel. An attack of gout was delaying his departure and Jean-Jacques was exasperatedly awaiting his arrival. Jean-Jacques' imagination was at work inventing some fresh disaster. His persecutors could not have failed to be struck by the coincidence between his own journey to Trye and Du Peyrou's journey to Holland where he had seen Rey, the publisher. At the same time he had written to Coindet asking for paper. This was enough to convince his persecutors that he was still writing. He advised Du Peyrou to be on his guard against both Coindet and Mme de Verdelin. Coindet was a conceited ass and Mme de Verdelin's tool: 'She deceived me for six years,' he exclaimed, 'but has not been able to do so during the past two. I pretend to notice nothing; I stifle my own feelings, and answer endearment with endearment. They are being false in order to destroy me, and I am being false in order to protect myself: but since this is of no avail, I feel that I cannot go on being false for much longer: sooner or later the storm must break.' He had now come to believe that the Prince de Conti, the Maréchal de Luxembourg, and Mme de Verdelin had no doubt been anxious to protect him, but that 'the two ladies' had also wanted to 'make a mock of him' in order to 'reassure their friend' M. de Choiseul. And 'their friend' never seemed to them to be sufficiently reassured. This was why 'the prince's entire household, the clergy, the peasants, in fact the whole neighbour-hood had been stirred up against him'. His pride had been provoked so that once again he would be forced to take flight. Thérèse, 'his sister', and the only friend he had in the world, had been right to hold him back.

> Where can I go? [he exclaimed]. Where can I find a safer refuge from my enemies? . . . On final reflection, I have decided to put up with everything and to remain here, whatever they may do. If all they wanted was to have me in their power they need only leave me here: for here I am bound hand and foot and at their mercy: yet everyone insists on luring me to Paris; I leave you to guess why. No doubt they are all in league with one another: they are bent on destroying me and bent on taking my life, in order to be rid once and for all of the need to keep a watch on me. It is impossible to suggest any other explanation for all that is hap-pening. As a result I shall be dragged from here only by main force. I shall endure all, humiliation, disgrace, ill-usage, and I have resolved to perish here. O God! if the public were informed of what is going on, how indignant the French would be to dis-cover that in order to appease the fury of a Scotsman they had become the satellites of the English, and that they themselves were being compelled to punish me for having sought refuge among them from the barbarity of their natural enemies!

There was no question of luring him to Paris: this was exactly what *they* did not want, because it was in Paris that he would be in the greatest danger. The truth was that nobody knew what to do with him. The authorities, who were themselves embarrassed, would have preferred to keep the whole matter quiet. If nothing was said he could be tolerated and allowed to live in peace. It was impossible, however, to grant him explicit authorisation to remain in France since that would have aroused opposition on the part of the Parlement, and Church, and all the upholders of tradition. And there was no knowing what consequences this might entail. He was mad! To attempt to elucidate the full significance of these words is a deeply moving but also perhaps a rather fruitless and preposterous task. Some readers perhaps have given up trying to follow him along the strange paths of his madness. I, for my part, cannot do other than go with him to the bitter end. It is not a question of love, or hatred, but simply of compassion; I have lived so close to him that his very madness now seems to hold no mystery for me, and to be almost natural and necessary. Like Nietzsche he was one of those organisms which can, and must, burst asunder. Some irresistible impulse had made him construct his work, and reveal to the world all the strangeness that was in him; now that the work was behind him, and he had proof of its power but also of its peculiarity, he was at once proud of it and afraid of it. He felt he was a man apart, alone and unique. All he wanted now was silence and tranquillity. Throughout the centuries his work would go on producing its effect. But for pity's sake could he not now be allowed to live and die in peace! The *Dictionary of Music*, the proofs of which he had been correcting for over three years, was finally ready to be brought out by Duchesne. At the last moment he wrote to the Chief Commissioner of the Paris Police, M. de Sartine, objecting to the publication of the work, until it had once more been submitted for censorship.

Since he had seemed disposed to leave for Italy, the Prince de Conti, embarrassed and uncertain of his influence, informed him through Mme de Verdelin that he would help him to obtain 'all possible facilities'. Jean-Jacques refused any such help. Since the Prince wanted him out of Trye, he would stay there. People would see who showed the greater steadfastness, his enemies in persecution or himself in suffering: 'My only expectation and my only hope,' he replied, 'is that my sufferings will come to an end, and it is a matter of indifference to me whether this outcome is achieved by nature or by men, and, in whatever way people may think fit to dispose of me, they will always be doing me less harm than good.' Early in October the Prince came to Trye.

Jean-Jacques ate at his table and the Prince instructed all the members of his household to treat Jean-Jacques as they would himself. He tried to explain to him that all the trouble had been caused by 'the silly, ignorant doings of peasants and servants'. Finally he urged him to be more explicit and to describe the nature of the plot which he felt was being hatched against him. Jean-Jacques refused to speak, remained inscrutable and declared that he would say nothing until he had left Trye. A madman is loath to relinquish his madness. However paradoxical it may seem, it was his madness which now ensured the balance and survival of his being. For him to cling to his conception of himself, at a time when life was being measured out to him so grudgingly, and so as not to feel completely vanquished, he had to believe in the reality of this appalling and mysterious conspiracy. Only the persecution of which he imagined himself to be the victim was worthy of him and saved his pride. The Prince, after leaving, wrote him a kind letter: 'I accept the state of ignorance in which you insist on leaving me, although I find your attitude in this respect less than reasonable; friendship must serve friendship in its own way and mine for you, though perturbed, has not been impaired and never will be.' Jean-Jacques for his part remained unconvinced and concluded that the Prince's visit might have brought about some change in the neighbourhood, but had produced no effect whatever in the château. 'The root of the evil,' he wrote to Coindet, 'which pursues its tortuous and subterranean course, has not been severed and never will be until the thread of my own life has been cut.' It had been decided that he would remain at Trye. Du Peyrou, having recovered from the attack of gout which had kept him in Paris, arrived at the beginning of November. His visit, to which Jean-Jacques had looked forward so eagerly, proved disastrous. After a few days Du Peyrou had a relapse and Jean-Jacques and Thérèse looked after him as best they could. But one night . . . Space is lacking to quote in full the extraordinary account, thirteen pages long, that Jean-Jacques sent to the Prince de Conti. There exists no more lamentable document about human nature. All the characteristics of the normal man reappear in the madman. The masochistic streak which had always made him wallow in his misfortunes led Jean-Jacques on that particular night to believe that Du Peyrou

P   213

thought that he, Jean-Jacques, had poisoned him. This was only to be expected of the wicked and 'vicious' man he was reputed to be: he was under suspicion of having poisoned his best friend. Du Peyrou's man-servant had convinced his master that this was the case. In vain Jean-Jacques implored them both in turn to speak out. Du Peyrou had uttered only 'indistinct, ambiguous, deceitful and falsely negative replies which his eyes and his manner belied'. The manservant had pretended not to understand, and Jean-Jacques had imagined he saw 'in his eyes that imperturbable assurance of the rogue which resembles the artlessness of innocence', and he had been obliged to 'give up trying to fathom the dark mystery'. All this had been perpetrated by his enemies. 'I know what my enemies are like,' he declared, 'and I know what they are capable of doing. They knew that M. Du Peyrou had been entrusted with all my documents, my secrets and my plans. That was enough to make me foresee that they would not leave me to enjoy his visit in peace. What I did not foresee was that instead of trying to prevent it taking place, they would succeed in turning it to their advantage.'

Madness is impossible to explain; the most we can hope is to recognise the impulses behind it. Now 'on that disastrous night, the most terrible night of his whole life', Jean-Jacques had tried to find a document which Du Peyrou has 'sent to him in England (we are still quoting from his letter to the Prince de Conti) guaranteeing his commitments in the event of death': on the back of this same sheet Jean-Jacques had signed a declaration whereby he relinquished all the benefits which might accrue to him through Du Peyrou. He had wanted to take the document to Du Peyrou there and then, but Thérèse, who was sorry for the sick man, had prevented him from doing so and had managed to persuade him to wait until the following morning. Such behaviour is obviously significant. When he saw that Du Peyrou was ill, he had been afraid what people would think if Du Peyrou should die while staying with him when he, Jean-Jacques, had in his possession the document which guaranteed him certain financial benefits. Jean-Jacques had invented the whole business, and the ramblings of a sick man who was himself delirious were hardly likely to bring him to his senses. His was, as always, the poor man's obsession with money. Money matters always made him lose his head. The following day he drew up a detailed 'statement of the business matters between himself and M. Du Peyrou'. He considered the agreement between them as being cancelled. But since he had already drawn the stipulated allowance for a year and a half, a total of 2,400 *livres*, he must return it to Du Peyrou. He was unable to do so immediately. However, the documents in Du Peyrou's possession provided a sufficient guarantee. Jean-Jacques' only reservation was that the documents and memoirs relating to his life should not be published while he was still alive. And Du Peyrou could take what was owing to him from the 6,000 *livres* which he had received from the Earl Marischal as capital for a life annuity of 600 *livres* which he was paying to Jean-Jacques. As regards the remainder of the 6,000 *livres*, Du Peyrou could dispose of them as he pleased with the consent of the Earl Marischal. . . . And Jean-Jacques concluded, settling rather too meticulously what each owed the other: 'Being thus freed from financial obligations towards M. Du Peyrou, I consider myself still indebted towards him for the services and kind and zealous attentions he has showered upon me, and for which I shall continue to feel all my life the gratitude they deserve, being unwilling for my part to take into consideration the distress he has caused me, nor the fact that I have in a sense saved his life against his will.'

As early as the 12th, Jean-Jacques wrote to the Prince: 'Du Peyrou is still convinced that he is going to die, and yet his condition is visibly getting better in spite of himself, as it were.' Madmen are not always devoid of humour. At the end of the month, Du Peyrou had completely recovered. The two friends quarrelled again, Du Peyrou protesting vigorously against the suspicion imputed to him by Jean-Jacques and refusing to break the contract. They got to the point of communicating with each other only by means of written notes. Poor Du Peyrou tried to give a common-sense explanation of what he had perhaps said in his delirium. A few days before, Jean-Jacques himself had told him some story about being poisoned at Dover where he had been served a dish in which hemlock had been used instead of parsley. The incident might have come back to him when he was in a feverish state. Jean-Jacques made some sour reply but the two friends were eventually reconciled. Jean-Jacques commented that 'Du Peyrou's mind might not have made such a good recovery as his body', which showed that he believed only in the madness of others. He wrote to Colonel de Pury at Neuchâtel to ask him to come and fetch Du Peyrou and accompany him on his return journey.

In Paris the *Dictionary of Music* was now on sale, and, as the good-natured Coindet reported, enjoying remarkable success. *Le Devin de Village* was also being performed, but Jean-Jacques feigned indifference to all this. He continued to botanise, with the help of Dillenius' dictionary, and sorted out his herbarium. As the days went by, he was more conscious, he said, of the emptiness of life, and surrendered himself more and more to indolence. He was 'eating his hay'. He had abandoned his intention of continuing the *Confessions*, and in a letter to the faithful Marianne he included a moving quotation from Metastasio:

> Sentirse, o Dio morir,
> E non poter mai dir:
> Morir mi sento!

> I have condemned myself [he wrote], to observing an eternal silence about my misfortunes, and I will do all I can to obliterate from my heart the memory and awareness of them. My final consolation is that their end is near, and since those people who seek to prolong them beyond my life-time are also mortal, that end will be only slightly postponed: eventually, however, time and truth will tell and whatever my contemporaries may do, my memory will not always be without honour.

The year drew to a close, and Du Peyrou left at the beginning of January. Jean-Jacques was not sorry: he had found him difficult to get on with, cold and incapable of real affection. The arrangements between them about Jean-Jacques' works remained unsettled. Jean-Jacques no longer had enough confidence in him to agree to being under any obligation towards him. However, he received two quarters of the pension from the King of England, and so he was sure of his daily bread.

He was bored and found solitude wearisome. Even the letters he received were few and far between. He was saddened by the fact that he no longer bore his own name. But the following lines by an anonymous poet which kind Marianne had copied out for him at least afforded him a moment of pleasure:

Rousseau, prenant toujours la nature pour maître,
Fut, de l'humanité, l'apôtre et le martyr;
Les mortels, qu'il voulut forcer à se connaître,
S'étaient trop avilis pour ne pas l'en punir:
Pauvre, errant, fugitif, et proscrit sur la terre,
Sa vie à ses écrits servit de commentaire:
La fière vérité, dans ses hardis tableaux,
Sut, en dépit des grands, montrer ce que nous sommes.
Il devait de nos jours trouver des échafauds;
Il aura des autels, quand il naîtra des hommes.

(Rousseau, ever taking nature as his guide, was the apostle and
martyr of humanity. Mortals, whom he tried to force into self-
knowledge, had become too debased not to punish him for so
doing: a poor, wandering fugitive who was outlawed in every
land, his life was a commentary on his writings. In the bold scenes
he depicted, proud truth succeeded, in spite of the great ones of
the earth, in showing us as we really are. In our day he could not
but end on the gallows. When the earth is peopled with true men,
altars will be erected to his memory.)

This was precisely what he thought of himself.

He had not abandoned his intention of going somewhere else,
perhaps to Dombes, so as to be nearer to Switzerland and the
mountains. In February the Prince de Conti informed him that
permission had been granted for him to do so. He must however
keep the name Renou and never on any account come within
the jurisdiction of the Paris Parlement.

Coindet, who had been promising to come to Trye for two
months, but who had been prevented from doing so by a
sprained ankle, finally arrived in February. But once again, as
in the case of Du Peyrou, the visit proved disastrous. The cause
this time was the Genevan controversy. The long battle was
drawing to a close. The Petit Conseil had made two conciliatory
proposals to the *Représentants*. Moultou had written to Coindet
about the matter and would have liked Jean-Jacques to intervene
and urge his friends to exercise moderation. Jean-Jacques, who
had been apprized of the matter by Coindet, replied in a long,
very carefully written letter which, were it opened by the police,
would allay the suspicions of the French police whose government was acting as mediator. He was careful to make it clear
that he was playing no part in Genevan affairs, was not in

217

correspondence with a single Genevan apart from D'Ivernois—
and even claimed, which was going a bit far, that, had people
listened to him, 'there would never have been any disagreement,
nor even any remonstrances'. After which, he gave his opinion
about the proposals put forward by the Petit Conseil, and it
was very conciliatory. Coindet, however, who inclined towards
the *Négatifs*, probably considered Jean-Jacques' opinion still too
favourable to the *Représentants* and therefore did not send the
letter on to either Moultou or D'Ivernois. It is not difficult to
imagine the kind of reception he was given on his arrival at Trye.
Jean-Jacques had reached a point at which he could no longer
tolerate any kind of contradiction. They quarrelled. Thérèse no
doubt added fuel to the flames. As Du Peyrou had noticed, she
expected 'so exclusive a devotion' from Jean-Jacques that she
could not bear any of his friends to be near him. No doubt the
truth was that Jean-Jacques was slipping away from her, that
the 'ménage' was breaking up and that she became a mere
servant again as soon as one of his old friends, some genuinely
cultured man to whom he could talk, entered the house, and
this must have been intolerable to her. Coindet went back to
Paris, and wrote ten letters to Jean-Jacques assuring him of his
affection and disappointment, but to no effect. Jean-Jacques
eventually replied that, given his fear of becoming lost in the
dark mysteries surrounding him, he was obliged to break off all
useless relationships, and never wrote again.

He was more alone than ever and was becoming panic-
stricken by his very solitude. He had never replied to Mme de
Boufflers who had not approved of his break with Hume. On a
sudden impulse he wrote to her once more: chiding her for not
having written to him and begging her to rescue him from the
abyss of humiliation in which he found himself plunged. He
no longer dared leave the château. He remained shut inside the
Prince's little garden 'which was no bigger than a pocket-
handkerchief, and as deep as a well'. In March, after being
informed by Conti and Mme de Verdelin that the Duc de
Choiseul 'was prepared to listen to what he had to say', Jean-
Jacques wrote a personal letter explaining the allusions in the
Contrat Social and justifying himself. He concluded: 'Being
certain that I had incurred your displeasure only through some
misunderstanding, I have always hoped that this misunder-

standing might be dispelled, and that I would at last be allowed some small share of your kindness'. And he added the post-script: 'Should you honour me with a reply addressed to me under the name of Renou, three words will suffice, *I believe you;* and I shall be satisfied.' It is not known whether Choiseul ever replied.

Deschamps, the lodge-keeper, who had been suffering from dropsy, died on the 7th April. During the preceding weeks Jean-Jacques had visited him and taken him wine, preserves and even on one occasion fish cooked by Thérèse, that the sick man had specially asked for.

But after Deschamps' death, Jean-Jacques became obsessed again with the same fixed idea which had tormented him during Du Peyrou's illness. The following day he wrote a wild letter which is still extant: 'Everything that I saw and heard during the course of that day, the ambiguous and tendentious remarks made by M. Manoury, the floor polisher, and the hairdresser, as well as those that were current in the neighbourhood, and in addition the deceased's manner towards me during the days preceding his death, all this made it clear to me that I was accused of having poisoned him.' He therefore insisted that the body of poor M. Deschamps should be opened up in order to prove that he had not been poisoned. Jean-Jacques wrote to the Prince saying that he wanted to go to Paris and face the conse-quences of the warrant for his arrest, or alternatively, give himself up to the authorities at Trye. The Prince de Conti arranged to meet him at Sandricourt on the road to Paris, and did what he could to calm him down and set his mind at rest. But he was bent on leaving. He wrote once more to Mme de Luxembourg and Mme de Verdelin, begging them to ask someone to intercede with Choiseul on his behalf. Where could he go in France? Ought he to leave France?

In the state of terrible 'uncertainty' in which he found himself, he invented fresh reasons for being anxious. A kind of duality began to take shape within him. Rousseau was beginning to pass judgement on Jean-Jacques. It was becoming apparent to him that he had never been as unhappy as he had been since he lived in comfort and had enough money for his needs. For a man such as Jean-Jacques to be rich was tantamount to living a lie. In order to be true to himself, he should aspire to poverty.

Being still full of resentment he refused to go back on what he had said to Du Peyrou about their agreements. He considered those agreements as having been cancelled and insisted that Du Peyrou should reimburse himself for the sums already paid to Jean-Jacques out of the capital given by the Earl Marischal. Du Peyrou replied that he had no right to do so without the Earl Marischal's permission. He added that he found it 'intolerable' that their quarrels should be made public in this way. This gave rise to interminable arguments between them, and on Jean-Jacques' side they were bitter, and disagreeable. He was ever thus—in the very act of renouncing his only reliable source of income, he referred, in the tones of a miser, to the money he was disdaining. To crown all, mad as he was, with nevertheless sudden flashes of insight into his own 'disorder', he accused Du Peyrou of having 'an unbalanced mind' and warned him against 'mental derangement'. This was how he explained Du Peyrou's 'changing attitudes' towards him. As regards his pension from the King of England, he believed that he had 'good reasons' for giving that up as well. On the other hand, he decided to make his old aunt at Nyon a small allowance of a hundred francs a year. On 26th April he wrote as follows to D'Ivernois:

> I am not asking your advice about the decisions I have taken. I am informing you of them: thus you may spare yourself any useless effort to dissuade me from them. It is true that weak, sick and disheartened as I am, I also find myself almost destitute on the threshold of old age, and unable to earn my living. No matter, Providence will come to my relief in some way or other. As long as I was poor, I was happy, and it was only when I lacked none of the necessities of life that I felt myself to be the most unhappy of mortals. Perhaps the happiness, or at least the peace I am looking for, will come back with my return to poverty.

It was as if he were aiming at some kind of self-destruction. He believed he was reverting to the Jean-Jacques he had been before he became famous, but this Jean-Jacques bore a strange ressemblance to the legendary Jean-Jacques, the man whom people had come to love through his books. The more humble he could make himself, the greater he would be. He wanted nothing more to do with his writings or his manuscripts. Du Peyrou could keep them on the understanding, of course, that none would be published during his life-time. The best course would have been to 'commit everything to the flames', and this is what he begged Du Peyrou 'urgently and emphatically' to do. The use of these insistent adverbs are a symptom of his self-deception. At the same time he was having other papers and other manuscripts that he had rediscovered taken by Thérèse to the Abbess of a near-by convent for them to be left in her safe-keeping. He wanted nothing whatever to be lost.

At the beginning of May, he again wrote to the Prince, saying 'that he wished to submit unreservedly to the judgement of mankind'. Once again the Prince begged him to retain the name Renou and not to 'show himself publicly in Paris', while he would busy himself with the search for another refuge. It was agreed that he would send a carriage to fetch him from Trye, and that he would give him lodgings in Le Temple during his stay in Paris. On the 10th June, Jean-Jacques left suddenly, after despatching a further letter to the Prince: 'Those who compose your household (I make no exceptions) have little ability to understand me: whether they take me for a spy or believe me to be an upright man, all seem equally to fear my gaze . . . my life and my heart belong to you, but my honour is my own: allow me to obey its call and leave your house tomorrow; I dare affirm that you must do so. Do not leave a scoundrel such as myself among decent people.'

CHAPTER EIGHT

The Shattered Consciousness (1768–1770)

He dashes first to Lyons, then to Grenoble—At Chambéry he visits 'Maman's' grave—Jean-Jacques, once again in the grip of fear, sets off for Bourgoin—The Thévenin affair—Thérèse joins him at Bourgoin—An inscription on the door of his room in an inn—He 'marries' Thérèse, and acts both as officiating priest and bridegroom—The night of November 9th. He pieces together the whole 'conspiracy'—A temporary respite from madness. Reflections on death—Jean-Jacques and Jesus—A fresh crisis in May 1769—He goes to Pougues to meet the Prince de Conti and at Nevers makes the acquaintance of the young Comtesse de Berthier—Letter to the young Comtesse about his children—'I am innocent'—His excursion to the Mont Pilat. He leaves a letter for Thérèse. The *petit ménage* in danger—In great secrecy Jean-Jacques resumes work on his *Confessions*—The letter to M. de Saint-Germain.

> 'For eight years I have searched for a soul among men; now I no longer search for anything, and my lantern has gone out.'
>
> Rousseau, *Corr.* XX. p. 36

HE SET OFF ALONE, while Thérèse remained at Trye. He went through Paris, but resumed his journey by coach without delay and on the 18th reached Lyons. There was no question of him staying any length of time there, since Lyons came within the jurisdiction of the Paris Parlement. He stayed with his old friends, the Boy de la Tours, the banking family. All he had brought with him was his herbarium and a few books on botany. With the Prince de Conti's agreement it had been arranged that he would go on botanising expeditions among the near-by mountains. The change of environment took his mind off his troubles, and for a few weeks he was restored to some kind of sanity. He even considered starting work again on the novel, *Emile et Sophie*, or *Les Solitaires*, that he had begun in the past, and he asked Du Peyrou to send the manuscript to him if he had not burned it. On 7th July he set out for the Grande Chartreuse along with four botanists from Lyons, and they spent a few days gathering plants. But as early as the 13th he came back, exhausted, to Grenoble, with the intention of staying there until his fate was decided. For a few days he was tolerably happy, and went on a few excursions. The people of Grenoble gave him a warm welcome; he was pleased to be recognised, to be Jean-Jacques Rousseau again instead of Renou.

He had a sudden notion of going back to Chambéry, to Les Charmettes, to see M. de Conzié again, and to visit 'Maman's' grave. Just before leaving, during the night of 25th July, at three o'clock in the morning, he wrote to Thérèse, what amounted to a kind of last will and testament. All his fears had returned. It was true he had a government passport, but he had been granted no 'safe-conduct by the *philosophes*'. He explained to her what she would have to live on if he failed to return from this expedition. 'With every passing day,' he wrote, 'I have more certain proofs that the watchful eye of malevolence is always upon me, and is awaiting me particularly at the frontier.' It would be better for him to face his enemies and bring matters to a head, rather than 'live constantly surrounded by their fawning and knavish satellites!' The last phrase was a reference to the agents of the Grenoble lieutenant of police. Jean-Jacques saw M. de Conzié but found him cold and distant, a transformation that had been brought about by that 'excellent magician' M. de Choiseul. He climbed up to the tiny cemetery at Lémenc. There she lay beneath the earth, the woman who had taught him how to love, who had supported and fashioned his divine indolence, his genius. What had become of those 'charming features', those 'beautiful eyes full of gentleness', that

223

'dazzling complexion', that 'entrancing bosom?' Her grave was overgrown with weeds. Soon it would no longer be possible to discern the resting-place of Dame Louise-Françoise-Eléonore de la Tour, Baronne de Warens. He recalled and mused on all that had happened, exactly forty years ago. He went back again to that Palm Sunday . . . with 'Petit' and 'Maman'. . . . He was still no better than an 'elderly child'. Why did hatred thus dog his steps? He walked back down to Chambéry and crossed the frontier again. Nothing happened. Neither the police nor the *philosophes* put in an appearance.

When he got back to Grenoble, he rented a small apartment in the Rue des Vieux-Jésuites, where Stendhal was to be born a few years later. His friends in Lyons had recommended him to a local barrister called Claude Bovier. He continued his botanical excursions. Later, in *Les Rêveries*, he described how he had nearly been poisoned (another instance of his obsession with poisoning) by eating the berries of a small thorny tree, under the very eyes of the aforementioned Bovier who made no attempt to stop him. When *Les Rêveries* eventually appeared the innocent Bovier was to make an earnest protest. A few days later, it so happened that a teacher of philosophy in the local school arranged a discussion about the contemporary *philosophes* and Jean-Jacques took fright. Believing that his 'persecutors' were after him, he left suddenly. Since he was banned from Lyons, he went to Bourgoin where his friends from Lyons could at least visit him. He had left his dressing-gown behind him in Grenoble and at the same time had taken the keys of the apartment with him by mistake.

He took a room at the Auberge de la Fontaine d'Or. He was both tired and scared. But there was no reason for him to be afraid. The Comte de Tonnerre, the governor of the province, was no doubt keeping a watch on him: but he was a kind man who was determined to let him live in peace. An absurd incident brought about a return of his madness. A certain Thévenin of Grenoble (according to a letter written by M. Bovier's son) was asking for the return of nine francs which he had lent Jean-Jacques ten years before one day when he had met him in an inn in Verdières-de-Jonc, near Neuchâtel. In return Jean-Jacques had given him letters of introduction to various people in which he had signed himself 'the eternal traveller'. Jean-Jacques spent several busy months trying to restore his honour. He pointed

out that ten years ago he had not even been in Neuchâtel, that
there was no such place as Verdières, that he had never had any
dealings with the people in question, that he had lent money,
but never borrowed any and so on.... Thévenin was summoned
to appear before the Comte de Tonnerre, and Jean-Jacques
went back to Grenoble in order to confront him. He wrote to
Neuchâtel and asked for duly attested evidence from the inn-
keeper. All these operations went on for weeks. Finally, in what
was tantamount to a report, he was able to prove to the Comte
de Tonnerre that Thévenin was just an impostor who had been
sentenced to penal servitude by the Paris Parlement. There
remained, of course, the fact, as he observed bitterly, that public
prejudice being what it was, he, Jean-Jacques, would continue
to be thought of as a frequenter of taverns who went about
sponging a few crowns here and there from any individuals
stupid enough to lend them to him. But at least his honour was
safe!

Thérèse was on her way to join him. He wrote to her at Lyons,
calling her 'my dear, good friend' and 'my child'. He described
in full his unhappy existence, the 'prison' in which she would
have to live.

> Everywhere [he wrote], I discover the effects of the machinations
> which preceded my arrival. I am everywhere an object of public
> hatred and derision, and I have found that those apparently
> most anxious to help me were in fact most eager to do me harm,
> and that people who behave decently on all other occasions,
> delight in transforming themselves into knaves as soon as there
> is an opportunity of playing me false.... It is certain, my child
> [he continued], that you would be well advised either to stay
> where you are or to return to Paris, for if you persist in following
> me, however pleasant it may be for me, it will only add to my
> difficulties, and you would have to be prepared to share all the
> hardships of the terrible fate which is in store for me, and from
> which I will not be allowed to escape until I die.... In depriving
> myself of your help in my physical and spiritual tribulations, I
> shall, I hope, be freed from them all the sooner: I can wish for
> nothing more, and so must you, if you truly love me....

This was enough to break the old woman's heart and she
hastened to his side. The letter ended with a mysterious sentence:—'It does not seem to me to be advisable for you to refer

to me here as your brother. . . . Let us be friends and relatives pending something better: I shall say nothing further on the matter for the time being.' We do not know what he meant by 'something better'. He had been well received at Bourgoin. He arrived on the 13th August and the 15th was the feast-day of the local saint. He was invited to the municipal banquet. He knew the mayor, M. de Champagneux, and was at once made welcome in a number of houses. But he was obsessed with the Thévenin affair which was still going on. He himself felt that his 'mind was affected', and did not know to whom he could turn. He was reluctant to cross into Savoy or Italy. He posted up the following inscription on the door of his bedroom in the inn:

> The attitudes of the various sections of the public towards me:
> Kings and the great aristocrats do not say what they think, but they will always behave magnanimously towards me.
> The true nobility who love glory and who know that I understand it, honour me and are silent.
> The magistrates hate me because of the wrong they have done me. The *philosophes*, whom I have unmasked, seek at all costs to ruin me, and will succeed in so doing.
> The bishops, proud of their birth and their rank, have a high opinion of me but do not fear me and honour themselves by showing me respect. The clergy, who are the creatures of the *philosophes*, hound me in order to curry favour with them.
> The wits take their revenge by jeering at my superiority of which they are well aware.
> The common people whom I idolised, see in me only an unkempt old fogey and a man wanted by the police.
> Women, deceived by two cold fish who despise them, betray the man who was most deserving of them.
> The Swiss will never forgive me for the harm they have done me. The Magistrates of Geneva know they have done me wrong, realise I forgive them, and would make amends if they dared.
> The leaders of the people, having climbed onto my shoulders, would like to hide me so completely that they alone would be visible.
> Writers plagiarise me and accuse me; scoundrels curse me, the rabble boo me.
> Decent, upright people, if there are still any left, quietly bewail my fate; I for my part thank God for it, if it can one day serve as a lesson to mortals.

Voltaire, who is jealous of me, will parody these lines. His coarse insults are the tribute he is obliged to pay me against his will.

Such was his summing-up of society: he was surrounded by enemies. Moreover, when he moved with Thérèse to a larger room where there were two beds, and forgot to remove the inscription, he got the impression that people had crossed out certain words and added others, to what purpose he did not know. However, he did not fail to send an accurate copy for the record to his friends in Lyons.

Thérèse had arrived on the 26th. Three days later occurred the strange ceremony during which Thérèse, 'his sister by the grace of the prince', became 'his wife by the grace of God'. He had invited the mayor, M. de Champagneux, and one of his cousins, M. de Rosière, to dinner without telling them of his intentions. When they arrived the two guests found Jean-Jacques and Thérèse suitably dressed for the wedding. Jean-Jacques himself officiated: Thérèse and he pronounced the customary 'yes'. According to M. de Champagneux, Jean-Jacques, in a state of great excitement, delivered a moving speech and everyone dissolved into tears. M. de Champagneux declared that he had never been so affected in all his life.

So it was that, in a room at the Auberge de la Fontaine d'Or, he 'married' Thérèse, who was henceforth known as Mme Jean-Jacques Rousseau. The ceremony had consisted of a pure act of his own will, recorded by two witnesses, without any other guarantee or any document to show for it. Proceeding by decree he changed everything, morality and laws, to suit himself. It matters little that the legal formalities were not strictly observed. This was the most genuine act he had ever performed. He was right in declaring to his friends in Lyons: 'I have never fulfilled any duty so gladly or so willingly. I owed at least this to the woman for whom my respect has only increased during an attachment which has lasted now for twenty-five years, and who has resolved to share all the misfortunes in store for me, rather than be parted from me.' In the confusion of madness, but with that lucidity that his 'misfortunes' had bestowed upon him, he reverted to the most humble yet at the same time the most powerful truth. He agreed to see himself only as an old man who was Thérèse Levasseur's husband. He had probably told more lies and been more secretive about Thérèse than about any other person. And yet, after all the fruitless ordeals, after so many desires and dreams, she remained: she was reality, the irreducible residue. In accomplishing this act he had shown himself to be loyal to what was most profound and most tragic in his life. They had been bound together by sensual pleasure and wrong-doing. They, and they alone, knew exactly what each other was worth. They forgave each other their trespasses, and were grateful for kindnesses shown. He was at last about to really become Jean-Jacques. Having renounced all fame, all the notoriety which had been associated with his name, all the ambitions of his vainglorious heart, all the young girls and all the ladies to whom he had spoken of love, Mlle Serre, Mme de Mably, Mme Dupin, and Mme d'Houdetot, he threw in his lot with a woman who was hardly able to read or write and declared that he belonged only to her. The memory of only one other woman remained in his dilapidated heart, the memory of 'Maman', who now lay in the cemetery at Lémenc, and who, perhaps, a few weeks previously, had suggested and advised the 'marriage'. 'Elderly child' that he was, he felt the same gratitude towards Maman and Thérèse. Besides, he informed everyone that although his union with Thérèse 'had become indissoluble, this did not change its nature which remained as chaste and brotherly as it had been for the last thirteen years.'

He was at this time living in an almost perpetual state of fear, convinced that 'those who controlled his fate' were pursuing a sinister plan to dishonour him. He imagined that he would soon be destitute. All the journeyings to and fro were using up his meagre savings; Thérèse had been allowed to join him, but to increase his financial embarrassment his enemies had seen to it that she came without her clothes and without even a change of petticoat. In two or three years' time he would not have a penny to his name. This was what they were waiting for 'so that they could force him to beg and accept dishonour in return for his daily bread'. Thérèse's trunks finally arrived. This suddenly reassured him and he decided to stay on at Bourgoin. I feel I am perhaps not giving the reader a very clear idea of what the unhappy Jean-Jacques' letters were like at this time. They were a mixture of gentleness, aggressive resentment and frenzy. His plans changed suddenly from day to day and I have the greatest difficulty in following his changes of mood. He wrote page after page, proving to M. de Tonnerre that M. Thévenin was an 'impostor', with the conviction that the 'cry of truth would sooner or later pierce the heavens'. He had become just a poor frightened man with eyes ablaze, wearing his virtue on his head like a sign. He could not even devote himself whole-heartedly to his botanical studies. However, his one joy was that he had discovered a few new plants, the *osyris* and the *terebinth*, the *hypopitis* and the *crepis fœtida*. He explains that he is neither free to stay where he is, nor to go where he wants to; he cannot even discover where people want him to be, nor what they want to do with him. He felt, indeed he knew, that the mere fact of his existence was a burden to everybody. What makes his madness still more terrible is that it expresses itself with such admirable eloquence, for never had he spoken or written so well. One idea after another passed through his mind. One moment he was prepared to ask to be transported to America—at another he wanted to go to Cyprus, or to Greece, where 'Turkish barbarity' would deal more kindly with him than 'Christian charity' had. He implored one of his friends, Laliaud, to 'take soundings', to enquire at the embassies. He was also quite prepared to go to the Montpellier area where at least he would find a friend, Moultou. Where could he escape from 'the Machiavellis and their friends'? At the beginning of November he received from the Duc de Choiseul the passport he had asked for and which authorised him to leave the kingdom. This time, he said, his mind was made up and 'nothing would change it'. He would return to England, and to Wooton. His determination was all the more unshakeable since the decision had been a terrible one to take. He instructed Laliaud to make enquiries of the English ambassador, but to do so confidentially. He would also be quite prepared to go to Minorca. . . .

And then on the night of the 9th November, all was changed.[1] He decided to remain in France. As he was to write later: 'For the first and only time, I believed I had pierced the dark mystery of the fantastic plot surrounding me. . . .' This realisation was the outcome of a whole series of circumstances; linking one thing up with another, he had a sudden flash of revelation and was

[1] He later gave an account of this night in a quite extraordinary letter addressed to M. de Malesherbes (23rd November 1776), Vol. XX of the *Correspondance générale*, p. 14.

convinced that he now understood the crux of the matter. In the first place he now grasped the truth of the Thévenin affair. Bovier had been acting solely on the instructions of the Comte de Tonnerre. The confrontation with Thévenin had been organised to put him, Jean-Jacques, to the test, to prove that he could be embarrassed and upset and made to lose his self-possession. Furthermore, a few days previously, 'a man who was said to be involved in an abominable attempt at murder had been arrested on the Dauphiné border', and this man had been going to travel by way of Bourgoin. In this connection the people surrounding Jean-Jacques had made mysterious remarks in an ostentatiously provocative way, and he was reminded of the terrible weeks in 1757 at Montmorency, when he had felt himself to be the object of the same furtive and suspicious looks. And on that very night of the 9th November, while he was sorting out his papers, in preparation for his journey to England, he looked through the collections of letters transcribed by himself in the past and he had alighted upon a gap of which he had been aware for six years, but to which he had never given any thought. Suddenly, everything had become clear, blindingly clear.[1]

The gap in question related to that same period of 1756–1757.

Imagine my feelings [he exclaims], when I observed that the gap occurred precisely at that period of which I had been reminded by the prisoner going through Bourgoin, and about which I would never have been led to think but for this incident. I was overwhelmed by the discovery; in it I found the key to all the mysteries surrounding me. . . . I concluded that the pledge to destroy me had been taken more than six years before, and that certain letters had no other purpose than to supply dates and geographical locations for the construction of the fraudulent system of which I was to be the victim.

Grimm, Diderot and Mme d'Epinay had started the whole thing, then Mme de Luxembourg had joined the conspiracy. Everything could be explained, his exile in England, Hume's machinations, the letter from Walpole, the mischief-making at Trye, and the Thévenin affair. They were all part of the same plan to dishonour him. So in the middle of the night he wrote to

[1] The papers in question had been returned to him at Motiers, as early as 1762, by Mme de Luxembourg.

the Prince de Conti to tell him of his discoveries and of his decision to remain in France and armed only with his innocence, to face all the plots that power, guile and injustice might hatch against it.[1] There lived in Bourgoin an old gentleman, called M. de Saint-Germain, who had the reputation of being upright and honest. Jean-Jacques was convinced that he was the very man he wanted, since he needed a witness, so he asked M. de Saint-Germain if he could call on him, and a few days later went and told him about his misfortunes, and his 'secret'. He continued to see him during the rest of his stay in Bourgoin.

Now that he had made up his mind, he lived for a few months in a state of relative tranquillity. In December and in January he was ill again: his stomach became so distended that he was unable to stoop, or put on his shoes, or even to breathe. He blamed the swampy nature of the countryside, and the bad water. But the real illness occupied his mind and made him forget his imaginary anguish. Thérèse too suffered from rheumatism. A local aristocrat, Mme de Césarges, offered them accommodation at Monquin a few miles above Bourgoin, facing the Alps. They moved there at the end of January. He had consulted a Swiss doctor, Professor Tissot, of Lausanne, who was one of his friends and agreed to follow a diet, but refused to take any medicines. He mistrusted those 'helpers of nature', as he called doctors. They destroyed nature more than they helped it. 'Sooner or later we have to die', he used to say, 'and nature's helpers cannot prevent death.' In order to be cured the important thing was 'to know how to be ill'. After a while the swelling subsided, and for a few weeks he devoted himself to botany. He was working on his herbarium and wrote letters to

[1] It must be admitted that he was very unlucky. Since he did not trust the post he had arranged for his letter to be taken to the Prince by one of his courtiers who happened to be passing through Grenoble, on his way back from Italy. As an additional precaution the letter to the Prince was sent inside a letter to Mme de Brionne. It is clear from the Prince de Conti's reply (*Corr. gén.*, XIX, p. 105) that the letter only reached him through another intermediary, a friend of the Comtesse de Brionne, at the beginning of April 1769. It would have been quicker to send it by post. Moreover the Prince himself declared that he had in the meantime received several other letters from Jean-Jacques. We can however imagine what a commotion such incidents caused in Jean-Jacques 'diseased mind'. There was nothing more the Prince could do in order to allay his fears.

other botanists and to the Duchess of Portland. He went walking, and in order to avoid stooping he used to examine lichens and mosses on the trunks of trees. . . . It seemed to him that he 'owed his life to plants', and as long as he could go botanising he was not unhappy. His great sorrow was that he did not have a spinet, but he often sang verses from Tasso to himself. The story of Olinda and Sophronia would reduce him to tears. He had moments of delightful enjoyment: we can imagine him in the spring-time in his large bedroom at Monquin. Two swallows had built their nest inside the window. As he said later to Dussaulx, he acted as 'window opener', and had to be constantly on duty. 'If I was not,' he wrote, 'the birds became very impatient. They would flutter around my head in the early morning with a great beating of wings until I performed the duties imposed upon me by the tacit agreement between them and me.'

Once again thoughts of death occurred to him, and affected him more deeply now that he felt himself to be so defeated by the circumstances of life. However, this time he did not make his will as on previous occasions, precisely perhaps because a deeper awareness of what might eventually happen made him indifferent to the things of this world. Thérèse, who felt anxious about the future as she usually did in such circumstances, had urged him to make a will. Now, however, he thought only of himself. And it seems that it was at this point that the idea of death made its solemn entry into his mind, from which it was to be hardly ever absent during the next nine years. He would never cease to dream of the compensation that he could not fail to be given in the after-life, and of the illustrious phantom he would become in the minds of posterity.

A certain M. de Franquières had written to him to consult him about his religious doubts. He replied in a long letter written in a wonderfully relaxed style: 'I cannot', he declared, 'form an opinion of the state of doubt you describe, since I have never experienced it. In my childhood my belief was based on authority, in my youth on feeling, in my mature years on reason: now I believe because I have always believed. . . . What grounds have I for re-opening the argument? Time is running short, my departure is at hand.' He laid no claim to being a fashionable *philosophe*: he clung to the ideas he had always held, to the evidence of his heart, to his 'innermost feeling', which was that of nature itself, a personal protest against the sophistry of reason.

> It is always pleasant in adversity [he concluded], to have some-one to witness that you did not deserve it: there is a feeling of pride truly worthy of virtue in being able to say to God: Thou who canst read in my heart, thou seest that it is as a just man and staunch of soul that I use the freedom thou hast granted me. The true believer who everywhere believes himself to be watched over by the eternal eye delights in boasting before Heaven that he has fulfilled his duties upon this earth.

And he gently tried to give back M. de Franquières his confidence and concerned himself once more with a fellow-being 'in those moments', as he himself remarked, 'when one is concerned with little else but oneself'. Meanwhile, Laliaud reproached him with 'being deliberately black'. He replied sharply: 'It is not I, Sir, who am being deliberately black, but others who are smearing me with blackness. But wait. In vain do they keep me away from the crystal springs; I shall find those springs when I am no longer in their power, and at a time when they least expect me to.'

As this admirable metaphor testifies, he had almost achieved a state of purity. In the lucid moments between his fits of madness, he seemed to be composing his own character as if it were his last and finest work. It was now, and only now, that he finally achieved the 'reform' that he had dreamed of twenty years before and which had always remained so incomplete. The inevitable chain of his life's events, the pursuit of fame, even his ideas and his need to express them as well as his frenzy, had always made it imperfect and precarious. But he had now almost achieved the simplicity that his books extolled. At the very time when his madness convinced him that the whole world, which had once loved him, now despised him as a hypo-crite and a 'wicked man', he strove to be that wise, simple and humble man that Europe had come to call Jean-Jacques. He was really turning into the Jean-Jacques that fame had fashioned. 'Given the present state of affairs', he wrote, 'and the way things are tending, I do not wish to be concerned with anything that might draw me out of myself or deprive my mind of that tran-quillity which is enjoyed by my conscience.' And again:

233

'Overwhelmed by the ills of life and the injustice of men, I joyfully approach that bourn beyond which such things cannot pass; and in the meantime I wish to be solely concerned, if I may, with coming closer to myself and with enjoying here a few moments of sweetness and peace while awaiting my final hour, between my help-meet in misfortune, my heart and God, who can see it as it is.' The final hour would be the hour of justice. Nietzsche, in moods of exaltation, turned to Dionysos, so Jean-Jacques turned to Jesus.

> O God! [he exclaimed], can it be that a just and ill-fated man who has been subjected to all the ills of this life and has not even been spared humiliation and disgrace, has no hope of compensation in the after-life, and has to die like a beast, having lived like a God? No, no, Jesus, whom this century has failed to appreciate because it was unworthy of understanding him, who died because he tried to change his base compatriots into an illustrious and virtuous people, that sublime Jesus, did not die completely on the cross: and I am but a weak and wretched man, yet one who is conscious of never having allowed his heart to be sullied by any guilty feeling, and this is enough to make the awareness of my approaching dissolution be accompanied by certainty about the after-life. The whole of nature assures me of this. Nature is not self-contradictory. I discern in it an admirable physical order which is never at variance with itself. The moral order must correspond to this physical order. Yet in my case it was upset during my whole life: it will therefore come into force with my death. . . .

At the end of May he went through another emotional crisis. He found his prison intolerable, and wrote to the Prince de Conti formally demanding either that he, the prince, should immediately grant him a hearing, or leave him free to choose his own asylum in France, which would involve travelling, or else send him a new passport which would allow him to leave France. 'If not,' he said, 'I shall dispose of myself as my heart prompts me to.' The prince pointed out to him that it was not possible for him to come to Paris, nor to wander at will through France. He himself, however, had to go to Pougues, a watering place near Nevers, at the end of June, and he invited Jean-Jacques to join him. Jean-Jacques was at Pougues on the 15th July but we do not know what passed between them. Jean-

Jacques returned to Monquin in a slightly calmer frame of mind, after lingering for a while on the way at Nevers and Lyons.

At Nevers he had met a young woman called the Comtesse de Berthier. She was twenty-two years old, 'dangerously provocative' with 'most disturbing eyes'. And the rustle of a silk dress had always touched his romantic old heart. The poor old man was not entirely immune to self-conceit: 'She may pretend to have forgotten', he wrote a few days later in the *Confessions,* 'but I remember. Having avoided this pitfall, I fear no further lapse, and I can vouch for my conduct for the rest of my days.' He was delighted when, during the succeeding months, she wrote to him complaining about being lonely; he did not fail to reply, and, on one occasion, he sent her an admirable letter: 'The inner void of which you complain,' he wrote, 'is only felt by hearts which are made to be filled: small hearts never feel any void because they are always full of nothing.' He urged her to breastfeed the baby she was expecting, extolled the charms of family life, then suddenly exclaimed:

But who am I to speak of family life, and children. . . . Madame, pity those whom a rigorous fate has deprived of such happiness; pity them in their unhappiness; pity them still more if it is accompanied by guilt. For my part, you will never find me distorting the truth and in my aberrations altering my principles to fit my behaviour; you will never find me falsifying the sacred laws of nature and duty in order to extenuate my sins. I would rather atone for them than excuse them: when my reason tells me that I have done what it was my duty to do in my situation I am less convinced by it than I am by my heart, if my heart is complaining and contradicting it. You may then condemn me, Madame, but listen to me: you will see in me a man who is the friend of truth even in his wrong-doings and who is not afraid to recall them whenever it seems possible that some good may come of it. Nevertheless I render thanks to Heaven for having inflicted the bitter experiences of life only on me, while sparing my children: I would rather they led an obscure and humble life without knowing me, than see them basely enslaved by the perfidious generosity of my enemies who would be eager to teach them to hate, perhaps even to hate their own father: I would much prefer to be a wretched father who neglected his duty through weakness and who bewails his sins rather than a traitor who betrays the confidence of a friend, and in order to ruin his reputation, divulges the secret with which he has been entrusted.

To write to her in this way he must surely have confided something of his secret to her. Whether he had or not, this letter, far more moving than the public statements he was busy preparing, testifies to his remorse, and to the fact that it was at the root of all his anguish. The young woman probably remained unconvinced by his arguments and was embarrassed by his confidences. Jean-Jacques accused her of 'shilly-shallying' and of having let herself be too much influenced by her nearness to Paris. She wrote back, but this time more kindly. This forgiveness granted by a young and almost unknown woman filled him with joy. 'Rose', he wrote to her, 'I believe you and I would believe you with still greater satisfaction if you had insisted less.' He went on to describe to her the purity of his heart: 'My position is without parallel; there has never been another case like mine since the world began. . . . Young woman, heed my words: whatever happens, whatever fate is being prepared for me, when you have been given a full recital of my crimes, and have been shown striking evidence, and irrefutable proof of them, and have had their obviousness demonstrated to you, remember these three words with which I end my farewell: I AM INNOCENT.'

But by anticipating events I have broken my own rule. . . . He had had serious arguments with Thérèse on his return from Pougues. Thérèse was peevish and he himself, after his trip, was perhaps less patient. The news he had brought back was not good: they had to stay at Monquin which was far from Paris. Thérèse was furious at having to live in the provinces so far from her native town. It is not clear what happened, nor what exactly were 'the wounds and lacerations' which Thérèse inflicted on his heart, at that time, and that he refers to in the *Confessions*. A few days later, Jean-Jacques went off on a botanical expedition to the Mont Pilat with three companions. He left behind, on the table, a letter addressed to 'Madame Rousseau', in which he described the great disaster threatening the *petit ménage*. Their union, which had lasted twenty-six years and which (he says in the *Confessions*) had 'given stability to his moral being', which was his last refuge and which he had recently solemnly confirmed by a marriage that he had entered upon in order to draw closer to himself, and to achieve the greatest possible simplicity of living, was in danger of collapsing and of coming to an end. Thérèse did not love him, or rather no longer loved him. 'My only concern,' he wrote to her, 'has been to try to make you happy. My dear friend, not only have you no longer any pleasure in my company, but you even have to make great efforts to stay with me for a while out of kindness. . . . If you were happy with me, I should be satisfied; but I clearly see that you are not, and this is what distresses me. . . . ' He reminded her of their recent promises and vows. He, for his part, had still the same desire—which was, he said, 'to end my days with you in the most perfect union, and to share the same bed when we have but one soul between us'. But she had said, and had constantly repeated, that she wanted to leave. So continuing in the same marvellously un-affected style, and changing from the formal you (*vous*) to the more intimate thou (*tu*) he wrote:

> You know the position in which I find myself—it is such that it could hardly be described, since no one would believe in it. I had only one consolation, but it was a delightful one: Dear friend, it was to pour out my heart to you. . . . It is certain that if you are not with me I am obliged to live absolutely alone, I can no longer carry on, and will soon be dead. But I would die an infinitely more cruel death if we were to continue to live together in a state of disagreement. . . .

He therefore urged 'his dear wife' to reflect during his absence, to 'sound her heart'. She could go and live for a while in some religious community or other. He would pay all expenses. The separation in itself might make them realise perhaps to what extent they were necessary to each other: then they would be reunited. But he did not want her to leave him in anger: 'Think,' he exclaimed, 'of what you owe yourself, of what you owe me, and of all we have meant to each other for so long. . . . We have faults to weep over and atone for: but Heaven be thanked we have no base or criminal deeds to reproach ourselves for: let us not by rash action in the last days of our lives wipe out the memory of the sweetness and innocence of our earlier years together.' He ended his letter with recommendations about what she should do should he happen to die during his journey. One curious sentence calls for comment: perhaps Thérèse had become more involved than he liked with certain monks at

Bourgoin. 'Let no monk,' he wrote,[1] 'meddle in your affairs in any way whatever. I am not telling you this through jealousy, and I am quite convinced that they mean no harm to your person. Nevertheless, pay heed to my warning, or you may be sure of meeting with nothing but disgrace and disaster for the rest of your life.' He urged her not to allow herself to be 'swayed by others' and added that should she ever find herself in difficulties, she should get in touch with Duclos, Mme Dupin, Mme de Chenonceaux and Du Peyrou. He signed his letter, not Renou, 'since that name had been disastrous to their love', but Jean-Jacques Rousseau.

Thus even the very restricted and modest mode of life he had chosen in order to escape from his misfortunes was threatened. He set off and was away for nine days: but the trip was disastrous. It rained and the mountain provided no specimens—it was too late for flowers, and too early for seeds. He found his companions stiff and formal. Sultan had a fight with another dog and got lost: he himself fell and sprained his wrist.

But when he got back to Monquin the faithful Thérèse was waiting for him and Sultan had proved no less faithful, having somehow or other managed to cross the Rhône and travel the twelve full leagues all by himself. A letter arrived from Conti who had been in touch with the authorities with regard to 'the unreasonable and distressing request' that Jean-Jacques had made to him, but had carried out the task 'with a sad heart'. Once again, he warned Jean-Jacques against 'his speculations' and his 'ideas'. He could do nothing more for him if he decided to carry them into effect and leave his present abode: and most

[1] Some rumour, whether serious or not, had been current about Thérèse and a monk. In his *Correspondance* (IX; 91) dated the 15th July 1770, Grimm wrote: 'Jean-Jacques Rousseau has been in Paris for a month with his house-keeper Mlle Le Vasseur, whom he has at last made his wife. He has abandoned the Armenian cloak and has resumed French dress. In this connection a story has been going around which is a libellous accusation against the virtue of Mme Jean-Jacques and even more so against the good taste of the man who formerly lived in sin with her. The story goes that her husband, having caught her *in flagrante delicto* with a monk, abandoned his Armenian costume there and then, saying that up till that time he had wanted to look outwardly different from others, since he did not believe he was an ordinary man, but now saw he had been mistaken, and was like everybody else. . . . '

important of all Jean-Jacques must continue to use the name Renou.

He had to resign himself to staying on at Monquin. He would have liked to have some musical instrument or other, a 'cello, or a zither, or better still a spinet, so that he could dream and compose. 'Music,' he wrote, 'is for me a real cure, and the only one perhaps which can have an effect on my condition. Provided I have an instrument, whatever it may be, and a little ruled paper, I can be sure of spending my days without boredom and without being greatly affected by anything whatsoever.' Mme Boy de la Tour arranged for a porter to bring him a spinet from Lyons. It was now the beginning of winter. Thérèse was busy looking after seven pullets and a cock which they would never be able to bring themselves to eat. She was in a cross mood and they felt their loneliness. They thought about their children and what life might have been like. 'Happy is the man who can watch his children grow up around him,' Jean-Jacques wrote in a letter to a correspondent who could not possibly guess the emotional stress underlying these words. Occasionally a visit from some friend who happened to be passing through the district, D'Ivernois and Moultou, for instance, provided a distraction. The room in which Jean-Jacques spent his time was like an ice-box. Thérèse lit huge fires, but in spite of this his fingers tingled with the cold. Yet he went on working. He even felt at one point that he had given up too much of his time to botany and thought of selling his herbarium and his books. In mysterious terms he confessed that he felt he had 'great and melancholy duties' he could not neglect without being untrue to himself.

In great secrecy, and without saying a word to anyone (there is no mention of it in any letter[1]), because he knew that the idea of the book was causing anxiety and alarm, he had resumed work on his *Confessions*, that portrait of himself which would serve as proof of his innocence in centuries to come. After giving

[1] On the contrary, he even wrote to Rey, on April 27th 1769: 'When you suggested to me that I should write my memoirs, I hardly imagined that this proposal to which I agreed without due consideration would involve me in the disasters which have occurred as a result of it. Never raise the matter with me again: if you love me, be sorry that you ever suggested it, and should you ever mention it to me again, do not expect to receive any reply.'

up writing his *Confessions* for a while, he had changed his mind: by remaining silent he would merely be playing into the hands of his enemies. He hid himself away like a thief in order to carry on with the work:

> I would give anything in the world [he said], to be able to allow the mists of time to engulf what I have to say, and, compelled to speak against my will, I am again reduced to secrecy, subterfuge and prevarication, and obliged to lower myself to the discussion of matters for which I was not at all suited by nature; the ceilings above my head have eyes, the walls around me have ears; hemmed about by watchful and malevolent spies, distracted and anxious, I hastily scribble a few disjointed sentences which I hardly have time to read still less to correct. . . .

Poor Jean-Jacques!

People sometimes ask: are the *Confessions* true? And the more we study his life, the more meaningless the question appears. The *Confessions* are all they could be, an absolutely sincere yet absolutely futile attempt to be truthful. Jean-Jacques sees himself and describes himself as he was able to see himself. He was absolutely convinced that he had always been the humble and disillusioned man with only a short time left to live that he was at the time of writing. The first six books could have a kind of poetic truth. The remoteness of the events described in them justified the use of the imagination and Jean-Jacques did not hesitate to embellish. But the last six books plunged him once more into the fray. He repeats in full the elaborate tale he had evolved as an explanation for his misfortunes, on the night of 9th November, as he went through the collection of letters he had received together with the copies of those he had sent: he was a gentle, easy-going man, who delighted in indolence and who was made for happiness. He was without even the seeds of error or sin because he had no ambition; he enjoyed his own being, such as it was. He had been plunged into the literary life by other people and even after achieving the greatest success, he had thought only of retirement. But something had always arisen to prevent it. Had fate been kinder he might have grown old along with Maman, at Les Charmettes. But he had been unable to stay there. He had been involved in the chaos of modern life. He was proud, admittedly, and had refused to bow to the arrogance of those in high places: he had despised money and refused a pension from the King of France. He had taken a mistress, Thérèse, it was true, but this was because he needed love. She was no more than a servant. If they had abandoned their children, it was because they could not do otherwise, because old Mme Le Vasseur had insisted, and also because it was 'the custom of the country'. He himself had believed himself to be acting like 'a member of Plato's Republic'. And what would have become of his children had they been submitted to the kind of life he had been forced to lead? Yet he still felt remorse. However, in *Emile* he had almost made public confession of his wrong-doing. Confession had washed away the sin. There was nothing more he could be accused of. It was of course true that Thérèse had not satisfied him completely, and that he had fallen in love with Mme d'Houdetot. . . . But his love had never been guilty, and yet it had marked the beginning of his misfortunes, since it was at that point that the conspiracy against him had begun. . . .

It is not the mistakes he makes in the detailed narration of events which matter most. The most serious thing is that the whole of his account is proof of the fact that he did not know himself, that we do not know ourselves. He is right to say that laziness had been at the root of all his work, and his whole life. But is laziness or frenzy the right word? He was so profoundly indifferent to everything which did not spring from within himself that he was never able to submit to the discipline of any profession, the restrictions of any rule, or the ordinary obligations of life: on the other hand he had been passionately absorbed in his day-dreams and had displayed an irresistible energy which kept him engrossed in his work and his 'visions' for months and even years, and which was oblivious of all obstacles. What is missing from his account is his passion and his genius. His genius was not without guile. He claims to be completely spontaneous, and impulsive, and perhaps he was in the small things of life. But his whole work bore witness to the greatest capacity for patience. He said he was incapable of secrecy. This was not so at all, however, when he thought that secrecy might serve his work, and ensure the success of his 'vision'. He had been able to keep silent, obstinately silent, and even to lie while writing the *Lettre à d'Alembert* and the *Lettres de la Montagne*. And he had never lacked a sort of rancorous tenacity when it came to ensuring the triumph of what he believed to be the truth. The botanising resident of Monquin had forgotten all that; he had lost his interest in such things, or at least thought he had. Yet, at the very moment when he was saying this, he was in fact secretly preparing the weapons which would bring about his final victory.

In itself the writing of his *Confessions*, by filling him with the conviction that he was a virtuous man with right on his side, produced a curious effect. It restored his confidence and courage. Suddenly about mid-January he made various decisions. In the first place he determined to resume his own name which he ought never to have abandoned; henceforth he would be Jean-Jacques Rousseau and not the M. Renou whom people affected to despise. He would leave Monquin. He wrote at once to Mme Boy de la Tour to ask her to help him with his removal. He would go to Lyons first of all and then wait and see. He would escape the dark trap which was being constructed around him. From then on he started to date his letters in a curious way: for instance, he would write: Monquin 17 $\frac{22}{1}$ 70, which should be read as 22nd January 1770—and he used as an epigraph in all of them four lines of bad poetry that he himself had composed:

> Pauvres aveugles que nous sommes!
> Ciel, démasque les imposteurs,
> Et force leurs barbares cœurs
> A s'ouvrir au regard des hommes.

(Poor blind creatures that we are! O Heaven, expose impostors and compel their barbarous hearts to open up beneath men's gaze.)

Occasionally the quatrain produced the wrong effect since the recipients of his letters believed it was intended for them personally. He explained that it was a general statement which had no connection with the people to whom he was writing 'but which was addressed only to those who allowed themselves to be deceived by power and taken in by impostors', and who would have less excuse for such weakness since they had been warned. Grimm maintained that Jean-Jacques added the epigraph to his letters as 'a protection, in the same way as nuns write: Hail Jesus!'

A kind of rage once more took possession of him 'when he saw that his fellow-men were beginning to hate him in return for the warm affection he felt for them'. He made preparations for his departure and wrote a long letter of farewell to M. de Saint-Germain. There exists no more tragic document on man. It can be regarded simply as an outline of his *Confessions*, yet the succinctness of his account coupled with the intensity of his emotion give the letter a moving and symbolical grandeur that has never been surpassed. In the last half-century Kafka, who was also overwhelmed by the fact that man seems to play the part of an accused prisoner at the centre of the universe, has described the trial of man in his novels. Jean-Jacques, being more conscious of his destiny than any other man has ever been, believed himself to be that prisoner at the bar. He had done M. de Choiseul no harm, except pay him a tribute which he had not understood. And from then onwards M. de Choiseul had imagined 'that the greatest anguish that could be inflicted on a proud soul fired by the love of fame was contempt and obloquy', and had organised this plan accordingly. Jean-Jacques had become 'the laughing-stock of the people, and the sport of the rabble'. He was surrounded by swarms of spies who carefully concealed what was good in him, while exaggerating what was bad. What initial crime could he have committed to explain all the others of which he was accused? This was an 'astounding enigma' that he was incapable of elucidating. Diderot, Grimm, Mme de Boufflers, Mme de Luxembourg, Choiseul, Tronchin and D'Holbach all hated him. Yet what had he done to them? He had been lazy, without ambition, and chaste. Before meeting Thérèse he had known no more than three women. There was of course the question of his children. But 'to sin was natural to man, even to the just man', and he had atoned for his sin. He had never been a rake. He had restored dignity to love by writing *La Nouvelle Héloïse*. 'Was that an example of the speech of the depraved?' He had loved solitude, and, whatever Diderot may have said, a wicked man would never want to live alone. He had perhaps wished for fame, but 'fame had never been the road to infamy'. And what had been the outcome of all this?

> Herein [he exclaimed], lies the profound mystery which I am forbidden ever to solve. . . . I was to be cut off from the society of men, even though I lived among them; for me everything was to be shrouded in secrecy, mystery and falsehood; I was to be made

a stranger to society, without seeming to be excluded from it, I was to be surrounded by an impenetrable wall of darkness, I was to be shut up as in a coffin. . . . I was not openly accused, arrested, or punished but a close watch was to be kept on me, I was not to be able to take one step without being followed . . . and hatred of me was to be so carefully spread abroad wherever I went that at every step, and with every object on which my eye alighted, I felt my soul being lacerated. This was not to prevent me being treated like Sancho Panza and being greeted everywhere with endless mocking bows and expressions of respect and admiration; for admiration in particular is the pass-word of traitors. Their compliments are tigerish because they smile at you at the very moment when they are about to tear you to pieces.

No effort had been spared to dishonour him in the eyes of the world: for instance, there was that portrait of him by Ramsay in which he really looked like a Cyclops and which had been widely circulated, whereas the portrait by Latour which was a much better likeness had been either suppressed or falsified. 'As they portray our faces, so with the same accuracy do they paint our souls.'

But he would speak out, he would throw himself at his enemies and defy them. He would at last find out what he was guilty of. In vain did M. de Saint-Germain advise him to be prudent, and remind him of the dangers he would incur.

Sir [he replied], I have lived my life and I cannot even see the possibility of anything which might still afford me a moment of true pleasure. On this earth, were I to be offered here below the choice of being what I want to be, I would reply: *dead*. None of those things which once charmed my heart any longer exists for me. If I still enjoy any respite while waiting for that moment which is so slow in coming, I owe it to my memory. . . . So far I have put up with misfortune. I have yet to learn how to endure captivity, pain and death; this is not so difficult as withstanding the jeers, the contempt and disgrace, the lot usually reserved for the virtuous among the wicked. . . . Everything you say to dissuade me from remaining in retirement, although distinguished by common-sense, truth and eloquence, has only served to strengthen my courage. . . . No, I can imagine nothing greater or finer than to suffer for truth. I envy the glory of the martyrs. My faith may not be in all respects the same as theirs, but I have the same innocence and the same zeal and my heart feels worthy of the same prize.

CHAPTER NINE

'The Trial' (1770–1774)

Bad weather keeps him at Monquin—On the 10th April 1770, he sets out for Lyons—The performance of *Pygmalion*—On the 8th June, he dashes off to Paris to start his offensive—He gives readings from his *Confessions*, but the campaign is a failure—He moves into the Rue Plâtrière—He chooses poverty—He is churlish and difficult with his former friends—His new friends, Corancez and Bernardin de Saint-Pierre—His advice is sought on the subject of the government of Poland and its proposed reform—He writes to M. de Sartine—He works as a music-copyist—Final meeting with Marianne—He begins to suspect everybody—An extremely curious book: the *Dialogues, Rousseau juge de Jean-Jacques*. He takes the manuscript of the *Dialogues* to Notre-Dame, but finds the entrance to the chancel shut.

> 'I am accused and yet I cannot find the slightest misdeed which might be laid to my charge. . . . What authority is conducting the trial?'
>
> Kafka, *The Trial*.

GENIUS IS ALWAYS naïve. Jean-Jacques' only crime was the strangeness of his thought and he did not realise the full extent of that strangeness. The truth was that he could endure neither his solitude nor the watch and check that was kept on him as a result of the warrant. He never mentioned the reasons for the

R   245

warrant. He imagined that his enemies were busy composing new works and ascribing them to him, but there was no need for this since *Emile* and the *Profession de Foi* were quite enough. His greatness lies in the fact that he was unable to tolerate a police supervision, a political situation that others tried to get the better of by craft. He argued and stated his demands on the basis of an ideal freedom, of an ideal man and of all that such a man could lay claim to. He was mad, of that there is no doubt, but his madness was no more than his sane thought, as it had been exacerbated by his ordeals. Jean-Jacques is not made up of two different men, a writer and a madman. If we are to understand him we must integrate his madness with his thought. In Nietzsche's case it may well be that madness was in a sense physiological and destroyed thought altogether. But all those who suffer from retention of urine do not necessarily become mad, and although Jean-Jacques' weak constitution predisposed him to aberrations, it was his virtue which drove him to madness.

Bad weather and snow kept Thérèse and him at Monquin for a few more weeks, and their situation was becoming unbearable. Thérèse had quarrelled with a woman whom M. de Césarges had put in charge of a farm: a veritable 'rogue in skirts' was how Jean-Jacques described her to M. de Césarges, whom he accused of not having any authority over his servants and of 'being submissive like all the others'. He refused to take any responsibility for the scandal he might be obliged to cause for his own defence and that of Thérèse. About the same time he received the collected edition of his works published by Rey and noticed that it contained interpolations and hitherto unpublished passages. He had written to the Duchess of Portland and sent her plants but had had no reply from her. It was not difficult to see what was behind all these incidents; his enemies were obviously at work. He was in a state of panic: when Du Belloy consulted him about one of his plays he wrote back: 'Nothing ever terrified me when it was open and above board, but in the darkness at present surrounding me I am terrified by everything, and I can see only the blackness of obscurity. When I was a child the most hideous sight could not frighten me, but a face concealed under a white sheet could throw me into convulsions; in this respect as in many others, I shall remain a child until I die.' Finally, about 10th April, the roads became more passable and a cart and post-chaise were able to reach Monquin. Jean-Jacques and Thérèse set off in the direction of Lyons, but Jean-Jacques refused to say where they would go from there. He would allow himself to be guided by 'honour and duty', 'the only voices he would listen to from now on'.

At Lyons he found his friends, the Boy de la Tour family, and their kindness soothed his nerves and took his mind off his troubles. He enjoyed a few weeks' respite. He put up at the Couronne d'Or, and devoted himself whole-heartedly to music. On Good Friday, he was able to hear Pergolesi's *Stabat*. A local music-lover called Coignet, who had written an opera, was introduced to him and Jean-Jacques read him his poem *Pygmalion*. Soon they were both hard at work. Coignet wrote music to accompany the poem and Jean-Jacques contributed two slow movements. Both *Pygmalion* and *Le Devin de Village* were performed at the Hôtel de Ville under the supervision of the provost of the guild of merchants. Jean-Jacques enjoyed the heady vapour of fame. News arrived that a statue was going to be erected to Voltaire, and M. de la Tourette, the botanist, was commissioned to collect subscriptions in the town of Lyons. Jean-Jacques at once sent him his contribution, adding that he had paid dearly enough for the right to be allowed to contribute to the fund'. Voltaire was put off his stroke and asked in offended tones whether 'a foreigner' should be admitted as a subscriber. His protest was however unavailing; an ounce or so of Pigalle's statue was undoubtedly paid for by Jean-Jacques, who, for once, had shown himself to be wittier than his opponent. But inevitably a letter from Monquin plunged him back into misfortune. The farmer maintained that he had gone off without paying for the eggs, butter and cheese that had been supplied to him. Jean-Jacques wrote a solemn letter to M. de Saint-Germain. It was the Thévenin affair all over again! However he was able to get the better of the farmer as regards every item. The farmer and his wife were summoned before M. de Césarges, confessed their knavery and were dismissed. Thereupon Jean-Jacques, rather inopportunely, assured the farmer of his 'fraternal commiseration'. 'Do you want to relieve your sufferings?' he asked him. 'Learn to suffer in peace, become patient and gentle: you will soon cease to feel wretched.' Far more than he realised, he was on the side of the masters.

He left Lyons on the 8th June, and passed through Dijon where he saw the Président des Brosses, and through Montbard where he saw Buffon and Daubenton. He was making for Paris with all possible speed. It was there that he had to fight his campaign to restore his honour. By Midsummer Day he had moved, with Thérèse, into their former lodgings in the Hôtel Saint-Esprit, in the Rue Plâtrière.

Paris was just as frivolous as ever. The Dauphin's marriage had just taken place and the Court was in a buzz of excitement because at the marriage ball the King had threatened that he would give precedence to Mlle de Lorraine over the royal princesses of France. The latter had therefore let it be known that they would be indisposed on that particular evening. Mlle Clairon and Mlle Dumesnil were contending for the rôle of Athalie. Torre and Ruggieri were preparing a new display of fireworks. Pigalle, who had returned from Ferney, was working on the statue of Voltaire. M. de Saint-Lambert, Sophie's friend, had just been elected to the Académie. On the 18th August by order of the Parlement, seven works were burnt in the courtyard of the Palais de Justice: they were *La Contagion sacrée, Dieu et les Hommes, Les Discours sur les Miracles de Jésus Christ, L'Examen critique des Apologistes de la Religion chrétienne, L'Examen impartial des Principales Religions du Monde, Le Christianisme Dévoilé,* and *Le Système de la Nature.*

A short poem said to have been written by a young woman of twenty was going the rounds. It ran as follows:

> Fille à dix ans est un petit livret
> Intitulé: Le Berceau de nature.
> Fille à quinze ans est un joli coffret
> Qu'on n'ouvre point sans forcer la serrure.
> Fille à vingt ans est un épais buisson
> Dont maint chasseur pour le battre s'approche.
> Fille à trente ans est de la venaison
> Bien faisandée et bonne à mettre en broche.
> A quarante ans, c'est un gros bastion
> Où le canon a fait plus d'une brêche,
> A cinquante ans, c'est un vieux lampion
> Où l'on ne met qu'à regret une mèche.

(At the age of ten a girl is a little booklet entitled: The Cradle of Nature. At fifteen a girl is a pretty casket which cannot be opened without forcing the lock. At twenty a girl is a thick bush and many a hunter comes up to beat it. At thirty a girl is like well hung venison and ready for the spit. At forty she is a stout bastion in which the cannon has made many a breach. At fifty she is an old lantern into which one reluctantly puts a wick.)

As regards serious political matters, Mme du Barry was contending for power with M. de Choiseul. This was the sort of society in which Jean-Jacques found himself, with his care-worn face and sombre thoughts. The police did not bother him. The Procureur-général had merely insisted that he should write nothing more, or at least publish nothing more. However, any ill-humoured councillor could, if he cared, demand that the warrant should be put into effect.

> The return of this extraordinary man [wrote Grimm], to a town in which he has spent most of his life, and which is the only town in the whole world which he finds congenial, has for some days provided a subject of conversation in Paris. He has appeared on several occasions at the Café de la Régence at the Place du Palais Royal: his presence drew a huge crowd, and the common people flocked to the square to see him pass by. If you asked these people why they had come, half of them would reply that it was to see Jean-Jacques. If you asked them who Jean-Jacques was they would reply that they had no idea, but that he was about to go past.

Jean-Jacques was asked to be more discreet and from then on he led a more secluded life.

> Also he frequents society a good deal—[we are still quoting Grimm]—and the salons of fashionable ladies; he has discarded his misanthropy at the same time as his Armenian garb, and has become polite and simpering. He also goes to supper at Sophie Arnould's house with the most exclusive circle of fops and courtiers, and it appears that he had chosen Rulhière as his guide. As for his profession, he has abandoned all literary activities until further notice, and has once more become a music-copyist; he admits that he was formerly a bad copyist because, he says, at that time he had a mania for writing books; but now that he has come to his senses, he claims to have no equal; he says furthermore that he must earn fifteen hundred *livres* a year with his copying in order to live in comfort. . . .

Grimm's account, if we disregard the disparaging tone, was reasonably accurate. Jean-Jacques was right to complain to his friends in Lyons that he was leading a life of frivolity, adding: 'I would much rather live entirely within myself than entirely outside myself' because during those first weeks he was much in society. He was delighted with the enthusiasm with which he was greeted. He was always excited by the heady incense of fame, even though he might later have regrets. The Prince de Ligne came to visit him and offered him asylum in Flanders. The Italian Players gave him seats for their performances. M. de Jussieu invited him to join him on his botanical expeditions. Everybody was anxious to see Jean-Jacques and this in no way displeased him.

Mme de Berthier, the young countess whom he had met at Nevers the previous year, wrote to him and he replied with alacrity and in a rather curious style:

> A meeting at the theatre would hardly be suitable because, although I have no wish to hide myself away, on the other hand I have no desire to show myself to the public view; but should it so happen that we were at the theatre on the same day and that I was aware of this, do not doubt but that I would joyfully avail myself of the pleasure of seeing you and would even call upon you in your box if I were sure that this would not cause you displeasure.

What a welter of dubitative statements! He never got any better: his old heart was always ready to start throbbing once more. In the end, it was agreed that he would not go to dinner, but would take coffee or chocolate with her one morning. The young countess however returned to the Nivernais, and that was the end of their romance. 'I feel,' he wrote archly, 'that since I must lose you so soon, it would be wrong to allow the need to see you to become a habit.'

From this point onwards his correspondence is less abundant. Not only did he write less, and quite often did not reply to the letters he received, he even sometimes refused to accept them in order to avoid paying postal dues. On the other hand there exists any amount of gossip and any number of picturesque but more or less accurate and more or less reliable anecdotes about his life during those years. They help us to catch glimpses of his various conflicting moods. It is however not always easy to assess their value. I shall mention only the most significant, those which reveal his character as we have seen it developing through the years. I shall try not to allow myself to be carried away by gossipy details, but to keep to the main stream of his life and his problems.

His success in society did not make him forget his one purpose in coming to Paris, which was to provoke his enemies and cause the truth to be revealed. He proposed to start an offensive. The agreements he had undertaken to observe forbade him to publish his *Confessions*, but on reflection it occurred to him that he could give readings from them. By the 20th July, he was writing to Mme de Nadaillac, the Abbesse de Gomerfontaine, to ask her to send back the first six books which he had left in her safe keeping. He took every possible step to ensure his victory by appealing to his acquaintances, Dussaulx, Corancez, and Mme de Genlis, to all his fellow-countrymen who happened to be in Paris, and even to the society people who lionised him. During the winter he gave various readings from his book at which Dorat, Dussaulx and the Marquis de Pezay were present. The last took place in May at the home of the Comtesse d'Egmont, the daughter of the Maréchal de Richelieu. Unfortunately we know very little about these extraordinary sessions, and can only imagine the poor man in his wig, his grey plebeian costume and his blazing eyes, proclaiming his virtues to a fashionable society which found them entertaining. What an astounding spectacle it must have been! The session which Dorat attended lasted from nine o'clock in the morning until three o'clock the following morning. Dorat himself was quite moved. After returning home, he wrote to his mistress saying how proud he was of having unashamedly wept at the confessions of a sage and sending his compassionate tears as an offering to the woman he loved. Even Dussaulx who was ill-disposed towards Jean-Jacques describes how, when he read the passage about how he had abandoned his children, his listeners at first lowered their eyes, but it was not long before they shared Jean-Jacques' emotion, for his profound grief aroused their pity. At the Comtesse d'Egmont's house, when Jean-Jacques had finished reading, he added in a toneless voice:

> I have spoken the truth. If anyone knows of anything which contradicts what I have just said, although he may have abundant proofs, what he knows is lies and deceit, and if he refuses to get to the bottom of them and to expose them with my help while

I am still alive, he loves neither justice nor truth. For my part, I hereby proclaim openly and fearlessly: if anyone, even without reading my writings, studies my temperament, my character, my behaviour, my tastes, my pleasures and my habits for himself and still thinks me a dishonest man, himself deserves to be silenced.

He himself says: 'At this only the Comtesse d'Egmont gave a start, but she very quickly regained her composure and remained silent, as did the entire company.'

A few days later he was asked to call upon M. de Sartine, the lieutenant of police. It is not known what exactly was said. M. de Sartine was a friend of Mme d'Epinay, who had written to him asking him to intervene: 'After thinking the matter over,' she wrote, 'I feel that you ought to speak to him yourself, kindly enough to give him no cause for complaint, yet firmly enough for him never to do it again. If you make him give you his word, I think he will keep his promise. Pray forgive me, but my peace of mind is at stake. . . . ' Jean-Jacques no doubt 'gave his word', and there were no more readings from his *Confessions*. He had given voice and now remained mute, dismayed by the silence which at once closed in around him. His enemies refused to fight, and the battle was lost.

At the end of December he had left the Hôtel Saint-Esprit and rented a small apartment on the fifth floor of a house in the same street. This was to be his last home.

According to the people who met him in the neighbourhood he was at this time a thin little old man with piercing black eyes, a fine yet strange face, on which the storm and stress of life had left its mark, always wearing a grey or reddish brown dress coat and a round powdered wig, who was still spry, although he walked with a slight stoop and with one shoulder lower than the other, who carried a little cane in his hand, and had a sad, preoccupied look, yet who could be suddenly charming when his face lit up in a smile. People whispered to each other that he was a very famous man whom the whole world was talking about and whom rich and famous people from all over Europe came to see, and that even so he lived like a workman, copying music at so much a page. With the remains of his savings that were in the hands of his friends, the Lyons bankers, he had bought furniture. Corancez, one of the new friends he had made, came to see him one day and found him beaming with delight in the middle of his room: 'All this belongs to me,' he said proudly. He had 'owed money to the upholsterer and had just finished paying him that morning'.

Bernardin de Saint-Pierre has given us a description of his *petit ménage*.

> Near him was a spinet on which he tried out tunes from time to time. Two little beds covered in striped cotton fabric, blue and white like the wallpaper in his bedroom, a chest of drawers, a table and a few chairs constituted the sum total of the furnishings. Hanging on the walls were a plan of the forest and park at Montmorency where he had once lived, and an engraving of the King of England, his former benefactor. His wife was sitting sewing: a canary sang in a cage hanging from the ceiling; sparrows came and ate crumbs at the open windows which looked out onto the street, and on the window-sill of the anteroom one could see window-boxes and pots, full of plants growing as Nature had sown them. There was a general and most pleasing air of cleanliness, peace and simplicity about this little household.

The 'reform', on which he had embarked somewhat too precipitately round about 1750, and which he had attempted again on so many occasions, had now at last been achieved. He had really become himself again, after all the experiences he had been involved in through his genius. He was as his father before him had been—a craftsman. He had started off as an engraver, and was ending up as a copyist, but he was exhibiting the same delight in work well done. He formed the notes with care. His mistake, like his father's, had been that all his life he had tended to proclaim rather too loudly: 'I am Rousseau, I am Rousseau!' and to insist on being recognised as Rousseau. It was this kind of frenzy which had resulted in exile for old Isaac. It had brought exile to his son, but fame and madness too. The same slight taint could be detected in the two succeeding generations.[1] All things considered, he remained true to the

[1] Corancez describes how, after Jean-Jacques' death, he met one of his first cousins, who had been brought up in Persia, where his father, Jean-Jacques' uncle, had spent his life. He bore an amazing resemblance to Jean-Jacques. He stayed in Paris for a while then left for Persia on a government mission. As he was about to leave he had a fit, in the forest of Fontainebleau, which showed that he was mad.

family pattern. All the Rousseaus had always been good crafts-men, of course, but they had been a little too intelligent and strange. He was happy to have fulfilled his destiny. He said to Bernardin de Saint-Pierre: 'I have neither risen above, nor sunk below the condition in which fate caused me to be born: I am the son of a craftsman, and a craftsman myself; I am doing what I did from the age of fourteen.' This was as it should be. He no longer had any desire 'either to rise or fall'.

He deliberately chose to remain poor. He took stock of his income and planned his life rigorously. At his wish the agree-ment with Du Peyrou was cancelled once and for all. His Swiss friends, Colonel Roguin, Romilly and his son-in-law Corancez had an opportunity to arrange for payment of the pension from the King of England to be resumed and thought fit to take advantage of it. Their efforts proved successful, and one day an extremely embarrassed Corancez went to Jean-Jacques' house with a bill of exchange for six thousand three hundred and thirty-six *livres*, which was the sum owing to him for the past few years. Jean-Jacques refused to accept any of it and requested Corancez not to interfere in his affairs. On his return to France he had refused to accept the pension, and when later he had tried to make amends for his behaviour the English court had disregarded his apology: now it was too late and General Conway could keep his money. He was therefore left with the following resources: three hundred francs a year royalties from Mme Duchesne for his *Dictionnaire de Musique*, a pension of six hundred francs from the Earl Marischal payable via Du Peyrou, and a regular payment of ten pounds sterling for the books that he had sold in England—in all 'an annuity of eleven hundred francs, only three hundred of which were absolutely reliable'. In addition he had in cash what was left of his life's savings, now that all his travels were over. Thérèse, for her part, had a fixed income of three hundred francs from the publisher Rey. That was all. He reckoned that he would have to earn about the same amount from his work as a copyist if he was to live in reasonable comfort. But he was the sort of man who could organise his life according to his means. He explained to Corancez that at meal times he was very fond of drinking wine unmixed with water. He had at first had the idea of dividing such wine as he could afford between his two main meals, but in this way he was never satisfied: 'What I have decided to do,' he concluded, 'is to drink water with one of my meals and keep all the wine for the other.' And he added: 'I may be poor but I am my own master.'

He had to work and so his solitude had to be safeguarded. Thérèse acted as his 'Cerberus' and kept watch in the anteroom. Being a Parisian she had a sharp tongue, and so it was no easy matter to get to 'her husband'. She opened the door to female clients, to the fine ladies who out of curiosity wanted to have music copied by Jean-Jacques Rousseau, but she gave them such a hostile reception that the fine ladies soon lost heart and, satisfied at having caught a glimpse of the famous genius, subsequently sent their lackeys. Discriminating between the various visitors was quite a different problem. All kinds of people came to see him, both French and foreign. She obeyed orders strictly, yet the orders she was given were undoubtedly muddled, since the master who gave them was himself torn between mistrust and pride. Pride opened the door but mistrust shut it again. The worst thing people could do was to fling themselves at him. 'The surest and speediest way of getting me to do something,' he said, 'is not to rush me into it.' And again: 'My golden rule is never to ask anything of those who are offering me something. I am as much moved by all that is freely given me as I am unmoved by what is forced upon me.' Such was his 'peculiarity'; he did not apologise for it, on the contrary he clung to it. He was withdrawn and surly as ever with his former women friends, Mme Dupin and Mme de Créqui. Henriette, the young girl who had written him such splendid letters on solitude, asked to see him. He replied that he only vaguely recalled her name and her letters, and could not think who she might be. He concluded: 'I need friends more than Henriette does, but I do not want them to choose me, I want to choose them.' Even poor Marianne, who had done so much for him at the time of his quarrel with Hume, fared no better. Apart from the fact that he mistrusted everybody, as he once explained to Bernardin de Saint-Pierre, he always dreaded meeting women whom he remembered as being beautiful. He did not like to see them growing old. As soon as Marianne heard that he had returned to Paris, she was anxious to see him. He was offended because she had not invited him. He let her write several times before finally replying in

September that 'his lodgings were not suitable for receiving visits from ladies'. 'And your visits,' he added, 'could not fail to be as embarrassing for my wife and myself as they would be boring for you.' Poor Marianne did not know what to think of such a change of tone. She immediately asked him to come to her house but he would not hear of it. Rather tactlessly she reminded him of their long correspondence and said, as a way of forcing his hand, that she was thinking of publishing it. Through Guy, the bookseller, she sent him the manuscript of a second letter which she had written in order to defend him against Hume. He remained quite adamant. It occurred to Marianne that Mme Rousseau perhaps objected to their meeting, and so she promised to give back the letters which she had received from Jean-Jacques to Thérèse herself, should something untoward occur, and for this purpose asked Jean-Jacques for Thérèse's Christian name and surname. Jean-Jacques replied very insultingly by simply writing, Thérèse Le Vasseur on a large sheet of white paper.

He had found a few new friends among the many people who had rushed to make his acquaintance, on his return to Paris. But things never went smoothly. Dussaulx, who had showered him with compliments and helped him to find somewhere to live, got on the wrong side of him. Before six months had passed they had quarrelled irrevocably. Dussaulx, who at that time was writing a work entitled *Le Portrait du Fourbe* (Portrait of a Deceiver), had the unfortunate idea of describing Jean-Jacques as the embodiment of honesty in order to contrast him with the deceiver in question. Jean-Jacques could only see this as a 'piece of diabolical guile'. 'The difference between you, Sir,' Dussaulx replied, 'and the author of *Les Provinciales*, is that the sight of the imaginary precipice which never ceased to terrify that great man hurt only himself, whereas your over-active and over-acute distrust wounds and casts a slur on all those who come near you.' They never saw each other again.

Yet in a sense he had a great yearning for friendship. When he broke with Dussaulx, he wrote to him:

> If I knew one man within reach whose heart was as open as my own, who shared my hatred of deceit and falsehood, who scorned, and refused to frequent those people to whom he dared not say what he thought of them, I would go to that man, and,

feeling certain that he would become my friend, I would abandon all others: for me he would be the whole human race. But, after ten years of useless searching, I am weary and I am about to put out my lantern. . . . I would never have believed that people could feel such pride in being traitors.

He had a vision of himself, should he live much longer, 'remaining in this world only to mourn for himself while he was still alive'. He felt that he had got beyond the age at which one could make new friends.

Two men, however, Corancez and Bernardin de Saint-Pierre, had the patience, loyalty and simplicity of heart to remain his friends until his death, throughout all difficulties. Corancez was no more than a decent, kind-hearted man, but he had a sort of genius of the heart. 'Self-regard' seemed to him to be at the root of all the bickerings between Jean-Jacques and his 'false' friends. 'It was their self-regard,' he wrote, 'which led them to visit Rousseau; it was their self-regard which was wounded by the manner in which they had to leave.' Corancez for his part had divested himself of all feelings of self-regard.

When he was himself [he says of Jean-Jacques], he had an extraordinary simplicity, which still retained some of the characteristics of childhood—he had the ingenuousness, the gaiety, the kindness and above all the shyness of a child. When he was tormented by a certain kind of humour which was present in his blood, he was so completely unlike himself that he in-spired, not anger, nor hatred, but compassion: this at least was the feeling I experienced for a long time: it only served to strengthen my affection for him.

And Corancez rightly adds, as a further explanation for all the quarrels: 'Those who sought him out were too engrossed in themselves and in the motives which had prompted them to visit him, to be able or willing to see the state he was really in, or at least to try to take it into account, because they had no real affection for him.'

Within the confines of his *petit ménage* he had now achieved a wonderful simplicity. But every encounter, every conversation was fraught with danger because there was no telling what might happen. There was always a fear, as Corancez said, that he would launch forth on the sore subject of his enemies. He did not belong to our world, or to 'our country' to quote Corancez's expression. His madness seemed to be indissolubly linked with his wisdom. We are reminded of the bright and shifting lights we see when we shut our eyes, or again of those strange illustrations in natural history textbooks in which a perfectly regular cell can be seen suddenly, and with no apparent reason, throwing out inexplicable tentacles, and expanding monstrously. So it was in Jean-Jacques' conversation and his letters: some word would suddenly set him raving, yet he was still the same man with the same soul.

His physical health had improved, and his bladder gave him less trouble. His illness was all in his head. He rose early in the morning to work at his copying: then he had breakfast and set to work again. He took the afternoon off, and went out or stayed at home according to the weather. He loved the sun, but disliked the rain. As he said laughingly to Bernardin de Saint-Pierre, 'I am exactly the opposite of the little man in the Swiss barometer; when he goes in I go out, and when he comes out, I go in.' If he stayed in, he would tidy up his plants and seeds very meticulously or improvise tunes on his spinet. He maintained that music was as necessary to him as bread. He composed songs which he was one day to call *Consolations des misères de ma vie*. He sent some of them to the Comtesse d'Egmont: 'Pray accept, Madame,' he wrote, 'the homage of an elderly Muse, which has been rejuvenated through the sole desire to please you. These songs, although composed late in life, should still contain a few moving and tender notes. Having been composed at your command, they were intended for you: I would have liked to turn them into hymns.' He was still incorrigibly artificial when addressing a lady. If the weather was fine he went to the Café de la Régence, or to the Café des Champs Elysées, or would go botanising in the direction of Romainville, or Saint-Cloud, or Le Pré-Saint-Gervais, carrying his hat under his arm or pinned to his coat by Thérèse, who accused him of losing everything.

He had promised to give up writing, or at least to publish nothing more, and he was keeping his promise. But what could he do if people came to consult him as if he were a village soothsayer—in fact, the Soothsayer of Europe? Only a few of his letters of spiritual guidance are extant. However, at the end of the year 1771, a Polish noble, called the Comte de

Wielhorski, came to see him. He was full of the recent disasters which had befallen his country and he came to ask Jean-Jacques, on behalf of a few of his friends, what means he could suggest to save Poland. Jean-Jacques agreed to reflect on the subject. His madness led him to believe that Choiseul had undertaken the Corsican expedition for the sole purpose of preventing him answering Paoli's call for help. He did not ask himself what authority the Polish nobleman living in Paris had to invite him to draw up a constitution for his country. He proposed to do for Poland what he had been unable to do for Corsica and wrote a whole book, entitled *Considérations sur le Gouvernement de Pologne et sur sa Réformation Projetée*, it being understood of course that he would not publish it and that the matter would remain between M. de Wielhorski and himself.

The starting-point of his work was a book by M. de Wielhorski which he had agreed to study. But his imagination was fired. In this instance a whole people and not simply one individual had turned to him for guidance. Everything had fallen into decay since the days of the Greeks and the Romans, as Saint-Just, one of his disciples, was soon to say. And yet, he exclaimed, 'they were human beings like ourselves: what prevents us being men such as they were? Our prejudices, our base philosophy, and the petty interested passions that stupid institutions, which can never have been invented by genius, have compounded with selfishness in every heart. When I look at modern nations, I see plenty of law-makers, but not a single legislator.' So the old man in his attic, the music-copyist, saw himself as a Moses, a Lycurgus or a Numa. Suddenly he recaptured the noble and authoritative style which had served him for the writing of the *Contrat Social*. Once more he was in full possession of all his powers of reasoning. Not a word in his lengthy recommendations betrays his anguish, or his obsession. The only signs of ageing are that he occasionally gives way to his mannerisms and his resentment, rehearses his pet ideas, as it were, and is a shade too eloquent.

Poland seemed to him to present a curious problem. It was a large and strangely constituted organism, made up of many dead limbs and a small number of disjointed ones, and yet it displayed all the fire of youth by 'daring to ask for a government and laws as if it had just been born'.

Jean-Jacques' memorandum, by its attention to detail and to concrete nature, allows us to grasp as it were the make-up of his political temperament. On the one hand he constantly urged prudence: 'Social changes,' he said, 'should only be made with the greatest caution. It may be easy to make better laws if you want to; it is impossible to make laws which men's passions will not misuse as they misused the preceding ones. . . . ' But on the other hand he had within him such a passionate desire to 'put laws above men', and thereby to change men's hearts, that he was in constant danger of unleashing the revolution which his prudence condemned. Before expressing his opinion, he filled himself with the 'spirit of ancient institutions' and his memorandum was merely intended as an application of that spirit. The lesson he drew was that, if Moses had been able to turn a wandering and servile mob into a free people 'that has remained intact and even unimpaired for five thousand years and still survives today in all its might, though the body of the nation has disappeared', if Lycurgus was able to create Sparta, and Numa to create Rome, this was because stable institutions have always been connected with austerity of manners and rigorous application of the law in a small and deliberately closed society, concerned only with itself. Each of them had imposed upon his people rites, ceremonies and customs which, although seemingly unimportant, in fact kept them continuously on the alert, increased their pride and their self-esteem, strengthened the bonds of brotherhood between citizens and fired them with a spirit of emulation which was to make them feared by all other nations. In this context Jean-Jacques is preaching the worst kind of nationalism. The word 'nation' occurs on every page: Jean-Jacques uses it with a prophetic fervour and authority which is truly alarming. As we read his memorandum about Poland we cannot help thinking of France, and of all that was stirring in France around Jean-Jacques at the very moment when he was writing. The only cure for Poland's misfortunes, he explains, was to make her aware of the kind of nation she was—a nation apart, different from others, and unique. This is the function of education.

Today [he wrote], there are neither Frenchmen, Germans, Spaniards nor even Englishmen, whatever people may say; there are only Europeans. All have the same tastes, the same passions, the same manners because none of them has been given a specifically national form of any particular institution; in the same circumstances, they will all do the same things: all will claim to be disinterested and will behave like scoundrels: all will talk about the public good and think only of themselves: all will preach moderation and will try to become as rich as Crœsus. Their one ambition is to live in luxury, their one passion is a passion for gold. Being certain that with it they can satisfy every whim, they are prepared to sell themselves to anyone who is willing to pay them. It matters little to them which master they serve or of which State they obey the laws. Provided there is money to be had and women to seduce, they are at home everywhere.... It is the function of education to fashion the souls of the people according to the national pattern and to direct their opinions and tastes in such a way that they become through preference and necessity passionately patriotic. When a child's eyes first open, his fatherland must be present to his gaze and he must be conscious only of it until his dying day. Every true republican imbibed the love of his fatherland, in other words the love of law and freedom, with his mother's milk. This love constitutes his whole existence; he has eyes only for the fatherland and lives only for it: when alone he is as nothing: if he loses his fatherland, he ceases to exist; and although he may be still alive, he is worse than dead. Education for nationhood is possible only with free men; only they can enjoy a common existence, and be truly bound by law. A Frenchman, an Englishman, a Spaniard, an Italian or a Russian are all more or less the same kind of person, who on leaving school is already trained in licence, that is to say, ready for enslavement. At the age of twenty a Pole ought not to be anything other than a Pole.

Many others besides the Poles were to hear these words. They heralded all the greatness, all the wretchedness which has been our lot for two centuries. The frail little man in his attic, intoxicated with virtue and eloquence, mesmerised by his memories, was prophesying and even preparing the way for the remarkable holocausts of the future. The ancient conception of the citizen which Jean-Jacques had discovered in Plutarch, at the age of ten, which had been fostered by the years he had spent in the small republic of Geneva and had been still further enhanced by exile and homesickness, found here its most rigorous expression. We shall not follow him in the analysis he made of all the details of the Polish constitution and the reforms which he proposed to introduce. What he wanted for Poland, he also wanted for all nations. 'No man in Poland, fulfilling a public function,' he wrote, 'should have any other permanent status apart from that of citizen: all the posts he holds should only be considered as tests of his ability and as stepping-stones to greater responsibility when he has proved his worth.' His aim was to leave things unchanged, and to preserve the structure of the aristocratic Polish Republic, but in fact he upset everything by making virtue and merit the criterion of classification and of social differences between citizens. He even went as far as to envisage the whole of the civil service as a kind of Order, whose members would wear distinctive badges, according to their various ranks. After a three year test period, the best in each branch would be honoured by the award of a gold plaque bearing their name and the inscription: *Spes patriae*, which they would wear on their right arm: they would be the 'servants of the State'. Among the latter, those who rendered the greatest services would be promoted to the rank of *Cives Electi* and would wear a silver plaque. From these in turn senators would finally be chosen and would wear a blue steel plaque bearing the inscription: *Custos legum*. Thus each man would wear his virtue on his sleeve and would leave no doubts as to his own worth, and the intrinsic value of the badge would be in inverse ratio to his virtue, whereas among enslaved peoples medals and ribbons are more garish in proportion as the men who wear them are less deserving. . . . He was carried away by his dreams, he was intoxicated with virtuousness and giving full rein to his eccentricity. He was inventing the republic as he had invented a system of musical notation. He was building the new city with all the fanaticism of a priest and the fantasy of a backyard inventor, and showing himself to be a forerunner of both Robespierre and Fourier.

In the whole work only one sentence reveals any anxiety on the author's part: but he has his answer ready. 'If it is objected that I am trying to turn Poland into a nation of Capuchins. . . . I will reply that that is only a French argument, and that joking is no substitute for reason.' He did not foresee that the French, before anyone else, would be consumed with a desire to be Capuchins, or, to put it more accurately, Jacobins.

He was completely absorbed in this great work, and did not

mention it to anyone. He was convinced that later, after he was dead, when the memorandum could be published, it would add to his fame. For some time now he had been using a different epigraph on the few letters he wrote. He now used the motto of Geneva, the motto of his fatherland: *Post tenebras lux*. But on the 15th January 1772, feeling that the darkness around him had become even more impenetrable, he suddenly wrote to M. de Sartine, the lieutenant of police. He explained that one further small incident had made his position intolerable. Many stupid rumours were being repeated about him; it was being said that he had broken with Mme de Luxembourg after accepting three hundred *louis* from her, that he was rich, and that he had no need to do music copying. He had made no attempt to deny these lies. But now people were saying that Duchesne's widow was making him an allowance of one thousand *écus* 'for a new edition of his writings which he himself had supervised'. He had made enquiries and discovered that it was not Duchesne's widow, but a certain bookseller called Simon who was in fact boasting that he had recently printed some of his writings, and that he had paid him well for them. He had gone even further and maintained that Jean-Jacques had come to see him and had corrected the proofs, etc. . . .

If all this were true, it would mean that he had gone back on his word, and so the poor scared man hastened to exonerate himself in the eyes of the authorities, calling upon them to take note of the falseness of the accusation, and played the toady yet once more. He was in a state of panic. He never wrote anything which arouses more pity in the reader than this letter. He apologised for the precious time that M. de Sartine would waste in reading it. He explained that he had given up trying to understand what was going on. But, he added, 'no human art can change the nature of things', and slander would not change his heart. After recounting the fresh lies which were being circulated about him, he wrote:

Although in myself I am the least important of men, I have through my exceptional position acquired enough importance to rest assured that nothing of what I do or do not do escapes your attention: that is one of my surest consolations and I must confess to you, Sir, that the advantage of living under the supervision of an upright and vigilant magistrate who is not easily

deceived, is one of the reasons which made me uproot myself
from the provinces where, penniless and exposed to the machinations of people who control my fate, I found myself the victim
of their henchmen, and of all the illusions whereby powerful
and scheming people so readily delude the public with regard to
an isolated foreigner, from whom they have succeeded in completely concealing all that concerns him, with the result that he
is left defenceless against the most outrageous lies.

He protested that he had never seen Simon, and did not even
know where he lived; he was even totally unaware, before the
existence of these rumours, that he had ever printed any of his
writings. He asked only one thing—that his letter should be
read. In a final paragraph, in order no doubt to anticipate
any suspicion that the lieutenant of police might have had
as a result of information given him by his spies, he was careful to inform him that another bookseller, Guy, was in the
habit of paying him frequent visits, the motive of which he did
not fully understand. Guy wanted to make a selection of his
songs; on the pretence of bringing Thérèse novels, he brought
with him 'huge bundles of pamphlets, which, with his frequent
comings and goings, made it seem as if he had a lot of business
to discuss with Jean-Jacques. . . '. The rumours, the lies, and
also this recent paltry piece of espionage, were all no doubt part
of the same scheme. Nothing happened. It even seems that
Sartine reassured him and that during the following months he
was released from his promise not to publish anything more. He
continued nevertheless to live in the same intense fear. The very
silence in which he was left, the way in which his complaints were
disregarded, only increased his anguish. The worst kind of trial
is the one which is indefinitely delayed. 'If anybody accuses
me,' he cried, 'of harbouring vicious feelings, of having made
reprehensible statements or of committing some unjust act, let
him come forward and speak out; I am waiting for him and
shall not hide.' But no accuser had ever come forward, yet the
rumours and gossip which were spreading *rinforzando*, now
resounded throughout the whole world. He was fighting in
vain against a faceless phantom which always eluded his grasp,
yet whose breath he constantly felt upon him.

He put the finishing touches to his *Considérations*. With the
return of spring—he loved the springtime—he resumed his

work and his walks. He found copying a very arduous occupation. It occurred to him at one moment that he might earn the extra money he needed to add to his income of eleven hundred francs by other means, for instance, by doing research anonymously for Panckoucke, who was compiling a kind of botanical encyclopedia, or better still by making miniature herbariums which M. de Malesherbes would have helped him to sell to rich dilettanti. But the Panckoucke affair fell through, and although he worked at the herbariums for a month or two, he soon realised that the money he earned was not worth all the trouble; the whole business merely involved him in a trying and hazardous correspondence with Malesherbes who offended him in a variety of ways, either by under-estimating the amount of work involved, or on the contrary by refusing to accept gifts from him. He went on eternally copying; according to his own estimate he did eleven thousand one hundred and eighty-five pages in seven years. According to what he considered his talent and trouble were worth, he asked for rather more than the usual fee, which was ten *sous* a page. At least during the first few years there was no shortage of clients. The welcome he gave them varied according to his mood of the moment. One man would comment on his 'delightful warmth' and be 'electrified' by his presence, while another would tell quite a different tale.

One day in April a woman came to see him. He said that it would be three months before he could return the four pages of music she wanted copied. He had not recognised her. It was Marianne, who, despairing of ever seeing him again, had resorted to the trick of visiting him as a client. She revealed her identity, but he still remained adamant about the three months. Marianne was in despair, especially since she had learned that one of her friends, Mme Pasquier, had been admitted on three occasions in connection with only one piece of music and invited to come back. 'I understand and will say no more,' she wrote, full of jealousy, to Jean-Jacques. She forgave him for having failed to recognise her: six years of sorrow had impaired her looks, whereas Mme Pasquier was 'very attractive'. She relied on Mme Rousseau, who had 'viewed her without distaste', to try and get the work completed more quickly. She did not succeed in seeing him again until June. And that was their third and last meeting. She had offered to go through on his behalf the pirated editions of his writings which were being published. He reflected on their conversation, and her very enthusiasm had appeared suspicious to him. He gave her to understand that he would not see her again and requested her to insist no further. She might have 'private reasons' for doing so, but he was 'for that very reason, relieved of any obligation to give in to her'. He complained that people had 'a mania for protecting him against his will'. She continued to write for three, perhaps four, years more but he never replied.

He was beginning to mistrust everybody. About the beginning of August, he gave up accepting letters if he did not recognise the handwriting. Postal charges were high. In addition he despaired of ever meeting the man 'for whom he had searched unceasingly throughout his whole life'. At the end of August the Marquise de Mesme invited him to her house. He replied 'that it was very kind of her' but that she 'belonged to contemporary society' and that he had decided not to go out of his way to meet anyone, and would make no exceptions. 'I have shone my lantern in all directions, but in vain,' he concluded: 'I have found no man, no human soul'. In 1773, of his past friends only two remained, the old Marquise de Créqui and Malesherbes. He had read his *Confessions* to the Marquise and she had wept at the accounts of the theft, and the sending of the children to the Foundlings' Hospital. She made the mistake of putting off a meeting they had arranged. This was enough to make him imagine that even she was influenced by the 'agents of darkness', and he never saw her again. She for her part thought that her tears had perhaps put him to shame. He also fell out with Malesherbes over some dried plants that the latter had sent back to him because he already had specimens of them in his herbarium. In his frenzy, in the depths of anguish and fear, and haunted by remorse, he got to the point of imagining and actually writing a very strange book. We are reminded of Nietzsche's *Ecce Homo* which he too wrote when he was about to become insane. But Nietzsche's song was one of triumph. Jean-Jacques' madness was no less aggressive, but his rebelliousness is expressive of defeat. He could have continued with his *Confessions*, which was the story of his heart. He had got as far as 'the beginning of the misfortunes in his life but', he said, he had 'neither the courage nor the strength to endure the contemplation of so many horrors'. In fact, he was incapable of being his own historian, of considering the facts in their right sequence, and of examining the various incidents impartially. He was too proud to give a detailed justification of his behaviour. So compelling was his anguish that he had to plunge immediately into the heart of the matter and say once and for all what 'his constant mode of life had been', and portray his soul as God had made it, for all eternity. So during the following three years he worked intermittently at this new self-portrait. It is an unwieldy and difficult book, and, as he himself admits, full of tedious passages, useless repetition, verbosity and confusion. 'Being unable to work continuously at so painful an occupation,' he explains, 'I applied myself to it for only very brief periods, putting down each idea as it occurred to me and then stopping, writing the same idea down ten times if it occurred to me ten times, without ever remembering what I had already written and only realising the fact on re-reading the whole, when it was too late to make any corrections.' However, critics have too often ignored this extraordinary testimony. Jean-Jacques' madness is not divorced from his thought. Unless we see it as an integral part of his thought, it is not possible to understand it. Remorse for a sin he had committed preyed on his mind to such an extent that it was inevitable that there should come a time when he did his utmost to convince himself and the world that he for his part could not possibly have been any one of the various kinds of wicked creature that all men are potentially. It was inevitable that he should become mad through his own virtuousness. As is always said, he no doubt suffered from persecution mania and it was exacerbated by his relationships with others. But the expression 'persecution mania' only explains the negative and defensive aspect of his madness which was much more a desperate assertion of his being.

By a kind of splitting up of his personality, *Rousseau* becomes the *Juge de Jean-Jacques*, as if he were another man or a brother who had led the same chequered existence but had not been destroyed by it. 'Since the dialogue form,' he says, 'seemed to be the most suitable for putting both sides of the question, I adopted it for that reason. In these conversations, I have taken the liberty of resuming my surname of which the public has seen fit to deprive me, and following the public's example, I have referred to myself in the third person by my Christian name to which it has been pleased to reduce me.' The work is made up of three *Dialogues* between Rousseau and a Frenchman, and would be excellently composed were it not marred by endless and wearisome repetitions. The *Dialogues* are a straightforward transcription of his broodings. The argument itself, in its simple, almost schematic, form is eloquent proof of appalling mental disturbance. He set himself to untie a knot. His object was to blazon forth the absurdity of the accusation brought against him by the whole world, an accusation according to which, were it true, 'a base soul' had been able to write books which were full of sublime virtue. At the beginning of the work neither Rousseau nor the Frenchman have ever seen Jean-Jacques. 'Rousseau' knows his works and admires them. The Frenchman has never read them, but he lists proof after proof of Jean-Jacques' villainy. What are these proofs? Well, the poor old man simply rehashes all the gossip which, so he believes, is current about his work and life. Rousseau decides to go and see Jean-Jacques. The Frenchman decides to read his works. In the second dialogue, Rousseau who has been to see Jean-Jacques describes what sort of man he is. In the third, the Frenchman, who has finally read Jean-Jacques' works, describes them and both confirm that the same virtue shines forth from both his work and his life. For the last time Jean-Jacques uses as an epigraph a line from Ovid that he had quoted in his first discourse and which sums up all his misfortunes: *Barbarus hic ego sum, quia non intelligor illis.*

He was the most famous of men, yet he lived as if he were the most obscure. The contrast alone would have been enough to bring about madness. The curiosity which his return to Paris had at first aroused had now waned. The shallow Parisians were forgetting all about him. Grimm was right when he said that in Paris the latest item of news could make people forget all about the heroes of the age. Either people paid no attention to him or, on the contrary, when they recognised him they began to watch him too insistently. The noise of his fame came to him only as barely audible muttering. He enjoyed none of the normal relationships that a man of his abilities ought to have had with his equals. During these same years, Diderot and Voltaire continued to think and fight alongside their old friends.

Whereas he, because of the decision he had taken never to write again, and the feeling he had that even if he wanted to he would not be allowed to do so, was left in a kind of sterile agitation. He was alone, shut away with his pride. His friends were his customers, his clients, people who wanted to see him while there was still some life left in him, and who brought him music to be copied. Everything either wounded or offended him. So off he would go; and it must have been a strange sight to see the little old man who had been Jean-Jacques Rousseau, walking along the road to Romainville or Le Pré-Saint-Gervais with his botanist's box and pruning knife. There at least he could breathe, 'away from city streets and the society of men', face to face with a world with which he could cope and which did not reject him and where he was in harmony with the heavens and God.

He was beyond hope, but he said he wished to understand

> ... the profound and universal silence, no less incomprehensible than the mystery concealing it, a mystery which has been maintained for fifteen years with a thoroughness that I refrain from describing, and with what amounts to miraculous success. This frightening and dreadful silence has left me without the slightest inkling of what is behind these strange happenings. My only guide has been guess-work and I have been able to make no guess that provides an explanation plausible enough to make me think I have divined the truth.

But he was making one more attempt, and trying methodically and soberly, with all the honesty of which his heart was capable, to explain the universal and inexplicable sentence that had been passed upon him. He was conducting his own trial, playing the part of both prosecutor and counsel for the defence. He had re-read Pascal's *Lettres Provinciales* and adopted their tone. His 'Rousseau' has all the fervour and passion of the Jansenist to whom nothing matters except truth. His 'Frenchman', who represents the heartless docility of public opinion, is as naïve as Pascal's kind-hearted priest. The *philosophes* are referred to as 'these gentlemen', just as the Jesuits were in the *Lettres Provinciales*. He uses the same irony as Pascal, only his is more sombre and more despairing because throughout the entire discussion it is he himself who is being discussed.

The book, for all its madness, occasionally has a kind of

Shakespearian grandeur. His two characters are himself—he is both 'Rousseau' and the 'Frenchman', and sometimes he hesitates between the different images of himself which are reflected by these two mirrors. Using the Frenchman as a mouthpiece, he explains how it all began, how the universal conspiracy against him was formed, and it is clear that the plot is nothing more than a figment of his remorse. Everything springs from his first, his real and only misdeed: the abandoning of his children. The Frenchman says:

> He himself had put his friends on the scent, by admitting that he was guilty of a serious fault, and confided this secret to them unnecessarily and superfluously, not, as the hypocrite said, in order to be over and above-board with his friends and to show himself to them exactly as he was, but rather as they themselves very sensibly point out, to put them off the track, deflect their attention, and discourage them from probing any further into the dark mystery of his character. This rash step on his part was no doubt an act inspired by Heaven to force the knave to put off the mask, or at least to provide them with the opportunity which they needed to force him to do so. Skilfully taking advantage of this opening to set their traps around him, they were clever enough to supplement his confidence by the confidences of his accomplices, who were soon no more than instruments in their hands. With great skill, a little money and lavish promises, they won over everyone around him, and thus gradually succeeded in being informed of his affairs just as well, and even better, than he was himself. Thanks to all their efforts they discovered and proved what they had sensed ever since his books became famous; the great preacher of virtue was none other than a monster burdened with secret crimes, who for forty years had concealed a scoundrel's soul beneath the outward appearance of a decent upright man.

Passages such as these are heart-breaking to read, just as he found them heart-breaking to write. This then was the root cause of his anguish; this was what he sometimes admitted to himself when he felt unsure of his virtue, in spite of all he had written and when he looked into his inner abyss, reflected on the 'dark mystery of his character', and relived the memory of the shameful years in the sordid squalor of the Le Vasseur household, when, impelled by his frenzy and his genius, he had put his own selfish interests before the most sacred duties. Remorse, and remorse alone, he claims, prompted and dictated his analysis. He claims that others have betrayed his secret and at the same time insists that it was he who had confessed in the first place. He knows full well that he has never made the public confession of which he boasts. He admits that the public could make neither head nor tail of the involved passages in *Emile* and yet considers that they ought to have prevented decent, upright people levelling reproaches against him. When the *Sentiment des Citoyens* appeared, he sought refuge in denials and lies, even though Voltaire's denunciation caused little stir. But he was so eaten up with remorse that he was disturbed even by the absence of comment; he became convinced that people were only keeping quiet because of a feeling of revulsion, and that the public now saw 'ostentation where before it had seen courage, baseness where it had seen simplicity, boasting where it had seen disinterestedness and absurdity where it had seen eccentricity'.

He then proceeds to describe what his life was now like and falls into delirium: people treat him as if he were a monster: they turn his friends against him, while instructing them to keep up a pretence of friendship. They surround him with spies. They have discovered the art of making Paris seem to him a place more appalling in its loneliness than caves and woods; in the midst of men he finds no one with whom he can communicate, no one to console, advise, or enlighten him, nothing that might help him to regulate his conduct, only an immense labyrinth through the darkness of which he is allowed only to glimpse confusing paths which lead him even further astray. Walls, floors and key-holes, everything around him was so arranged that he was kept under continual supervision. A record was kept of everyone who came to see him. He could not go into a public place without attracting attention and being stared at, although people kept their distance and never spoke to him. And that year, the Swiss dummy who was always burned in the Rue aux Ours on the national holiday, had been made in his likeness, and dressed like him, etc., etc. . . . . Everybody's one aim was to debase him.

The Frenchman does not know that the 'Rousseau' to whom he is talking is Jean-Jacques himself. The passage in which 'Rousseau' describes to him what he found in Jean-Jacques' works is particularly moving: 'You know enough about my destiny,' he explains, 'to realise that it has allowed me very little opportunity to enjoy the good things of life; I have enjoyed neither the possessions that men set store by, nor those which I myself would have appreciated; you know how dearly life has made me pay for that fame so avidly desired by men, and which, even had it been purer, would not have been the sustenance my heart needed.' He relates all the misfortunes he had endured, and describes how, when friendship proved to be a vain illusion, he had to 'retire within himself'. It was at this point that he had discovered Jean-Jacques' books. And 'he alone,' he added, 'seemed to me to show men the road to true happiness, by teaching them to distinguish between reality and appearances, between natural man and the artificial grotesque man that our institutions and prejudices have put in his place. ... My confidence was renewed by finding one single man who thought like myself!' And would he, like everyone else, have to submit to public opinion and stop believing both in Jean-Jacques and in himself?

Passages such as these approach the sublime. He looks at himself from every angle, and sometimes sees himself as a monster, sometimes as virtue personified. What is his conclusion to be? The 'Frenchman' at once dogmatically affirms that 'an individual who has no human qualities, is not worthy of being treated as a man'. 'Rousseau' is unwilling to set himself up as a iudge: 'To carry out so hazardous a duty with so much confidence,' he says, 'a man must feel himself to be as infallible as a God . . . '.

> Every morning before daybreak [he adds], when I hear the bells of Saint-Eustache ringing for the Magpie Mass[1], they seem like a very solemn warning to judges and to all men that they should be less rashly confident in their understanding, that they should oppress and despise the weak less, and believe a little more in innocence, and take a rather greater interest in it, sparing to a greater extent the lives and honour of their fellow-men and lastly to ask themselves sometimes with misgiving if their excessive zeal in punishing crimes does not lead them to commit quite appalling ones themselves.

[1] Translator's note: a reference to a story according to which a thieving magpie almost caused the condemnation of a servant girl.

The second dialogue opens on a less sombre note. 'Rousseau' has seen Jean-Jacques in the flesh, and describes him to the 'Frenchman'. The man he has seen is not the monster that had been described to him, the 'hideous Cyclops' who appears in Ramsay's portrait which was painted at Hume's orders, nor is he 'the ludicrous, grimacing wretch' in the engraving made by Fiquet at the instructions of the *philosophes*. The elderly writer draws a final portrait of himself. The person 'Rousseau' saw was a little man who appeared even smaller by keeping his head bowed; he had little, deep-set, short-sighted eyes, very bad teeth and features that had been affected by age . . . but were the same as those of the tutor in *Emile*. 'If behind his countenance Nature has hidden a scoundrel's soul, no better hiding-place could have been devised.' Jean-Jacques the man corresponds to his books. He is 'solitary' through choice. Diderot's pronouncement: 'only the wicked man lives alone' is absurd. No, 'self-regard, the root cause of all wickedness, is stimulated and exacerbated in society where it has been bred, whereas in solitude it dies through lack of nourishment. No self-sufficient man can possibly wish to harm another.' Jean-Jacques is self-sufficient. At this point the elderly writer describes himself in his 'normal everyday life': he is precisely the reverse of the Jean-Jacques presented by the *philosophes*; he is of all men the one whose character is derived most completely from his temperament alone. He is as nature has made him; education has had but little effect on him. Had his faculties and his strength suddenly developed at birth, he would have appeared practically identical with the person he was in maturity and the one he now is after sixty years of suffering and wretchedness; time, adversity and mankind have altered him but little. His body is growing old and bowed, but his heart remains ever young; he still has the same likes and dislikes, the same passions as in his youth, and right to the end of his life he will be an 'elderly child'.

And he was delighted with the idea of this unconquerable childlike quality which he felt within him. 'He is either all fire or as cold as ice; when he is lukewarm he is nothing.' He has always liked himself and still does, but this self-love is not self-regard. It simply means that he takes every opportunity to extend and strengthen his consciousness of his own being. His heart needs to attach itself to others, 'since our true self is not completely within ourselves . . . and man is so constituted in this life that he can never properly enjoy his own being without the help of others'. He is given to imagining and dreaming. His concern is with being and not with appearances. He has something of the Oriental in his make-up. 'True, he is not capable of abstract reasoning, but his enjoyment is thereby enhanced: he never misses a moment's enjoyment and he is happy as soon as he is alone.' He believed himself to be a simple man 'as transparent as crystal'.

He could now no longer control the inexhaustible flow of words. How had this harmless, childlike man become a writer? 'Inadvertently, and without ever having conceived any such aim . . . an Academy had posed a wretched problem. . . . His heart, warmed by the thought of the future happiness of mankind and by the honour of contributing to it, had endowed him with language worthy of so great an undertaking.' He had given up writing, because by now he had said all he had to say: he was not a churner-out of books. From now on he would earn his living by copying music. 'I sell the work I do with my hands,' he proclaimed, 'but the productions of my soul are not for sale. They owe their strength and elevated tone entirely to their disinterested character. If I wrote for money my writings would be worth little and would earn me still less.' Whereupon he went into the tiniest details, counted up the pages he had copied and explained his budget. . . .

And that was the man that the *philosophes* were hounding, the man they wanted to 'make undesirable in every country on the face of the earth', and 'the illustrious Diderot, who does not soil his hands with paid work and disdains small profits, is considered by the whole of Europe no less virtuous than he is disinterested: whereas Jean-Jacques, the copyist who asks ten *sous* a page for his work in order to eke out a living, is a Jew universally despised for his rapacity! He continued to harp on this theme for three hundred pages. Hatred and slander had turned the whole of the present generation against him, as if it were suffering from a 'spiritual epidemic', a 'sort of contagious disease' or 'universal jaundice'. All the evil came originally from the *philosophes*. Being great imitators of the methods of the Jesuits they were their keenest enemies, doubtless through professional jealousy; and now that they rule minds with the same authority and skill as the Jesuits showed in directing consciences, and being at the same time more subtle in that they are more skilled in concealing their actions, and gradually substituting philosophical intolerance for the previous form, they are becoming as dangerous as their predecessors, without anyone noticing this. It is they who instil into the new generation the most hateful prejudices and the most cruel feelings in respect of Jean-Jacques. Here he thought fit to prove that he had never committed rape or robbery or murder by poisoning, as he had been accused of doing. But he had resigned himself to his fate. The aim of the *philosophes* was to drive him to despair.

> By means of heinous but veiled attacks, by means of mob pressure, whisperings, sneers, looks either cruel and fierce or insulting and mocking, they have succeeded in hounding him from every assembly, theatre, café and public place: their ultimate aim is to drive him from the streets, to imprison him in his own home, to keep him in a state of siege there through the agency of their henchmen, in short to make life so painful for him that he can no longer endure it.... But in making their calculations they doubtless forgot what a resource is offered by innocence and resignation. He seems to be rejuvenated through the calmness of his soul, and although he is now quite without hope in the world of men, he was never further from despair.

The third dialogue provides a kind of counter-proof. The 'Frenchman' has by now read Jean-Jacques' works, and this experience has cured him of all his preconceptions. He has made extracts from them which show only too clearly how writers, doctors, kings, aristocrats, rich men, women and the English have all been in league together against poor Jean-Jacques. His only crime has been his excessive love of nature and of truth. At this point 'Rousseau' once more explains the underlying motives of the plot to the Frenchman. The elderly Jean-Jacques, peering through the mists of madness, discovered the true reasons for the opposition between himself and his former friends. The truth was that they and he had never had the same conception of the order of the universe, the value of inner feeling and the 'usefulness of religion'. He appended a note to this last phrase: 'A fine and very necessary book could be written under this title. But the task could not be worthily fulfilled either by a clergyman or by a professional writer. The kind of man needed no longer exists in our age and will not reappear until a long time hence.' On this particular issue at least, he was not mistaken: in the final analysis God, or the idea that men had of God, had been the motive force in all these quarrels.

He spent a long time working on the dialogues, in 'genuine anguish of heart'. When he had finished he did not know what to do with them. There was no question of publishing them. But where would he find someone, not in league with his persecutors, to whom he could entrust the manuscript? It was then, he wrote, 'that my soul, carried away by its own innocence and their guilt, soared up to the fountain-head of all order and all truth, to seek there resources no longer available to me here below'. He would entrust the manuscript to God himself, by placing it on the high altar in Notre Dame, and the stir caused by this act might even bring it to the notice of the King. He made his arrangements very carefully, going several times to Notre Dame to study the lay-out of the chancel and the general situation in the church. He decided that he would go on a Saturday afternoon because he had noticed that this was a day when the chancel remained empty. He had re-copied the whole manuscript in his best handwriting, and added the following superscription:

A document entrusted to Providence. God of justice and truth, protector of the oppressed, receive this document that I place on thine altar, and entrust to thy providence an unfortunate outsider who is alone, friendless and defenceless on this earth, insulted, mocked at, slandered, betrayed by a whole generation, on whom for the last fifteen years inflictions worse than death and indignities hitherto unknown among men have been showered, without his ever having been able to discover even their cause. I have been refused any explanation, I have no communication with my fellows, and can no longer expect from men, embittered by their own injustice, anything but injury, lies and betrayal. Eternal Providence, my only hope lies in thee: take, I pray thee, this document in thy care and put it into young and faithful hands which will transmit it unadulterated to a better generation. May that generation in lamenting my fate learn what treatment was meted out to a guileless, inoffensive man, who was opposed to injustice but endured it with patience, and who neither did evil nor returned it, nor ever wished it to be done. I

276

know that no man has the right to expect a miracle, not even if he is the obscure and innocent victim of oppression. Since one day order will be re-established, it is enough to wait. Therefore, if my work has been wasted, if it is to be handed over to my enemies and, as seems inevitable, destroyed or defaced by them, I shall nevertheless place my trust in my work although I do not know at what time and by what means it will come into its own: and after doing, as was proper, what I could to help this outcome, I await the future with confidence, I put my faith in thy justice and resign myself to thy will.

For the benefit of mankind, he wrote the following on the first page:

You at whose disposal heaven has put this manuscript, whoever you may be, and whatever use you may have decided to make of it, and whatever your opinion of the author, that unfortunate man entreats you, in the name of human compassion and the sufferings he has gone through in writing it, not to dispose of it until you have read it in full. Reflect that this favour which is asked of you by a heart broken by suffering is an act of fair-mindedness imposed upon you as a duty by heaven.

He had completed his preparations. On the 24th December 1776, on the stroke of two, he went to Notre Dame. He tried to enter by a side door so as to go straight to the altar, but the door was closed. He entered by another door leading into the nave. He then saw that the chancel was surrounded by railings and the gates in these railings were closed. He had never seen the railings before. During his thirty-six years in Paris the space around the chancel had always seemed to him to be open and free. At this he suddenly felt faint: Heaven was in agreement with men. He left the church and wandered about all day until weariness and the oncoming of night forced him to return home, exhausted with fatigue and dazed with grief.

CHAPTER TEN

The Solitary Walker (1774–1778)

Pleasant days devoted to music and botany—Bernardin de Saint-Pierre: Arcadia—Jean-Jacques takes the *Dialogues* to Condillac who does not understand—He hands out the letter 'to every Frenchman who still loves justice and truth' in the streets—His frenzy abates round about August 1776—He yields to his fate—Thérèse and he are ill. They engage a servant—The accident of the 24th October 1776—He starts work on *Les Rêveries d'un Promeneur Solitaire*—Wisdom, peace—He reflects on whether or no he had been entitled to take as his motto: *Vitam impendere vero;* the fourth 'promenade'—He grants himself absolution—Pure awareness of existence—He pleads his case for the last time—He leaves for Ermenonville. He dies on 2nd July 1778.

> He often quoted to me the words spoken by Fontenelle on his death bed: "What of all you have done has given you the greatest satisfaction?—Never having exposed the smallest virtue to the slightest ridicule."
>
> Bernardin de Saint-Pierre

WE MUST NOW, however, retrace our steps: the extracts quoted in the last chapter cannot give a complete picture of the man he now was. According to the mood of the day or the hour, he

278

could either be in a frenzy or meekness itself. He was mad only when he launched forth on to what Corancez calls the sore subject of his enemies. He had only two passions left, botany and music, both of which helped to foster the dream he had always had of a sweet and innocent life. He loved botany, he said, because 'it was the ideal subject for a lazy and sensuous man'. Mme Delessert, his friend in Lyons, had a daughter. It occurred to her to keep her lively mind amused by training her powers of attention by the study of varied and agreeable objects such as plants. This seemed an excellent idea to Jean-Jacques, and while composing a botanical dictionary for his own amusement he wrote the mother and daughter eight long letters, admirably simple, colloquial and lucid in style, which amounted to an elementary course in botany.

About 1775 his interest in his herbariums waned, and did not revive until 1777. But he never lost his 'thirst for composing'. 'Music,' he said, 'was as necessary to him as his daily bread'. Corancez very unwillingly supplied him with words, grumbling about Jean-Jacques' 'despotic demands'. So together they composed the duet *Tircis et Dircé* and fragments of the opera *Daphnis et Chloé*. It is a rather curious fact that he took words from any source—only the tunes he composed mattered to him. No doubt his songs are the best guide to what one might call his inner climate during those years. I regret that I am not sufficiently musical to give an adequate explanation of their naïve charm. At least I can feel how both their melody and rhythm correspond to those of his last prose work, the smooth, nostalgic monologue of the *Rêveries*. He was still free to sing as he liked, but he could only write under supervision. Music helped him to be himself again for the last time. Music, the art which transcends words, concepts and people, allowed him to rise above polemics and controversies and to express his enjoyment in his own being. He made music the repository of his final confidences. He did not try to use it as a final means of attracting attention and putting himself in the lime-light. The Comédiens Français had decided to perform *Pygmalion*, and one evening in October 1775, they called upon him to ask his permission to do so. It was late and Jean-Jacques refused to allow them in, and they had to come back the following day. He declared that he neither agreed to nor objected to the performance and that he would refuse his share of the proceeds. The play was given on the 1st November with Coignet's music, as it had been at Lyons, and was a tremendous success. He took no interest in it, since he no longer wanted, in any sense, to be an author. He looked upon music as being purely a source of pleasure. Corancez had arranged for him to meet Glück, a new musician who was delighting Parisians. He copied music for him and saw performances of *Iphigénie*, *Orphée et Eurydice* and *Alceste*. He was a passionate admirer of his until one day it occurred to him that Glück, by translating the libretto of *Alceste* from Italian into French, had wanted to take sides against him and to contradict what he had said about the unsuitability of the French language as a medium for singing. From then on, he never saw him again.

He was fortunate enough to enjoy one last friendship. Bernardin de Saint-Pierre had returned to Paris almost at the same time as he had, and in many ways was strangely like him. Rulhière had brought him to the Rue Plâtrière in June 1771, and the two men had instantly felt drawn to each other. One was as mad as the other; both liked to live cut off from society; both had the same passion for Robinson Crusoe. Bernardin was a man of about thirty-five. Like Jean-Jacques he had started to write rather late in life, after travelling all over Europe and the world in search of an island where poor and virtuous men like himself might at last find refuge. He was a philanthropist yet unsociable, affectionate yet irascible. Like Jean-Jacques he considered he had not been given his due, and that the odds had always been against him. Society had wounded and humiliated him. He loved 'the muses who offer consolation for the past and reassurance for the future'. In 1773 he was to publish his *Voyage à l'île de France*, but the book brought him neither the fame nor the financial rewards he was hoping for.... Their relationship nearly foundered at the outset. Bernardin had brought back a whole sack of coffee from Mauritius and having discovered in the course of conversation that Jean-Jacques liked coffee, he thought fit to send him a small packet. Jean-Jacques wrote back at once that he was being a little forward: 'As I am not in a position to give presents, my habit,' he declared, 'in order to avoid the embarrassment of social inequality, is not to frequent people who give me presents.' Bernardin would either take back his coffee, or else that would be the end of their friendship.

Finally, the two men, who were both equally impecunious and touchy, came to an arrangement. In exchange for the coffee Jean-Jacques presented Bernardin with 'a root of ginseng' and a treatise on ichthyology which had been sent him by a Montpellier naturalist. In this way 'they were quits'. It was agreed that subsequently, whenever they were together, each would pay exactly half of the expenses incurred. In winter Bernardin sat and talked with Jean-Jacques by the fire, and in summer he accompanied him on his walks. Both were equally critical of the world and its ways. Yet Jean-Jacques did not offer to read the *Confessions* to Bernardin. Although he told him that he was married to Thérèse, he never revealed that he had had children by her. The two men, who suffered from the same sense of dissatisfaction, were both keen to maintain the same illusions, including those about themselves. They quarrelled on several occasions, but always patched up their differences. 'When I am sad, I have to be alone. My ill-humour,' Jean-Jacques confessed, 'gets the better of me. . . . I can keep it in check for a while, then there comes a point when I can control it no longer and it bursts forth against my will. I have my faults. But if you value someone's friendship you must take the rough with the smooth.' Bernardin, like a good disciple, noted down their conversations, which were marked by great sweetness of mood when they were out in the country far from the city streets. They shared the same religious hope: 'My heart tells me that *something* is owing to me,' said Jean-Jacques, 'but it is not in man's power to give it to me.' And Bernardin, echoing Jean-Jacques' emotion and pointing to the whole order of the world around them, replied: 'There is *someone* here. . . . ' So they walked on well pleased with each other. Jean-Jacques would have liked Bernardin to write a supplement to *Emile*, but he failed to persuade him to do so. At the time, Bernardin was thinking of writing about 'a society which owed its happiness only to the laws of nature and virtue'. They talked about it for weeks. The disciple adopted the master's noble conception of happiness which had filled *La Nouvelle Héloïse* and *Emile*, They were both poor and both felt the same nostalgia: '*Soli cantare periti, Arcades*'. They communed in their dream of an ideal country and Bernardin used their conversations in writing one of the *Etudes de la Nature*. His last letter to Jean-Jacques evoked these memories, and ended with the following two lines that Virgil's Gallus addresses to the Arcadian shepherds; one word had been altered;

Atque utinam ex vobis unus tecumque fuissem
Aut custos gregis, aut maturae vinitor uvae.

It would be enough, were there space, simply to reproduce here the 'story of the preceding manuscript' that Jean-Jacques added to his dialogues to give an idea of the profound mental disturbance that he experienced during the first months of 1776. He was still wondering to whom he could entrust the book that Notre Dame had rejected. After he had got over the first shock, he decided that the rejection was a 'heaven-sent blessing', because, if his plan had been carried out, his book would surely have found its way, not into the King's hands, but into those of his worst enemies at court. An elderly writer, l'Abbé de Condillac, with whom he had been acquainted long ago in Lyons, when he was employed as a tutor in the house of M. de Mably, then later at Diderot's in Paris, happened to be staying in the capital. Jean-Jacques saw this as a sign on the part of Providence. He managed to discover where l'Abbé de Condillac was living and took the manuscript to him, in 'an ecstasy of joy', feeling sure that the veil of darkness would at last be removed, now that the manuscript was in his hands. This was a strange idea. Old Condillac[1] who had an alarmingly clear brain, mistrusted 'imaginative minds', their 'fictions', their 'romances', their 'castles in the air', and their 'animal spirits' which make them mistake illusions for realities. He read the *Dialogues* and, so Jean-Jacques tells us, 'spoke to me about the manuscript as he might have talked about a work of literature . . . he suggested certain changes of order that would ensure a better presentation of the subject-matter . . .'. It is obvious that the excessively prudent Condillac was deliberately ignoring the drama of the situation. Jean-Jacques reflected that he had been very obtuse in confiding in a Frenchman who quite obviously could not be expected to admit the iniquity of his own country. However, he left the manuscript in Condillac's keeping. But another traveller happened to come along and this seemed a further sign on the part of Providence. He was a foreigner, a young Englishman, Brooke Boothby, who had been a neighbour of his at Wooton.

[1] Cf. Vol. I, p. 170.

Jean-Jacques 'thought he saw the finger of God in this'. He hastened to make a further copy of his manuscript. Boothby had to leave before it was finished, but he was at least able to take the first dialogue with him. A few days later, Jean-Jacques being unsure of the reliability of these well-known people to whom he had entrusted his manuscript, since it was clear that his perse-cutors allowed him to have communication only with people working for them, had a new idea: 'This was to write a sort of circular addressed to the French nation, to make several copies of it, and, in the course of walks, or in the streets, hand them to those strangers whose features would appeal to him most.' Here is the text of this pathetic circular:

> *To every Frenchman who still loves justice and truth.* Frenchmen! O nation once kind and gentle, what have you become? How you have changed towards an unfortunate foreigner who is alone and at your mercy. . . . Why must so public a scandal be an impene-trable mystery for me alone? Why so many machinations, ruses, betrayals, and falsehoods to hide the transgressor's crimes from himself when he must be better aware of them than anyone; if it is true that he has committed them? If, for reasons which are beyond me, you persist in depriving me of a right which has never been refused to any criminal, and have resolved to crowd the rest of my sad life with anguish, mockery, and shame, without allowing me to know why, without deigning to listen to my complaints, my reasons, my lamentations, and without even giving me leave to speak, my only defence will be to offer up to Heaven a heart which is without guile and hands innocent of all evil, asking that same Heaven not, O cruel people, that it should revenge me and punish you, (Ah! may it rather keep you from all unhappiness and all error!) but that it should soon provide my old age with a more secure refuge where your attacks can affect me no longer.

All this suffering and eloquence did not touch a single heart. He walked through the Tuileries watching the faces of the passers-by and going up to those which seemed to him to be the frankest and kindest. People refused to take his circular. 'All of them,' he says, 'after reading the superscription, To every Frenchman who still loves justice and truth, declared with an ingenuousness that made me laugh in spite of my suffering that it was not meant for them.' After this he sent copies to strangers who had written to ask if they could come to see him. He made

283

them promise that if they replied they should tell him what his crimes were. We have one of these letters that he sent to a lady living in Saint-Haon. Such replies as he received were, he says, 'contorted and ambiguous'. People were at a loss to understand. He thought they were 'pretending to be unaware of a secret to which, through the most amazing circumstance, he was the only man in the whole of Europe not to hold the key'.

Then, about the beginning of August, something extraordinary happened to him—his madness left him. He gave up struggling against what seemed to him to be the inevitable. He ceased to hand out copies of his circular, but he still intended to show it to people he knew, because he felt he must do everything possible to see that truth prevailed. Should he find some man capable of responding to his appeal, he would surely not fail to recognise him and would entrust all his papers to him. But he had no hope of this and even felt 'released from the anxiety of hope' and ended the 'story' of his *Dialogues* with the following words:

> Whatever men may do, Heaven will in time accomplish its work. I know not when, nor how, nor by what means: what I do know, is that the supreme Judge is powerful and just, and that my soul is innocent, and that I have not deserved my fate. That is enough for me. To abandon myself henceforth to my fate, no longer to struggle stubbornly against it, to allow my persecutors to dispose of their prey as they will, to be their plaything for the last sad years of my life without offering any resistance, to surrender to them even the honour of my name and my future reputation, should it be Heaven's wish that these things should be within their power, such is my final resolve; whatever may henceforth happen will leave me unmoved, let men do what they will. I have done what it was my duty to do and although they make my life a torment, they will not prevent me dying in peace.

Was this madness, or was it wisdom? Madness is close to reason, and at times completes and fulfils it. Let us say that there is a kind of plenitude of consciousness which sets a man apart from all other men. They thereupon decide that he is mad and he himself is unable to bear the continual and frightening glare which is directed upon him.

The elderly couple were growing old. For a few years he had enjoyed reasonably good health, but now several things were wrong with him. He had difficulty in working and it was not long before he had to give up copying music. Thérèse too was weary and suffered from attacks of rheumatism. They had to engage a servant, but no doubt neither Thérèse nor he were easy to work for. They employed no fewer than eleven servants in fourteen months. They had to pinch and scrape, since now that he had given up his work as a music copyist, they only had an income of one thousand four hundred and forty *livres*. The Duchess of Portland sent him some seeds of exotic plants as if he were a wealthy man. He returned the box unopened and replied with careful politeness that he 'had not a square inch of ground in which to put parsley or pinks, still less African plants'. In February 1777 he handed or showed to people a new circular in which he asked them to help Thérèse and him find refuge in some home or other, in exchange for which they would hand over such ready money and income as they possessed. In his usual way he rather overdid the pathos in his circular. He was rather too skilful in his complaints. Comte Duprat, a nobleman of Auvergne, found lodgings for both Thérèse and him for eight hundred *livres* in the Clermont area. He very nearly took this offer; however, if he went there he did not want to be obliged to attend mass, or to change his name. Finally he abandoned the idea, since Thérèse did not want to go so far away from Paris.

On the 24th October 1776 'an event as sad as it was unexpected' helped him to progress still further towards peace and tranquillity, because its consequences made hope even more remote[1]. The story is well-known. On that particular day he had gone for a walk in the Charonne and Ménilmontant area. He had spent the whole day wandering through the autumn countryside, gently day-dreaming about his unhappy but

[1] It is not certain how the phrase 'an event as sad as it was unexpected' should be interpreted. However, I think that there is no doubt but that it refers to the fall he had coming down the hill at Ménilmontant, on the 24th October 1776. You have only to read the first two *Promenades* to realise that their whole pattern is determined by the accident which governs the sequence of ideas.

The words 'unexpected accident' in the second *Promenade* echo the words in the first: 'an accident as sad as it was unexpected' and the end of the second *Promenade* is merely a development of the phrase: '. . . has now at last obliterated this faint ray of hope from my heart . . . etc.'

innocent life. At dusk, he was walking down the hill at Ménil-montant when M. de Saint-Fargeau's carriage came rushing down at full speed. He did not have time to get out of the way and a great dane which was running alongside the carriage bumped into him and he fell flat on his face. Night was falling when he recovered his senses. He experienced, so he says, 'a most agreeable sensation'. He was aware only 'of his diaphanous being' without even knowing who or where he was. His upper lip was cut, he was spitting blood and his whole body was bruised. But thanks to the excitement of his feverish state he was able to return to the Rue Plâtrière by way of the Temple. When he appeared in the doorway with his blood-stained face, Thérèse's cries suddenly made him realise what had happened to him. Corancez and Bernardin came to see him during the following days, and the kind-hearted Marianne and others wrote to him. He remained oblivious to these marks of affection. Meanwhile the story of his accident spread through Paris, and the *lieutenant de police* made enquiries. Rumour had it that he was dead. A few weeks later, in a newspaper called the *Courrier d'Avignon*, he read a paragraph expressing ironical pity for him 'for having been knocked over by dogs'. Other scraps of gossip also came to his ears. There was talk of a subscription for the printing of the manuscripts he had left behind him. It was then that he realised what kind of 'funeral oration' he would be honoured with when he really died, what kind of 'trumped up documents' his enemies were holding in reserve. Even the man on whom he had set all his hopes, the 'one man' who would have exposed the conspiracy, did not exist. He, therefore, resigned himself to his fate: 'God is just,' he decided, 'he wants me to suffer, and he knows that I am innocent. That is why I trust in him. My heart and my reason cry out that I will not be mistaken in my trust.'

Two months later towards the end of December he took a sheet of paper and noted down the first words of his last work: 'Here I am alone on earth. . . . ' He imagined himself back again on the paths around Ménilmontant no longer anything but a solitary wanderer gently day-dreaming about his ill-starred but innocent life and happy in his day-dreams. He had been con-demned to this solitude by the men he loved. He would no longer argue with them or try to defend himself. He felt 'at peace in the depths of the abyss, a poor unfortunate mortal, yet as impassive as God himself'. He felt himself to be 'on this earth as if he were on some strange planet'. He was of no account among men. Henceforth he would concern himself only with himself, putting his thoughts finally in order before going to meet his God. This was how he came to write the *Rêveries*. He was never quite free of anguish and fear, but his one purpose was to die in peace. He was wholly absorbed in his memories; they were uncertain, but their very uncertainty helped him at last to become the person that he thought he had been. The most extraordinary thing was his conviction of having been a model of wisdom. Perhaps all of us, as we grow older, come to believe in some remarkable piece of fiction that we have constructed about ourselves. According to the story he told himself, his youth had been one long spontaneous search for faith. His ambitions and frenzied passions had been forgotten. He believed that he had allowed himself until the age of forty to be a success, and that after that he had lived very deliberately from day to day more or less in retirement and without heed for the future. He had despised literary notoriety: he had patiently worked out his own philosophy and had always held on to it, and even now his sole aim was to learn 'how to leave this life, not as a better person for that (was) not possible, but as a more virtuous one, than when he had entered it'.

One day he came across a newspaper article at the head of which the author, the Abbé Royou, had written: '*Vitam vero impendenti*, R. . . . ' This seemed to him to be no more than a piece of sarcasm and it prompted him to ask himself how far he had been right to choose the phrase as his motto. It was his declared intention finally to settle all his accounts. He spent a whole day 'examining himself on the question of falsehood', 'subjecting himself to close scrutiny', and then wrote the fourth *promenade*. Except for the business of Marion's ribbon, about which he once more declared his guilt, he did not think that he had too much on his conscience. Even this particular lie had been a consequence of embarrassment—but a truthful man never serves truth better than when he is called upon to sacrifice himself for it. He had tried to become precisely that sort of man. Admittedly, during the course of a dinner party only a short time before, a woman had asked him if he had ever had any children and he had 'replied shamefacedly' that he had never been so fortunate. But that again had only been through embarrassment, and because he felt himself surrounded by malevolence and prejudice. To respect his motto fully he would have had to be devoid of shyness. On this score he had been perhaps too confident in his abilities. But he would try again, modestly, to improve. But when all was said and done, once again and for the last time, he granted himself absolution.

It is pathetic to watch him also for the last time tricking himself and quite unconsciously asking himself only those questions to which he can give a triumphant reply. He argued, split hairs endlessly, and conducted what appeared to be a most scrupulous discussion of each issue. He made innumerable fine distinctions, but only to arrive at a declaration of the general truth of his *Confessions* and to insinuate that he had often omitted to reveal all the good things about himself that he might have done. All things considered, he was sure that 'one day he would be judged less severely than he had judged himself'.

This was his final outburst of pride, his last declamatory statement. No doubt it is not so very important to know whether or not he told any definite lies, but it would be interesting to know, and one wishes he had said whether he was able to look into the depths of his heart without a feeling of uneasiness, whether, in that region to which other people's eyes cannot penetrate, he was in truth what he set himself up to be and what he was supposed to be, or whether, instead, he did not find there something which caused him shame and embarrassment, a sort of organic lie, that kind of lie which is perhaps inseparable from life and of which no living creature is innocent.

He felt he had the right to enjoy his own being. He discovered that the emptiest days in his life had been the happiest; they had not been the days of effort and application during which he had thought out, written and constructed great masterpieces, but days of *far niente* when a strange combination of fortunate and unfortunate circumstances had allowed him 'to devote himself to idleness'. The most fruitful time had been the time he had wasted. What lyrical days he had spent on the Ile Saint-Pierre, to which he had been exiled by persecution. On this earth, perhaps, even an unhappy memory was more real than happiness. He could still hear the plash of the waves on the island shore. Memory revived the day-dream, and the day-dream revived his memories. He was 'pleasurably aware of being alive, without taking the trouble to think'. There was no longer any distinction between past and present. He was outside time and already in eternity. 'What is it that one enjoys in such a situation?' he asked. 'Nothing outside oneself, nothing except oneself and one's own existence; as long as this state endures, one is self-sufficient, like God.'

He could not avoid the admission that he had hardly ever done anything else but follow the inclinations of his nature. And that no doubt set a limit to his virtue, if true virtue consists in mastering one's inclinations. But at the same time, all that he could discover within himself was a feeling of 'universal benevolence', and in a world filled with decent people he would have had no desire but to act virtuously. The uncertainty into which he had been plunged by the hypocrisy of society had made him resolve to avoid all opportunities for action, and to shun his fellow-men so as not to have to hate them. But had he possessed Gyges' magic ring which conferred invisibility, he would have had only one desire: 'It would have been to see every heart filled with satisfaction; only the sight of public felicity could have touched my heart with a lasting emotion, and the ardent desire to contribute to that felicity would have been my most constant passion.'

This was the tenor of his soliloquy, and it brought peace back into his heart. Occasionally he would compose some new song. One day, Corancez brought him Desdemona's song from the tragedy *Othello* as a present from his wife:

> Au pied d'un saule assise tous les jours
> On l'entendait qui pleurait ses amours
> Chanter le saule et sa douce verdure.[1]

He had promised to set to music any words that Mme Corancez might send him. But to do so he would have had to read Shakespeare's play, and he had sworn that he would never read

---

[1] *Othello*, Act IV, Sc. iii:
> The poor soul sat sighing by a sycamore tree
> Sing all a green willow;
> Her hand on her bosom, her head on her knee,
> Sing willow, willow, willow.

anything again. It was a great problem to decide whether to break faith with himself or Mme Corancez. In the end he decided to read Shakespeare and wrote music for the willow song, the melody and words of which served to express his own nostalgia. In the spring of 1777, he had also taken up botany again and this pursuit, by providing a 'recreation for his eyes', gave him respite from 'the awareness of his sufferings'. 'On those days when I see no one', he wrote, 'I no longer think of my fate, I am no longer conscious of it, I no longer suffer.' But once again he was to be obliged to come up against men. . . .

One day in December 1777 someone brought him D'Alembert's recently published eulogy on Mme Geoffrin, which contained the words, attributed to Mme Geoffrin: 'I wish one question could be put to all those unfortunate wretches who are about to suffer the death penalty for their crimes: Did you love children? I am sure their answer would be no.' Jean-Jacques had no doubt that these lines were intended for him and once more his mind was filled with remorse, and he added a chapter, a whole extra 'promenade', which was nothing more or less than a final plea on his own behalf, to a book that had been intended solely as an expression of happiness. He had always loved children, and only the day before how delighted he had been to see that his landlord's two little boys were not afraid of his 'aged countenance'. And two years before, had he not embraced a small child he had met when passing through the village of Clignancourt, and had he not retraced his steps to embrace the child once again and give him a Nanterre cake! And what about the other occasion at La Muette when he put his hand into his slender purse to buy wafers for a whole school of little girls. . . . Pathetically he produced one proof after another. As far as his own children were concerned, he had been unable to act differently, being surrounded by a family which would have turned them into monsters, and he forced himself to add: 'I would do the same again, and with far fewer misgivings, should the need arise.' But his heart overflowed and he went on: 'Oh, if only I could have experienced for a few moments those pure caresses which come from the heart, were they bestowed only by a little child dressed in a frock; if only I could see in some eyes, delight and pleasure at my presence. . . .'

Two months, three months went by and he was still among

the living. On the 12th April 1778 he was awakened by the loud pealing of bells, and his room was flooded with happiness and with memories. He got up and wrote the last pages he ever penned: 'Today is Palm Sunday, and it is exactly fifty years since I first made the acquaintance of Mme de Warens. At the time she was twenty-eight years old, having been born in the first year of the century. I was only seventeen . . . this first encounter determined the course of my whole life. . . . Never a day goes by but I remember with tender delight that unique and brief space of time during which I was able to be myself, to the full, without adulteration or impediment, and during which I can truly say I lived. . . . ' He was not deceived by the fervour of his memories. All his life he had been the man moulded by that woman whom he had addressed as 'Maman', and it was only right that his final words should have been a last tribute to her. Nothing is pure, and fifty years before the relationship between 'Petit' and 'Maman' had not been entirely pure. Both of them, in the first flush of conversion, had been too prone to believe that acts were unimportant, and that intentions were paramount —they had equated a form of quietism with innocence—but however they might have erred, they had at least borne witness to the fact that wherever there is a soul, there is positive fervour, and Jean-Jacques' fervour had been so sincere and so strong that it had carried all other souls along with it.

That was to be the last page he ever wrote. The chapter remained unfinished, but his accounts had been finally put in order. We can pass over the rest of the story rapidly, in the same way as he lived it. Since he had given up his music copying, he was afraid, as old people often are, of being in want in the last phase of his life, and he would have liked to find a more secure and less expensive refuge for Thérèse and himself somewhere in the country. Corancez offered him a house at Sceaux, being unable to spend his holidays there that year, because he would be busy in Paris. Jean-Jacques at first hesitated, then accepted. But, at the same time, through a doctor whom he had consulted on Thérèse's behalf and his own, he was offered accommodation at Ermenonville by M. de Girardin, who, with his wife, had been among his clients when he was a music copyist. On the 20th May he suddenly set off, alone, to investigate the possibility, without notifying anyone, neither Corancez, nor Bernardin with whom he had arranged to go to Sèvres on the following day. He took a post-chaise to Louvres, where he was met by M. de Girardin's carriage. He drove through the forest where the trees were 'so fresh, being free of smoke and dust'. He insisted on getting out of the carriage and walking and was delighted to discover the lake and the waterfall. The Marquis, the Marquise and their children came out along the drive to welcome him. He wept for joy. It was arranged that a thatched cottage would be built for him in the orchard, but meanwhile he was established in a little pavilion, in front of the château. Two days later, Thérèse received instructions to pack her belongings at once and to bring the furniture.

Early in June, he heard of the death of his old enemy Voltaire and was deeply affected by it. When M. de Girardin expressed surprise at this, Jean-Jacques answered with admirable lucidity 'my existence was linked to his: now that he is dead I shall not be long in following him'. And indeed the two men were now free to die because the ideas they had scattered were throbbing throughout the atmosphere of the century like invisible particles of dust. Preparations were complete; the systems and weapons were ready. The deep silence in the surrounding woods was deceptive because the storm was about to burst.

It seems certain that for a few days at least he was quite happy. He had found at least one place in the world that was arranged according to his ideas and his preferences. M. de Girardin being an enthusiastic reader of La Nouvelle Héloïse had embellished nature with precisely that degree of order and disorder which appealed to Saint-Preux and Julie. He might well ask himself who or what strange destiny had led him to this place. Looking around him he could contemplate nature as he wished that nature should be. Had he been capable of irony, he might even have noticed some affectation in these wild yet carefully man-made landscapes and regretted the extremes to which disciples so often go. But we may be sure that he remained oblivious to this. The year before, the Marquis de Girardin had published a little book on landscape gardening which included the following lines: 'Here in a remote and deep-set hollow, calm pure water forms a little lake, and the moon before sinking below the horizon, gazes long and lovingly at its own reflection there. Its shores are lined with poplars: far away in the shade of their restful foliage, can be glimpsed a little philosophical monument. It has been raised to the memory of a man whose genius illuminates the world. He was subject to persecution because he wished to rise above vain grandeur by being independent. Quiet and calm are the features of this sweet retreat.' Whether Jean-Jacques had read these lines or not, he must surely have felt that, while still alive, he was present in a place dedicated to his genius, and in the garden of his fame.

The accounts left by Lebègue de Presles, the Marquis de Girardin and Magellan provide us with a few last glimpses of him. He had decided to make a herbarium with the plants from Ermenonville, and he went on walks to gather them. He was accompanied by the Marquis' second son, a boy of twelve whom he referred to as his '*gouverneur*' (tutor or guardian). He chatted with the village priest, the Abbé Brizard, and with poor people to whom he distributed alms. He dined at the château and after dinner would sing the Willow Song accompanying himself on the spinet. After nightfall he would listen to music played on flutes and oboes by performers hidden in the groves in the park. One evening Magellan, the navigator, gave an eyewitness account of the Lisbon earthquake and Rousseau was reminded of his disputes with Voltaire. Such was his humour that he was very soon again a prey to scruples. Perhaps he was afraid of not being free enough, or perhaps he felt the very kindness of his hosts as a weight upon them. A young Norman aristocrat, M. de Flamenville, whom he had seen in Paris, asked if he could pay him a visit and when he came, offered him a small estate on the sea-coast in Normandy opposite Guernsey. He could live there 'for nothing' and would be 'free to be fully himself'. Jean-Jacques listened to the proposal and true to his habit of always complaining handed M. de Flamenville the letter he had written more than a year before asking for asylum in some hospice. But the matter went no further.

On the 2nd July—I shall follow the Lebègue de Presles' account, which is the simplest and most credible—he had risen very early, as was his wont, and had gone for a walk. He came home about eight o'clock and had breakfast with Thérèse and the maidservant. He then sent Thérèse to pay a bill that he had received from the locksmith. He was about to go to the château to give the Marquis de Girardin's daughter a music lesson when he suddenly felt unwell. On her return Thérèse could hear him groaning as she came upstairs.

He complained first of very disagreeable pricklings on the soles of his feet, then of a sensation of cold along his spine as if some icy liquid were running down it, and then of extremely violent pains in his chest and his head which came in waves; he showed he was in pain by putting both hands to his head, and said he felt as if his skull were being split apart. His life came to an end during one of these attacks and he fell from his chair to the floor. He was immediately lifted up again but he was dead, and the surgeons, whom it had been impossible to bring earlier, could not revive him, either by bleeding him or using sal volatile, cupping glasses, etc. . . .

Thérèse was the only person to witness his death and the various accounts she gave do not all tally with each other. She used to tell the story to the people who came on pilgrimage to Ermenonville: perhaps she made some small profit out of it and altered some detail or other at every telling. She was not lacking in either guile or imagination. It was she who supplied Moreau le Jeune with the subject for his print which shows Jean-Jacques sitting in an arm-chair at the open-window and addressing to Thérèse the edifying words: 'Be comforted, you can see how pure and serene the heavens are; well, I am on my way there.' She was constantly attributing further last words to her late husband. But as Lebègue de Presles says—although he himself uses her account—'Mme Rousseau, who was alone with him, was too agitated and upset to remember the exact terms of the moral and religious observations that her husband may have made; if indeed he was able to make any in view of the disturbance of mind necessarily entailed by the destruction of the organism and the cessation of life.' In 1798 she was convinced that Jean-Jacques had died on the 3rd of July and not on the 2nd. She may also have forgotten his final statements, because she added: 'He died with my hands clasped in his and without uttering a single word.'

The next day, the doctors from Senlis carried out an autopsy and diagnosed the cause of death as an attack of serous apoplexy.[1] Houdon and a number of Italian practitioners also came and

[1] The theory that Rousseau committed suicide cannot be sustained (cf· Dr. Lacossagne, *La Mort de J.-J. Rousseau*, Lyons, 1913).

made a death mask, which was to preserve his countenance for posterity. His face had already begun to swell. One of his eyes was more open than the other and gave an impression of winking. But art would remedy these details.

In the evening of Saturday the 4th of July, at eleven o'clock, the body was carried to the Ile des Peupliers at the far end of the lake. Romilly his elderly compatriot was present, Girardin tells us, so that the Genevan form of the burial service should be properly observed; Corancez and Lebègue de Presles were also there. Peasants from the village and the surrounding countryside stood along the shore holding torches. The night was wonderfully calm and clear. By midnight, there was nothing left but the quivering silence, a long reflection in the water, the trees and the sky; everything and nothing.

CHAPTER ELEVEN

Ile des Peupliers

The great problem of sincerity—Rousseau never achieved self-knowledge or did so only partially—Sincerity and truth—Voltaire and Jean-Jacques—Jean-Jacques' message—The pattern of the imagination and the pattern of action.

'You know, Madame, that his Julie when dying expressed the conviction, which is consequently his own, that a soul, once it has departed its earthly body, can return to haunt this earth, and perhaps remain close to its dear ones, and, by some inward communion similar to that practised by God, can make its way into their very thoughts. And indeed that soul whose last breath was expressive of kindness and love seems still to wander around these shady groves and to merge with the souls of all those who come here to dream of love and friendship.'

From a letter written by
René de Girardin, 1778

IT WAS ALL OVER: he was now dead and buried. I have made the journey to the Ile des Peupliers, because it is here that he still remains for all those who know something about him and have some feeling for him, and not in that icy palace to which the Revolution transferred his bones, and where posterity is only grateful to the glorious dead in so far as it can subordinate their thought to its own. The living are not in the habit of giving something for nothing. Even the fame they bestow on the dead must justify them in being what they are. . . . I have been unable to land on the island and perhaps it is just as well. The empty tomb is there across the water a few yards back from the shore between the tall flames of the poplar trees. When I ask myself how much I have been able to grasp of the reality that was Jean-Jacques, I see that something remains elusive.

For ten years we have lived together in a strange and some-times extraordinary intimacy. I have inspected and investigated everything about him so inquisitively, indiscreetly and relent-lessly that I have felt obliged to ask his forgiveness. But I would have liked to know the whole truth. I am now better informed about his life than about my own. One can never know one's own life, or rather there is almost always something within us which does not wish to become aware of itself. I have been able to live inside him at a level where one thing merges into another, where sincerity can be seen turning into hypocrisy, and where, if one were dealing with oneself, one would be unwilling to look. One of my ambitions when I started on this perhaps absurd undertaking was for once to find out everything about a man. I think that I have made some progress towards such knowledge. When we try to study ourselves we are de-ceived at every step by self-regard, self-interest and the instinct of self-preservation; one can acquire a rather better knowledge of human nature, by lovingly and scrupulously examining someone else's life if he has written a lot about himself and if, through the circumstances of his life, a great many other documents are also available.

Ten years' work on a single man, with the sole aim of dis-covering how sincere he was! I can still hear the sarcastic remarks of one of my friends. Every time I related to him one of Jean-Jacques' adventures, weaknesses or mistakes he would say: 'Of course! he's like everybody else.' I sensed that the comment was a condemnation of myself. What was the use of taking such pains to prove the obvious? I was constantly getting lost in incidental details which, into the bargain, were of the most glaringly naïve character. In my friend's view I would only have been justified if I had worked out the logical pattern of Jean-Jacques' mistakes, deduced some universally valid concept from the error of his ways, and stated the law governing his passions and the vicissitudes of his life. But on the contrary I think what kept me at my task was the impossibility of generalising and the inexpressible emotion I experienced at every stage in the work, on discovering that the mistakes and passions which made my hero appear similar to 'everyone else' nevertheless had the great distinction of being unique. Each individual is unique, and his uniqueness constitutes his dignity and, whatever his nature, makes him worthy of lengthy study. I may have started with the naïve intention of passing judgement on Jean-Jacques, but I soon lost sight of that. And my attitude towards him became marked by that forgiveness that we necessarily feel towards anyone with whom we live.

He who has written at such length about himself did not achieve self-knowledge, or did so only partially. How did he fail to see from the outset that he was caught in a contradiction from which there was no escape? Yet although in the very first lines of his *Confessions* he had written: 'Each individual only really knows himself', he had been careful to add: 'if indeed anyone can be said to know himself; for how can we properly define a human being only in terms of the relationships within him without comparing him with anything else.' How did he fail to realise that in his case this term of comparison would be lacking? He disregarded the problem, feeling that he was 'a being apart', and assuming that he possessed powers of frank and sincere self-examination and self-analysis hitherto unknown. He alone was capable of painting 'that inner world that remains unseen when the painter is portraying a person other than himself, and which the subject is unwilling to reveal'. Thus he was sure that by writing his *Confessions* he would supply mankind with the comparison that was lacking. He failed. The document is unreliable, and has even been slightly falsified. It is simply one more portrait of the artist which takes its place along with a hundred others, that we gaze at in turn in order to discover the true features of mankind and so see ourselves. This may be of little consequence. The novelty and greatness of the undertaking lay in his passion for self-knowledge. He studied himself with all his might for five or even ten years, admittedly cheating now and again as he looked into his mirror so as to make his reflection bearable for himself, yet at the same time bringing to light what he felt was the truth about himself. And then suddenly in London in February 1766, when he got to the point of seeing the kind of person he had become, he was unable to go on, he could not bring himself to write any more, and he abandoned the work. There could perhaps be no clearer indication of his determination to be truthful. It is quite easy for us critics and biographers to tell the whole truth and to put everything into place. We are not emotionally involved. But he was reduced to silence. This is the difference between a commentary on a life and that life as it is lived. One of the beauties of the *Confessions* is that the book had to remain unfinished. By means of his style he had imposed a harmonious pattern on the story of his life, but it was progressively more difficult to maintain as he drew nearer to the present and finally it became totally blurred. So profound was his anguish that he could no longer clearly apprehend his being in this world. The darkness was deepening both around him and within him. Between other men and himself the shadows were now too dense. His mind was confused by anger and resentment. He had got beyond understanding, explaining or confessing, there was nothing for it now but to go on living and suffering. His intolerable sufferings and anguish could still make him cry out as in the *Dialogues*, and he would proclaim his innocence and virtues to the whole world. But he would never be quite sure about them, and when he came to die, like everyone else there were still many features of his personality of which he was still unconscious. The faces of the dead often have a puzzled look.

He had been the victim of a rather magnificent illusion in thinking he had been, and still was, an example of natural man, and in imagining that he could discover within himself the human soul as it had been before it was disfigured by knowledge and social passions, as the statue of Glaucus was defaced by time and weather. He had lived as much as possible on the fringe of society, his sole concern being to remain himself, and to despise or correct any alteration that had been made in his heart through traditional misconceptions, 'passion which imagines itself to be rational', 'the understanding in a state of delirium', social ceremonies and social errors. He had wanted to revert to being, as God had first made him, a 'creature acting according to sure and invariable principles', in a 'state of heavenly and majestic simplicity'. But in fact society has no fringe, there is no way of escaping from it, and by dint of struggling against society he had only succeeded in turning himself into a wild eccentric or a crazy old man, whom children pointed to as he went past, almost like a character in a novel, and his own dreams were like 'the dreams of a man in a fever', which, as he himself declared, could go to the making of a very fine book. *Vitam impendere vero.* His sheer desire for truth had made him depart from the truth. There was no denying that his motto was ambiguous. The truth about man is not in any single man; it is in all men, and just as much outside us as within us and no one has the right to set up as a prophet.

'One must be oneself,' was his constant cry.... But what is the 'self'? A small, closed world, which is in the first instance terribly circumscribed and limited. It is important not to make a God of it. There was a lack of irony in his approach to himself.

His old enemy, Voltaire, had said in connection with Pascal: 'The expression, *looking only at ourselves*, has no meaning'... and again. '... I repeat that to think of oneself independently of the phenomena of nature is to think about nothing at all, precisely nothing: this should be properly understood.' Truth is outside ourselves, outside memory, suffering and resentment. Sincerity is not enough. Integrity is also needed and to achieve it the self has sometimes to be put aside. Sincerity is no more than a relationship of the self with the self, and if the self which has been taken as a point of reference is a flattering image, or an illusion, the relationship is always false, and the subject is constantly prone to error..., if not to lying. The biggest liar may be the greatest idealist. We are never more inclined to idealise than when we are studying ourselves.

The tomb is empty, the leaves of the poplar quiver, but their quivering bears witness for no one in particular. It is merely an effect of the passing wind which signifies that everything goes on as before. Yet I am convinced that something of the great anguish I have tried to describe will always remain.... 'Nothing at all, precisely nothing.' Voltaire is very emphatic because he finds it difficult himself to observe the moderation he preached. He knew perfectly well that when Pascal and Rousseau were thinking about themselves, they were reflecting on something. They were not, as a matter of fact, reflecting independently of natural phenomena because that is not possible. In that case why pretend to accuse them of doing so? It is impossible to dissociate oneself from nature and society. In spite of all, and however proud the effort, to think of oneself is to think of everybody else, because in the last resort they are no more than poignantly similar 'selves'. Hence the persistent resonance produced in our minds by the *Pensées* and the *Confessions*.

The same man who decreed that one should be oneself, also said that everything should be related to the common people. These apparently contradictory demands are in fact an exact definition of his life, his thought and his work. I have tried to follow in detail and day by day, the thoughts about happiness of an unhappy man, and those of a man in the crowd about the problem of human dignity, as well as his attempt to live a genuine life. Jean-Jacques may not always have been a truthful man, but he always tried to be truthful. This is the most we can achieve. When society is so powerful and noisy, nothing is more precious than the counsel of a man who helps you to rediscover your primitive nature and to hear, deep down, the fundamental note of certainty and hope. The world is saved in each passing moment by nothing other than the mania for truth which survives in a few consciences more demanding and sensitive than the rest, and because of that, unconquerable.

When he was dead his friends and enemies in the literary world argued with each other about his nature and his worth. Those who had known him best and were afraid of his eloquence, hurriedly put their versions of events down in writing or got their secretaries to do so in order to protect themselves against the *Confessions*. The guerilla warfare between rival susceptibilities went on for a few years as long as there remained survivors, however unimportant, of the tragi-comedies which had been enacted at L'Ermitage, Motiers, Wooton, Paris and anywhere else that fate had led him. But fame was at work in another way, and its beams which had sometimes been deflected from him during his last years were again concentrated on him now that he was dead. He himself had sensed how closely his thought was linked to the history of his times. He used to say that 'revolutions' would have to occur before justice could be done to him. And the fact was that the new world which came into being turned him into a prophet and a mascot. Myths grew up around him; hawkers sold portraits of him, and his features were used to decorate snuff-boxes, paper-weights, plates and serving-dishes. It even happened that enemies were reconciled in the confusion of battle, so that small-scale models of the busts of Voltaire and himself by Houdon could be seen standing at either end of the same mantelpiece. Ermenonville and the Ile des Peupliers became places of pilgrimage for the whole of Europe.

He had not been endowed at birth with any special tendencies towards truthfulness, and neither the accidents of his childhood nor the adventures of his youth were enough to make him have any reverence for it, given the fact that he was so idle, impulsive and imaginative. Had he been a little more frivolous, a little less shy, rather less absorbed from the outset in his own dreams, he might have become one of those intellectual, erotic, or literary adventurers of whom there was no lack in the eighteenth century. In the long run misfortune, humiliation, obstacles and failure were if anything, stimulants to his genius. By arousing his inborn stubbornness they forced him to be Rousseau, like his father old Isaac who had also banished himself from Geneva with the cry: 'I am Rousseau, I am Rousseau'. Jean-Jacques became 'Rousseau' regardless of the price that had to be paid, 'Rousseau' in the eyes of the whole world and soon no longer had any doubts that he, Rousseau, alone embodied truth in a world where everything was falsehood. From that point onwards his destiny was of no common order. Casanova, the Chevalier d'Eon, Grimm, Caraccioli and so many others, had entertained their contemporaries while amusing themselves. In Rousseau's case both entertainment and amusement were excluded. On occasions he was guilty of error and could be mistaken in the day-to-day events of his life, in his friendships and his amorous passions. He was never mistaken in his work. But some tenderly brooding impulse always brought him back to himself, and through an admirable effort of self-creation he finally became the man he was in his books. It was then that an anxious, exhausted and moribund society was struck by the extraordinary coincidence between his work and him-

self. The writing of each of his books, far from being a mere
game, had been a commitment of his whole being, and innumerable men and women who had forgotten how to live,
thought they could learn the technique of life from them and
read them in the same spirit as poor Marianne whom he had
so neglected. They saw him as a kind of saint or guru, as the first
of the poor to find his voice. It was as if death had purified
everything about him. He had his apostles both true and false.
The memory of all those who had ever been close to him became
worthy of preservation. Maman and Claude Anet were made
the subject of edifying reminiscences. His fame was much more
than that of a writer; it was the fame of a man who had delivered
people from confusion of spirit, and pointed the way to a new life.

Of course this man was also an author and he knew all the
tricks of the trade. Anyone looking carefully at his books would
have noticed that they were written in two different tones,
according to two very different rhythms, the pattern of the
imagination and the pattern of action. As a dreamer he was
without parallel, and could waft the reader away in his dream.
Full, deliciously melancholy sentences charmed the mind,
obliterated the world, carried you back to a paradise of illusions
and memories, and restored you to simplicity and greatness. But
other sentences, sharper, sterner and more forceful, and gleaming like sword-thrusts, inspired you with confidence and
courage. It was as if he used the gentle approach so that, in the
very next moment, he might better subjugate the reader, who
was held captive by the alternating rhythms. Voltaire and
Diderot who were envious of him called him a charlatan. The
reason was that they had been among the fortunate of the
century, their revolutions had all taken place only within their
brains, and they had never felt that profound longing of the
soul to which Jean-Jacques' message provided an answer. This
message announced rebirth. To read him was to be transformed
mysteriously into the 'new man' that he had instructed *Emile* to
become. Everything was collapsing but his readers could hope
and dare. All those pages that had been written by a sad unhappy man were charged and bursting with hope. They caused
the heart to bound and swell. They had about them a resonance
which was a constant reminder that man's consciousness is
creative and it makes him an image of God so that he has

within him, at every moment, the power to change the world. . . .
I must leave him at this point, although I find it difficult to do so. It seems to me that I still have everything to learn and express about him. Having reached the end of my long study, I feel I have made no great discoveries. I am left with the sustaining joy of having proved that men may not be what they are and what necessity makes of them, but that they can be what they achieve and what they will themselves to be.

Index